COMPUTER ORGANIZATION AND THE SYSTEM/370

COMPUTER SCIENCE SERIES

Computers: A Systems Approach, Ned Chapin
Computer Architecture, Caxton C. Foster
Advanced Programming, Harry Katzan, Jr.
APL Programming and Computer Techniques, Harry Katzan, Jr.
APL User's Guide, Harry Katzan, Jr.
Computer Organization and the System/370, Harry Katzan, Jr.
The Anatomy of a Compiler, John A. N. Lee
Numerical Analysis for Computers, John A. N. Lee

COMPUTER SCIENCE SERIES

COMPUTER ORGANIZATION AND THE SYSTEM/370

Harry Katzan, Jr.
Assistant Professor of Computer Science
Pratt Institute

VNR

Van Nostrand Reinhold Company
New York Cincinnati Toronto London Melbourne

Van Nostrand Reinhold Company Regional Offices:
New York Cincinnati Chicago Millbrae Dallas

Van Nostrand Reinhold Company International Offices:
London Toronto Melbourne

Library of Congress Catalog Card Number: 72-153191

Manufactured in the United States of America

Published by Van Nostrand Reinhold Company
450 West 33rd Street, New York, N.Y. 10001

Published simultaneously in Canada by
Van Nostrand Reinhold Ltd.

15 14 13 12 11 10 9 8 7 6 5 4 3 2

PREFACE

The announcement on June 30, 1970 by the IBM Corporation of the System/370 family of computers as a compatible successor to the highly successful System/360 series established the 360/370 design philosophy as a point of reference in computer technology.

This book has two main objectives: (1) to present an introduction to computers and programming using the System/370 as the primary vehicle; and (2) to present an introduction to the System/370 for people experienced in computer science. The book is oriented toward this end and the material is covered in three major sections, including ten chapters, and three appendices. Part One, entitled *Computer and Programming Concepts*, introduces computer systems and devices and programming systems and languages. Part Two, entitled *The Structure of System/370*, covers the System/370 computer architecture including data channel organization and input/output. Part Three, entitled *System/370 Systems and Devices*, describes the System/370 Models 135, 145, 155, and 165, direct-access storage, and input/output devices. The appendices cover: microprogramming, emulation, and compatibility; System/370 operating systems; and a survey of storage hierarchy systems.

The book is intended for the general audience and no specific background, other than an interest in the subject matter, is assumed. The book can be used in three situations:

1. As a general reference for systems programmers and data processing management.
2. As a professional development book for engineers, scientists, system analysts, and programmers.
3. As a textbook for a college or industrial course in *Computers and Programming.**

The book is not intended for use as a System/370 reference manual, but rather as an introduction to its structure and functional capabilities.

It is a pleasure to acknowledge: the cooperation of the IBM Corporation in granting permission to reproduce various figures and illustrations;

*A teacher's manual is available from the publisher for cases where the book has been adopted for classroom use.

the pertinent comments and suggestions on the manuscript by Mr. Morton B. Lurie; the expert editing of Mrs. Karen Boikess; and the careful attention of Mrs. Alberta Gordon and her staff at Van Nostrand Reinhold Company. Again, my wife Margaret deserves special recognition for typing the manuscript and providing a liberal amount of patience and understanding.

Harry Katzan, Jr.

May 1971

CONTENTS

PART ONE: COMPUTER AND PROGRAMMING CONCEPTS

1 COMPUTER SYSTEMS AND DEVICES

1.1 INTRODUCTION

A well-known computer advertisement reads somewhat as follows: "Machines should work. Men should think." Therein lies the essence of computer design and organization. The *raison d'etre* of a computer is to perform a specified class of tasks and the nature of those tasks determines, to a large extent, how the computer is designed and used. Today, most computers are classed as general-purpose computers—which means that they can execute a variety of operations in a prescribed sequence using the functional units of the computer system to satisfy the needs of a given application. It follows, obviously, that as the complexity of a system increases, so does its generality. The process of synthesizing a complete computer system from functional units is referred to as *systems architecture*. Although the architecture of a computer, in itself, does not solve any problems, it *does* provide the functional capability for solving problems. The design of an information retrieval system, for example, must contain an appropriate number of mass storage devices. Similarly, a complex physics problem often requires a computer that can execute arithmetic operations at a high rate of speed.

Another factor that contributes to the generality of most computers is that they are designed to perform basic operations, such as addition, shifting, and data movement. The process of constructing meaningful sequences of basic operations has given rise to a relatively new form of human activity—computer programming. Provided that the functional capability exists in a computer system, a computer program, composed of basic operations, can be developed to perform any definable task within the realm of information processing. Naturally, a complex information processing task usually requires a complex computer program and a simple task frequently requires only a simple program.

This book is concerned with the structure of computers and their functional capability. The art of computer programming, however, is not ignored and many computer topics are introduced from the programming point of view. Also, the second chapter is devoted entirely to programming systems and languages. The remainder of this chapter covers computer systems and devices and emphasizes the functional units that comprise a total computer system.

After this brief introduction, the reader who is experienced in computers and data processing can go directly to Chapter 3 and the System/370 computer. The curious reader may wish to explore the remainder of this chapter and Chapter 2 where more fundamental topics are covered.

1.2 BASIC COMPUTER SYSTEM CONCEPTS

System Components

Much like its human counterpart, the digital computer contains functional components for storage, control, processing, input, and output. All general-purpose computers have components of this sort but differ in the physical characteristics of each. As depicted in Figure 1.1, the control and processing units comprise the *central processing unit*, which controls and executes the basic instructions of the computer. Information (which includes computer instructions and data) is stored in *main storage* and a *secondary storage* device is frequently available for overflow and for holding intermediate results. Input and output units encompass a wide variety of devices ranging from low-speed cards or keyboard entry devices to high-speed magnetic rotating devices (such as drum storage) and wideband data transmission facilities. Although all input to and output from the computer system is controlled by the central processing unit, hardware devices (called *input/output data channels*) are usually available for transferring data between main storage and input/output units independently of the central processing unit, allowing the processing of data to continue.

The Forms of Computer Instructions

The programming of a computer involves the specification of a series of instructions that effectively tell the computer the precise operations that it should perform. As mentioned previously, the computer instructions

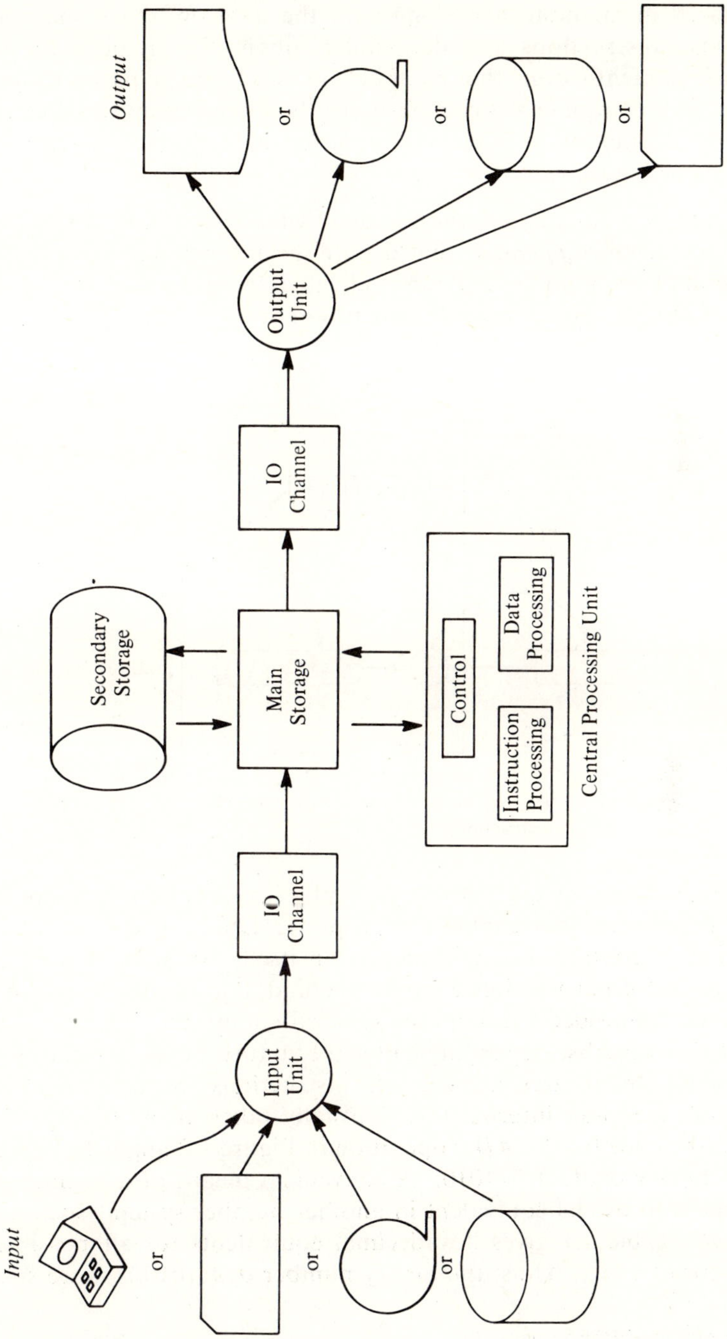

Figure 1.1 Representative components in a computer system.

are stored in main storage along with the data on which the computer operates. Instructions and data differ, obviously, in both format and numeric content—even though they are both coded numerically. The format of a computer instruction varies between computers but requires a minimal amount of information, listed as follows and conceptually depicted in Figure 1.2:

1. An *operation* that tells the computer what function it should perform.
2. One or more *operands* that denote the information upon which the computer should execute the indicated operations.
3. *Modifiers* that augment the operation or operands.

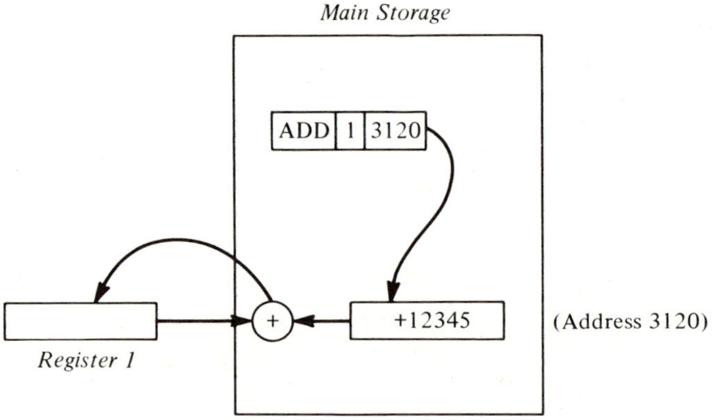

Figure 1.2 The general form and meaning of computer instructions.

An operand can be the address of a physical location in main storage (as in Figure 1.2) that contains appropriate data or it can be an item of information contained in the instruction itself. In some computers, the instruction format requires a single operand, and in others, two or more operands are needed. In addition, several computers* allow instructions of different lengths, depending upon the nature of the operation that is performed. In all cases, however, the instructions are represented in computer storage in an internal form—usually taken to be binary. For example, the code for the *ADD* operation in Figure 1.2 might be represented by the binary digits 01011010. A convenient means of denoting a binary number is to use its equivalent in another number system, such as *hexadecimal*. Table 1.1 gives hexadecimal equivalents for all possible combinations of 4 bits. Thus, the binary number 01011010 is more succinctly

*One of which is the System/370.

TABLE 1.1 HEXADECIMAL EQUIVALENTS FOR ALL POSSIBLE COMBINATIONS OF 4 BITS

Hexadecimal	*Binary*
0	0000
1	0001
2	0010
3	0011
4	0100
5	0101
6	0110
7	0111
8	1000
9	1001
A	1010
B	1011
C	1100
D	1101
E	1110
F	1111

expressed as 5A in the hexadecimal number system. Although mnemonic operation codes, such as *ADD*, are in widespread use, they serve only to facilitate programming and are not directly executable by a computer. The nature of symbolic operation codes and programming languages is covered in the next chapter on programming systems and languages.

The Form of Computer Data

Data are usually dependent upon a particular application and most computers permit data to be stored in a form that facilitates internal representation and computer processing. Fixed-point values, such as +25 or −12.3, are stored in a binary signed magnitude form (see Figure 1.3) or in

+	25
0	0 0 0 0 0 0 0 0 0 0 0 0 0 0 0 0 0 0 0 0 0 0 0 0 0 0 1 1 0 0 1

Figure 1.3 Fixed-point number represented in binary signed-magnitude form.

a decimal number format (see Figure 1.4). Figure 1.4 uses the concept of a *byte*, which contains 8 bits and can hold one character of information or two decimal digits; it is covered in a subsequent section of this chapter. When performing arithmetic on fixed-point data, the programmer must

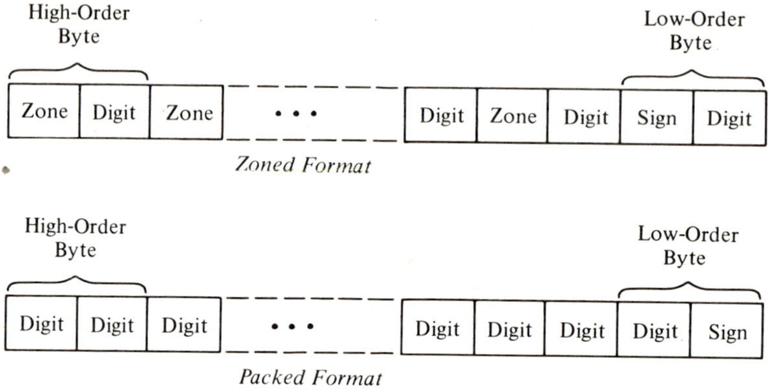

Figure 1.4 Decimal number format.

keep track of the decimal point himself and the circuitry of the computer knows nothing of an implied decimal point.

So-called engineering or scientific notation, such as 3×10^8, is known as floating-point notation in computer terminology and most computers have built-in operations to effectively use floating-point data. Figure 1.5

Figure 1.5 Floating-point format.

Figure 1.6 The value 3×10^8 in simplified decimal format using an excess-64 biased exponent.

gives the general form of floating point format and Figure 1.6 represents the value 3×10^8 is a simplified decimal format. Ordinarily, floating-point format would require a sign for both the number and the exponent; however, a biased exponent* is frequently used to eliminate the need for a sign in the exponent field. Two other types of data are frequently encountered: character data and logical data. Character data is usually stored in a variable-length byte format (see Figure 1.7) and logical data are frequently stored as one or more binary digits (bits).

*A biased exponent refers to the practice of adding a large positive value to the exponent so that it is always positive, eliminating the need for a sign position.

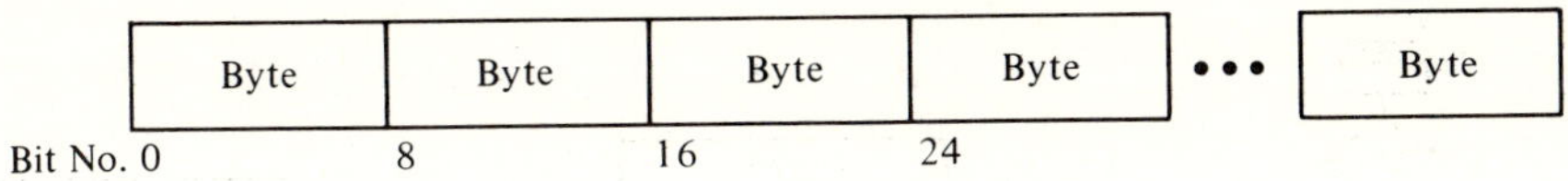

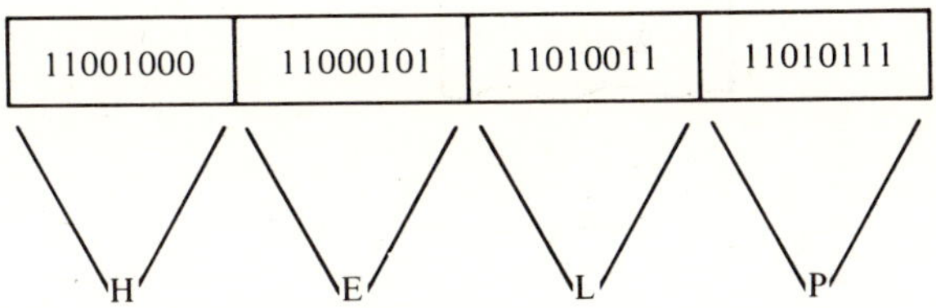

Figure 1.7 Variable-length byte format for character data.

Stored Program Concept

Modern computers use the concept of a stored program, which means that computer instructions and data must be placed in main storage before they can be operated on by the central processing unit. However, instructions and data can be stored on other media when not in use. In the latter case, information can be saved on a storage device for long periods of time or temporarily while the central processing unit is executing another program or using other data.

Instructions and data are both coded in the same form internally to the computer and have the same general appearance—a sequence of bits. If the central processing unit is directed to an item of information when it requires an instruction, then that information is regarded as though it is a computer instruction. Similarly, if the central processing unit is directed to information when it needs an operand, then that information is regarded as data. Normally, an item of information is *not* used as an instruction *and* as data. Usually, there is no specific area of storage for programs (i.e., a sequence of computer instructions) and for data, although each type is frequently grouped together for convenience and for operating efficiency.

The stored program concept has several advantages. First, the central processing unit has access to information at electronic speeds—compared with electromechanical speeds inherent in other devices. Second, programs can be changed readily by simply reading a new set of instructions into storage from an input device. Lastly, a series of instructions can be developed that can effectively modify itself—thus providing a great amount of flexibility.

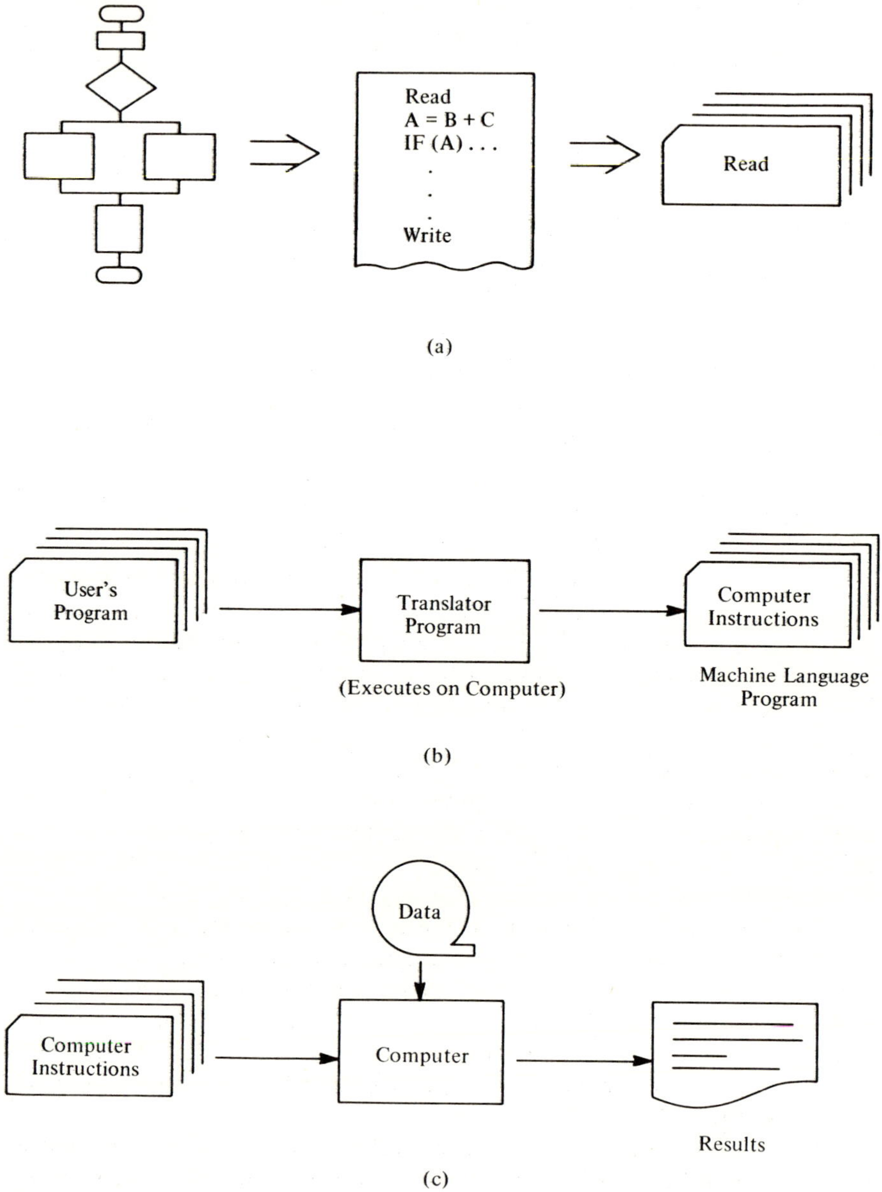

Figure 1.8 Programming and operating concepts. (a) Program preparation. (b) Translation to computer instructions. (c) Execution of user's program.

Programming and Operating Concepts

A fundamental knowledge of the steps involved in developing and running a computer program (i.e., having it executed by the computer) is necessary for an understanding of basic computer concepts. Much of the material is amplified in Chapter 2 in the context of programming systems and languages. The development process is depicted in Figure 1.8 and is summarized as a list of distinct steps.

1. The user prepares his program (often regarded as a series of statements) in a programming language (such as FORTRAN or COBOL) or a machine-oriented language (called assembler language).
2. The program is translated to computer instructions and data by another computer program, called a compiler or an assembler.
3. The user's program is loaded into the computer by a loader program and execution of the user's program is initiated.
4. The user's program reads data from an input device, performs calculations, and writes results to an output device. The classical scientific computer program reads a small amount of data, performs numerous calculations, and writes a small amount of output data. On the other hand, the classical business data processing program is known to read and write large amounts of information but performs few calculations. Obviously, most computer applications fall somewhere between these extremes.

The realm of computer applications has become quite diversified to the extent that: (1) Input and output devices may be located miles from the computer and are connected to it via telephone lines; (2) several users' programs can share the same computer system; and (3) computers now have sufficient speed and flexibility that they can be used in conjunction with physical processes on a real-time basis.

The effectiveness of a total computer system is a function of four important factors: (1) The basic speed of the circuitry from which the functional units are constructed; (2) the internal organization of the functional units; (3) the manner in which the functional units are combined to form the total system; and (4) the programs available for using the computer. Each of these factors is emphasized in the remainder of this chapter and in the other chapters of the book.

1.3 MAIN STORAGE

To a large extent, the functioning of the entire computer system is based on the organization and implementation of main storage. Several characteristics are of particular interest: (1) The physical storage media; (2) the manner in which storage is organized and accessed; and (3) the physical arrangement of storage elements.

By definition, main storage must be directly addressable by and must operate at speeds approaching that of the central processing unit. Information is stored as bits (i.e., binary digits) and a bit can be physically implemented in expensive high-speed circuitry or by a less expensive lower-speed physical process such as magnetic cores, thin film, or plated wire. The most widely used means for implementing main storage is with magnetic cores* and the name *core storage* is often used synonymously with the words main storage.

Organization and Addressing

The function of the *storage unit* of the computer is to hold instructions and data and each item of information is located at a specific place in main storage; that location is termed its *storage address*. The manner in which storage is organized determines to a great extent how a specific location is addressed. In early computers, storage was organized on a *word* basis with each word being composed of a finite number of digits.† Each word was assigned a physical address and that word could represent an instruction, a data item, or a fixed number of characters. Figure 1.9 depicts typical word formats in a representative word-oriented computer. Currently, most word-oriented computers are used for scientific applications since the processing of nonnumeric or variable-length data tends to be cumbersome.

The storage organization used with the System/360 and System/370 computers, as well as others, is both byte and word addressable; it provides for more efficient use of storage, allows high effective input/output rates to be sustained, and facilitates computer programming. With this type of storage, the basic addressable unit is an 8-bit byte—a unit that can represent one character, two decimal digits, or eight data bits. It follows that a sequence of bytes can be combined to form the following:

1. one of several different fixed-sized words;
2. variable-length character data;
3. variable-length decimal data;
4. fixed- or variable-length logical data.

Figure 1.10 depicts address formats for byte-addressable storage. Data are always located by the address of their leftmost byte and the length

*A discussion of magnetic storage devices can be found in almost any book on programming or on computer design. A good suggestion might be C. Foster, "*Computer Architecture*," Van Nostrand Reinhold Co., New York, 1970.

†Usually, a word is considered to be composed of binary digits; however, on some computers, a word is regarded as a fixed number of decimal digits—each suitably encoded.

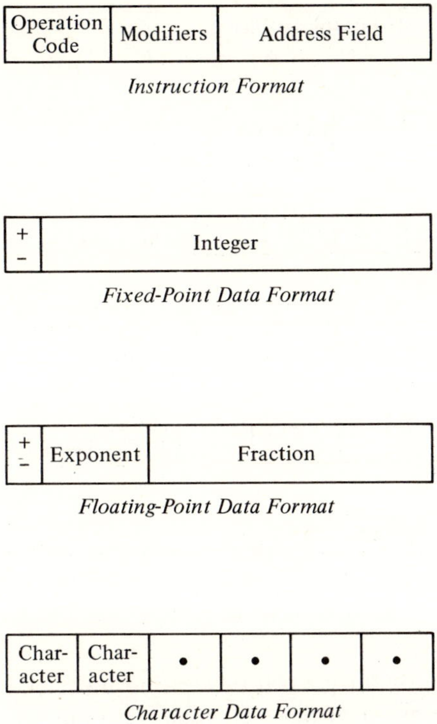

Figure 1.9 Typical instruction and data formats in a representative word-oriented computer.

and type attributes are implicit in the computer operation that uses those data. The fixed-point data format uses half and full words and rarely exceeds the size of a full word in length. The need for an exponent requires at least a full word to represent a floating-point number with double words being used when a higher precision fraction is desired. An extended precision floating-point number that uses 128 bits is also available on the System/370. Computer instructions that operate on variable-length data specify the address of the first (leftmost) byte of each operand and the length of at least one of the operands in bytes, regardless if characters or packed decimal digits are being represented.

Large Capacity Storage

Large capacity storage* (LCS) is high-speed addressable bulk storage. LCS is usually combined with main storage to form a hierarchy of storage

*Also known as large core storage.

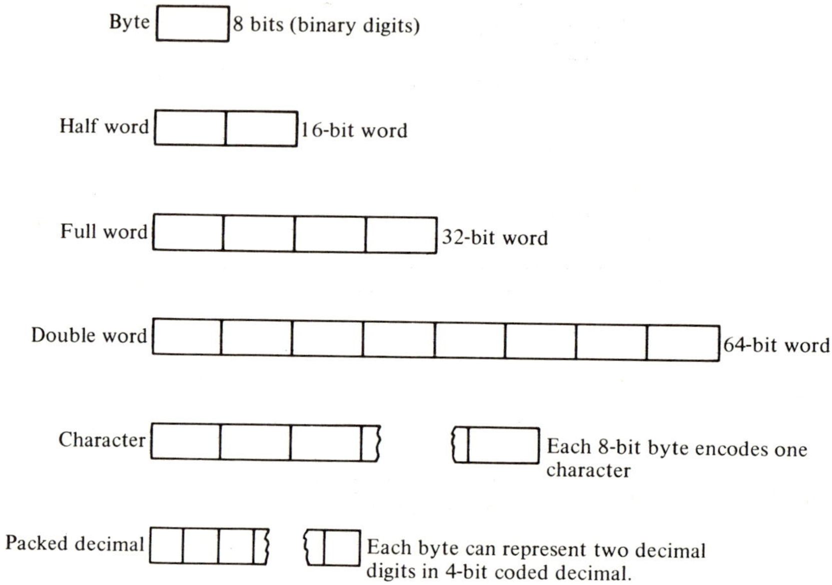

Figure 1.10 Address formats in byte-addressable storage.

directly addressable by the central processing unit. Addresses in LCS are regarded as an extension of main storage—although the time required to obtain information from large capacity storage is considerably greater than from main storage. When executing instructions out of LCS or using data that are stored there, performance of the central processing unit is degraded in the sense that execution times would be lower if the same information were held in main storage. For some applications, it is efficient to transfer instructions or data to main storage before processing, and in other cases, the overhead involved is not justified. Sophisticated algorithms have been developed for allocating large capacity storage and for determining the manner in which it is used.

Scratch Pad Storage

Another level of storage that is occasionally used is known as *scratch pad storage*. Scratch pad storage is a relatively small part of main storage that is implemented by using a very fast storage technology—such as thin film.* The scratch pad storage locations are known to the programmer who can use them to best advantage for improving system performance.

*Thin film storage (or memory, as it is called) is manufactured by depositing very thin spots of a metallic alloy on a ceramic plate. The metallic spot is used much like a magnetic core and allows for much faster switching times.

A frequently used application is to reduce the time required for an iterative procedure by executing the loop from scratch pad locations. When scratch pad storage is limited, it is often used by the operating system control program* for critical functions.

Access

One of the critical factors in the design of a storage system is known as *access time*—the time required to obtain a fixed amount of information from storage. When ferrite cores are used as the storage technology, access is governed by the storage cycle time which involves a read-out and a write-back. The write-back is required because it is necessary to reset the cores to zero during the read-out process. Consider Figure 1.11. At

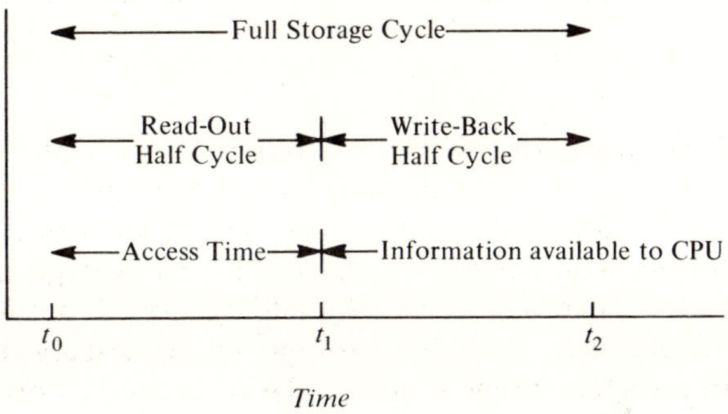

Figure 1.11 Access and storage cycle time.

time t_0, the central processing unit sends a control pulse to the storage unit to initiate a storage cycle. At time t_1, the information is available to the central processing unit and processing may proceed. The time fron t_0 to t_1 is called the *access time*. The write-back takes the time from t_1 to t_2 during which the storage unit is said to be busy. This restriction is often relieved by interleaving storage as described in a subsequent section.

Usually, the write-back of information immediately follows the read-out of that information from main storage. Some high-performance computer systems allow information to be altered by one or more computer operations before it is written back—a process known as a *split cycle*. In general, however, the write-back is completed before another read-out is initiated.

Synchronous and Asynchronous Operation

When the central processing unit and main storage operate in conjunction with each other in real time, the system is said to operate in the synchro-

*Control programs are discussed in Chapter 2.

nous mode of operation. Each storage cycle is synchronized with a central processing unit execution cycle. In the synchronous mode of operation, the entire system operates at the speed of the slowest unit. Moreover, when a central processing unit or storage unit operation requires more than one cycle, the other is forced to remain idle. Although a system that operates synchronously is easier to design, it effectively forces the central processing unit to operate at storage speeds.

The next advance beyond synchronous operation was to uncouple storage and the central processing unit allowing each unit to operate independently of the other. This design philosophy—called *asynchronous operation*—allows the functioning of the storage unit and the central processing unit to overlap so that the execution of one instruction is effectively overlapped, in time, with the access of data for a subsequent instruction.

Interleaving

When improving the performance of a computer system, the designer first considers the basic speed of the components and circuitry. If the state of the art has been pushed to the limit in that regard, the designer seeks improvements through functional organization. In storage organization, speed enhancements can be achieved by adding storage modules that can be accessed in parallel. The full storage cycle, discussed previously, applies only to a single storage module. Thus, multiple storage units can be cycled independently—provided that control circuits are available for each.

Consider a main storage organized as two independent arrays. The first, *Array 1*, contains all the even-numbered addresses, and the second, *Array 2*, contains all the odd-numbered addresses. Storage locations alternate between the two arrays, and, in this case, storage is said to be *two-way interleaved.* If sequential locations are accessed, as in Figure 1.12(a), then the overlap exhibited in Figure 1.12(b) could be achieved through interleaving. By effectively eliminating the write-back portion of the storage cycle, the average storage cycle time for two-way interleaving is reduced, theoretically, to one-half of its previous value. Some high-performance computer systems have used up to 16-way interleaving allowing simultaneous access to 128 bytes of information.

Buffer Storage

Another technique used to compensate for the mismatch in operating speeds of main storage and the central processing unit is buffer storage. A similar technique known as input/output buffering is frequently used to interface the relatively slow speeds of input/output units to the higher speeds of main storage and the central processing unit.

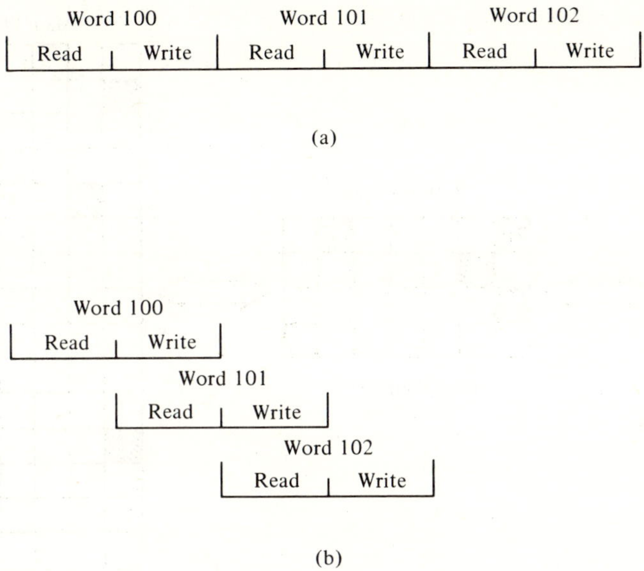

Figure 1.12 Sequential access to interleaved and noninterleaved storage. (a) Conventional storage (not interleaved). (b) Two-way interleaved storage.

Buffer storage is an extremely fast storage module, implemented in high-speed circuitry,* that is used as a buffer between the central processing unit and main storage. The characteristic features of buffer storage are that it is organized into fixed-size blocks† of information, as is main storage, and that it permits nondestructive read out. The first time that the central processing unit references a block (usually it references only a part of it), the entire block is moved from main storage to the buffer. Subsequent references to that block need only access the buffer, resulting in a substantial improvement in system performance. Since computer instructions and data tend to "cluster" in main storage, it is estimated that over 90% of all storage accesses can be made from the buffer in a typical system. Figure 1.13 depicts a typical buffer storage system. The contents of the buffer are maintained dynamically by a buffer control unit, using an appropriate algorithm, and its operation is completely transparent to the programmer. The details of buffer storage management in different computer systems tend to differ with respect to specific features. In general, however, the complexity of the replacement techniques is related to the performance requirements of the computer system.

*Such as bipolar monolithic chips mounted on a solid logic technology (SLT) substrate.
†A typical block might contain 32 bytes of information.

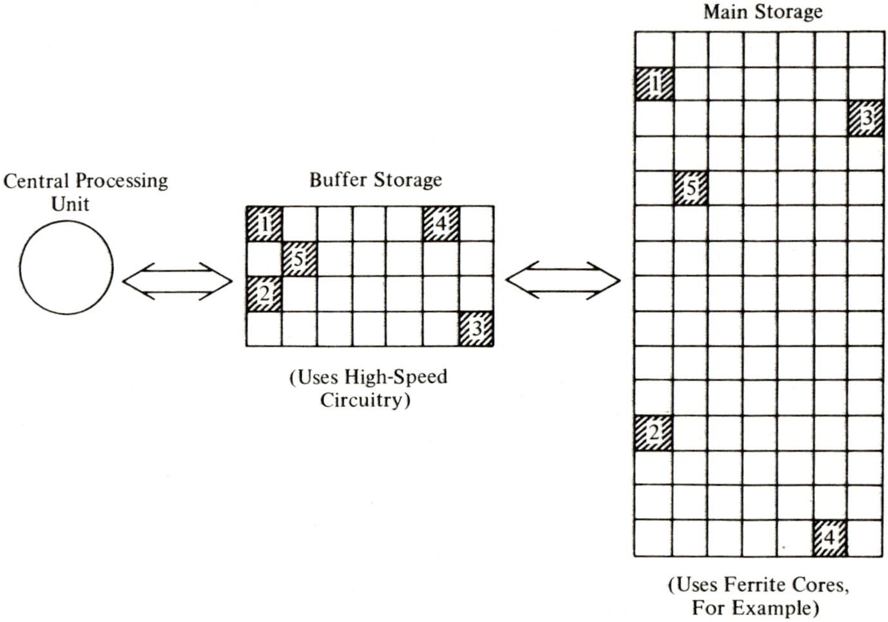

Figure 1.13 Buffer storage.

Storage Protection

Modern computer systems provide operating programs that effectively allow several users to share the same machine—a technique referred to as time-sharing or multiprogramming. When different programs share the same main storage, a storage protection mechanism is usually available to prevent one program from making storage accesses to a space occupied by another program.

A method of implementing storage protection is to divide main storage into blocks* and to associate a *storage key* with each of these blocks. Associated with each active program is a *protection key*, which is the same size as the storage key. When the keys match or the protection key is zero, then a storage operation into that block is permitted. Otherwise, the storage operation is inhibited and an alarm signal is raised. A fetch protection bit is frequently implemented along with the storage key. If the *fetch protection bit* is zero, protection applies only to a store operation. If the fetch protection bit is one, then protection applies to a fetch operation as well as to a store operation. Usually, the assignment of storage protection keys is managed by the computer system's operating program. Figure 1.14 depicts some representative cases of storage protection.

*System/370 uses 2048-byte blocks for storage protection.

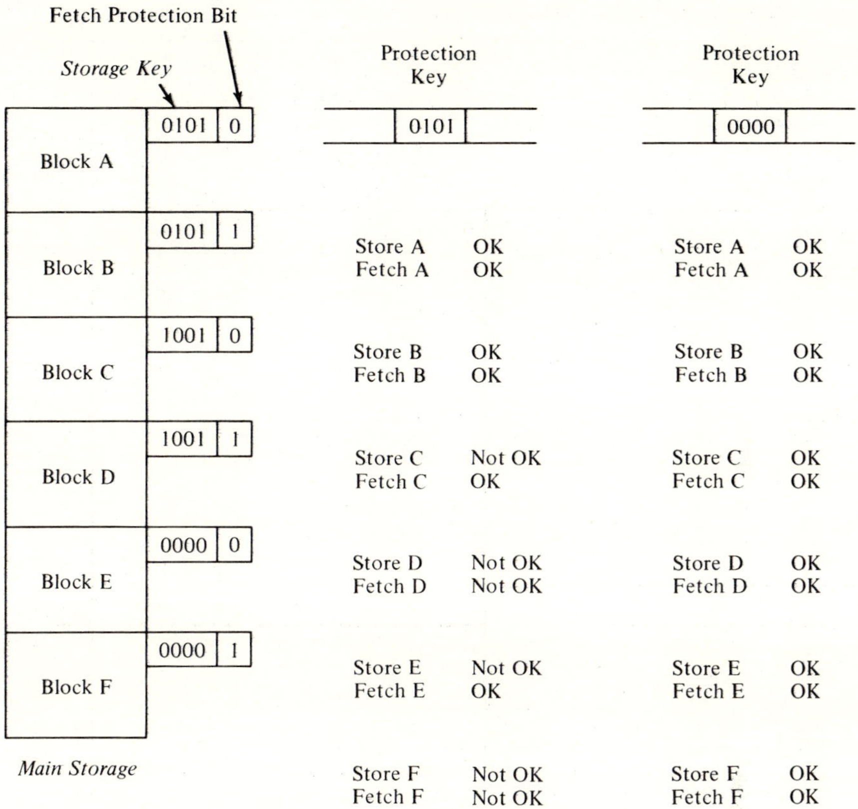

Figure 1.14 Storage protection.

Codes and Data Representation

No introduction to main storage would be complete without an example of how information can be represented in storage. Assume the characters |H|E|L|P| |+|1|3|(| | were punched into 10 columns of an IBM card and these 10 characters were read into byte-addressable computer storage beginning with byte location 83 by an appropriate input operation. The card and storage forms are depicted in Figure 1.15 and use the card-storage equivalents given in Table 1.2. Clearly, each byte combination of 8 bits possesses a related combination of card punches even though many bit patterns do not correspond to printable characters. Thus, any information that can be represented in computer storage can also be recorded on an external medium. For example, consider the fixed-point number 117 stored as the half word (2 bytes) 0000000001110101 in byte-addressable computer storage (see Figure 1.16(a). That information could be punched into an IBM card as punch combinations 12-0-1-8-9

TABLE 1.2 CARD STORAGE EQUIVALENTS[a]

Bit Positions 4, 5, 6, 7	Second Hexadecimal Digit	Digit Punches																	
			00				01				10				11				Bit Positions 0,1
			00	01	10	11	00	01	10	11	00	01	10	11	00	01	10	11	Bit Positions 2,3
			0	1	2	3	4	5	6	7	8	9	A	B	C	D	E	F	First Hexadecimal Digit
			12				12	12		12	12	12		12	12				Zone Punches
				11				11	11	11		11	11	11		11			Zone Punches
					0		0		0	0	0		0	0			0		Zone Punches
			9	9	9	9	9	9	9	9									Digit Punches
0000	0	8-1	(1) NUL	(2) DLE	(3) DS	(4)	(5) SP	(6) &	(7) -	(8)					(9)	(10)	(11)	(12) 0	8-1
0001	1	1	SOH	DC1	SOS				(13) /		a	j			A	J	(14)	1	1
0010	2	2	STX	DC2	FS	SYN					b	k	s		B	K	S	2	2
0011	3	3	ETX	TM							c	l	t		C	L	T	3	3
0100	4	4	PF	RES	BYP	PN					d	m	u		D	M	U	4	4
0101	5	5	HT	NL	LF	RS					e	n	v		E	N	V	5	5
0110	6	6	LC	BS	ETB	UC					f	o	w		F	O	W	6	6
0111	7	7	DEL	IL	ESC	EOT					g	p	x		G	P	X	7	7
1000	8	8		CAN							h	q	y		H	Q	Y	8	8
1001	9	8-1		EM							i	r	z		I	R	Z	9	9
1010	A	8-2	SMM	CC	SM		¢	!	(15)	:									8-2
1011	B	8-3	VT	CU1	CU2	CU3	.	$	,	#									8-3
1100	C	8-4	FF	IFS		DC4	<	*	%	@									8-4
1101	D	8-5	CR	IGS	ENQ	NAK	(	)	_	'									8-5
1110	E	8-6	SO	IRS	ACK		+	;	>	=									8-6
1111	F	8-7	SI	IUS	BEL	SUB	|	¬	?	"									8-7
			12				12				12	12		12	12	12		12	Zone Punches
				11				11				11	11	11		11	11	11	Zone Punches
					0				0		0		0	0	0		0	0	Zone Punches
			9	9	9	9									9	9	9	9	

Card Hole Patterns

(1)	12-0-9-8-1	(5)	No Punches	(9)	12-0	(13)	0-1
(2)	12-11-9-8-1	(6)	12	(10)	11-0	(14)	11-0-9-1
(3)	11-0-9-8-1	(7)	11	(11)	0-8-2	(15)	12-11
(4)	12-11-0-9-8-1	(8)	12-11-0	(12)	0		

Control Character Representations

ACK	Acknowledge	EOT	End of Transmission	PF	Punch Off
BEL	Bell	ESC	Escape	PN	Punch On
BS	Backspace	ETB	End of Transmission Block	RES	Restore
BYP	Bypass	ETX	End of Text	RS	Reader Stop
CAN	Cancel	FF	Form Feed	SI	Shift In
CC	Cursor Control	FS	Field Separator	SM	Set Mode
CR	Carriage Return	HT	Horizontal Tab	SMM	Start of Manual Message
CU1	Customer Use 1	IFS	Interchange File Separator	SO	Shift Out
CU2	Customer Use 2	IGS	Interchange Group Separator	SOH	Start of Heading
CU3	Customer Use 3	IL	Idle	SOS	Start of Significance
DC1	Device Control 1	IRS	Interchange Record Separator	SP	Space
DC2	Device Control 2	IUS	Interchange Unit Separator	STX	Start of Text
DC4	Device Control 4	LC	Lower Case	SUB	Substitute
DEL	Delete	LF	Line Feed	SYN	Synchronous Idle
DLE	Data Link Escape	NAK	Negative Acknowledge	TM	Tape Mark
DS	Digit Select	NL	New Line	UC	Upper Case
EM	End of Medium	NUL	Null	VT	Vertical Tab
ENQ	Enquiry				

Special Graphic Characters

¢	Cent Sign	-	Minus Sign, Hyphen
.	Period, Decimal Point	/	Slash
<	Less-than Sign	,	Comma
(	Left Parenthesis	%	Percent
+	Plus Sign	_	Underscore
|	Logical OR	>	Greater-than Sign
&	Ampersand	?	Question Mark
!	Exclamation Point	:	Colon
$	Dollar Sign	#	Number Sign
*	Asterisk	@	At Sign
)	Right Parenthesis	'	Prime, Apostrophe
;	Semicolon	=	Equal Sign
¬	Logical NOT	"	Quotation Mark

[a] Courtesy of IBM Corporation.

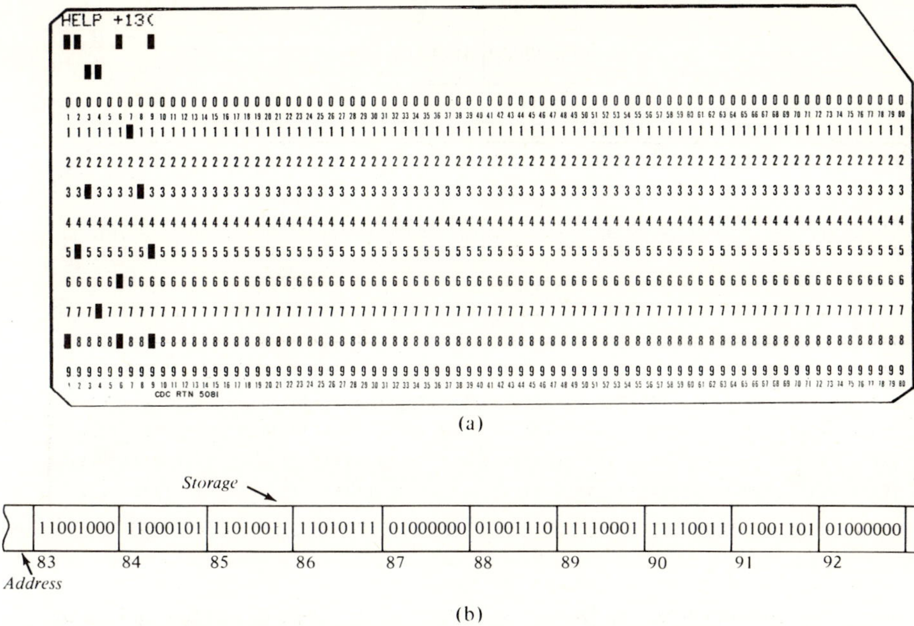

Figure 1.15 Representation of ten characters from a punched card in byte-addressable computer storage using IBM Extended Binary Coded Decimal Interchange Code (EBCDIC). (a) Punched card created with the IBM 029 card punch. (Courtesy of IBM Corporation.) (b) Representation of the first ten characters of the above card in byte-addressable computer storage beginning with location 83.

and 12-11-0-5-9 (see Figure 1.16(b), even though neither combination corresponds to a standard printable character.

1.4 CENTRAL PROCESSING UNIT

The central processing unit (CPU) controls the operation of the entire computer system. All storage references, calculations, and input/output operations are either performed by the CPU or are initiated by it. The CPU is directed, in a sense, by a series of computer instructions, developed by a programmer, that reside in main storage. The CPU can only operate on instructions stored in main storage and instructions stored elsewhere must be loaded into main storage before they can be used by the CPU. The form of a computer instruction has been described previously; the manner in which it is used is described here.

In support of its basic function—that is, to decode and execute computer instructions—the central processing unit includes four major com-

00000000	01110101

(a)

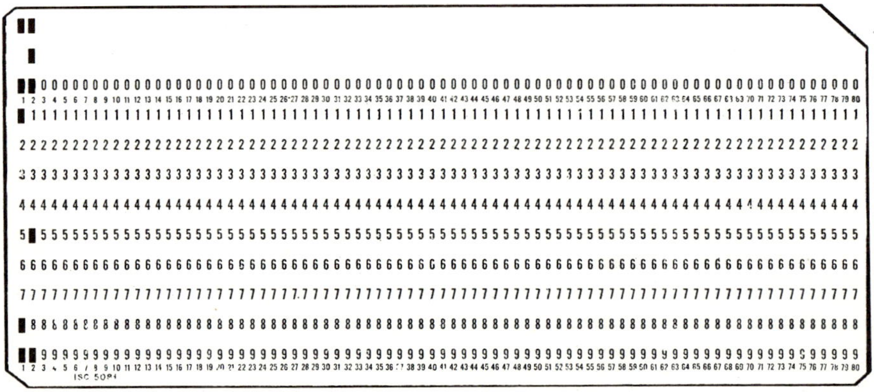

(b)

Figure 1.16 Representation of fixed-point information in computer storage and on an external medium. (a) Half word (2 bytes) representation of the fixed-point number 117 (117 to base 10 equals 165 to base 8 which equals 01110101 to base 2). (b) Representation of the above half word on a punched card using the storage-card equivalents in Table 1.2.

ponents: a control unit, an arithmetic and logical unit, local storage, and several functional elements used by the entire CPU.

Control Unit

The control unit obtains instructions from main storage, decodes them, calculates addresses of operands, prefetches instruction operands, generates internal signals to the arithmetic and logical unit so that appropriate operations are performed, and keeps track of the program address. Computer instructions relating to sequence and control, in many cases, are also processed by the control unit. In most computers, instructions are decoded and executed in a sequential manner. In high-performance computers, however, instructions are frequently obtained from main storage and decoded ahead of time, allowing the arithmetic and logical unit(s) to operate at optimum speed.

Arithmetic and Logical Unit

The arithmetic and logical unit contains the registers and circuitry necessary to execute the fixed-point, floating-point, logical, and variable-length operations of the computer. To some extent, the level of sophistication of the computer is reflected in the arithmetic and logical unit. For example, some high-performance systems contain multiple subunits for fixed, floating, and logical operations so that execution can proceed in parallel.

The basic design of the computer is also reflected in the addressable registers used to hold intermediate values during data manipulation and to maintain index values during addressing. The terminology "addressable registers" denotes a temporary storage location, implemented in high-speed circuitry, for holding fixed-length computer words. A register of this type is directly addressable, either explicitly or implicitly, by a computer program. Addressable registers are classed as *local storage*.

Local Storage and Addressing

In general, three methods exist for temporarily storing intermediate values during data manipulation operations. The first method involves *no* addressable registers and requires that all operations operate from *storage to storage*. Since most operations require two operands, two storage requests and a store are required for each operation—a technique considered to be inefficient of computer time, except when variable-length operands are involved.

Another approach is to have a pair of registers: an *accumulator* and an extension to it called a *multiplier-quotient* register, which is included for use in multiplicative and shifting operations. The accumulator and multiplier-quotient registers can hold either fixed-point, floating-point, or logical operands but require that frequent intermediate "stores" to main storage be made during execution of a program so that other operations can use the registers. Figure 1.17 shows how an addressable register is used. Clearly, all calculations are made with the contents of that register as one of the operands and all "loads" and "stores" are made to or from it.

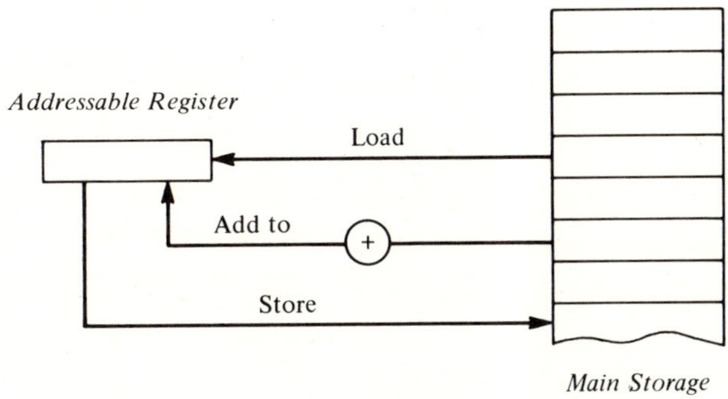

Figure 1.17 Use of an addressable register.

The last method in widespread use provides several distinct registers for use in fixed and floating-point operations, thereby reducing the number of intermediate "stores" to main storage. The System/370, for example, provides 16 4-byte fixed-point registers (called general registers) and 4 8-byte floating-point registers.

When addressing consecutive locations in storage or selecting an element of an array, it is frequently desirable to maintain an index and add that index value to a base address to determine an actual storage location. This technique facilitates programming by requiring only that the index be changed when it is desired to reference another storage location with the same instruction. In computers with single accumulators, another type of addressable register called an *index register* is used to hold index values. The number of the index register is maintained in the modifier portion of the computer instruction and the contents of that index register are added to the address field (contained in the instruction) by the control unit to form an *effective address*. The effective address is then used to reference main storage as depicted in Figure 1.18. When index registers are built into a computer, appropriate computer instructions are available for loading, storing, and modifying the contents of those registers.

In computers with several addressable registers, fixed-point registers are frequently used for indexing, eliminating the need for special index registers. This design philosophy facilitates the execution of arithmetic opera-

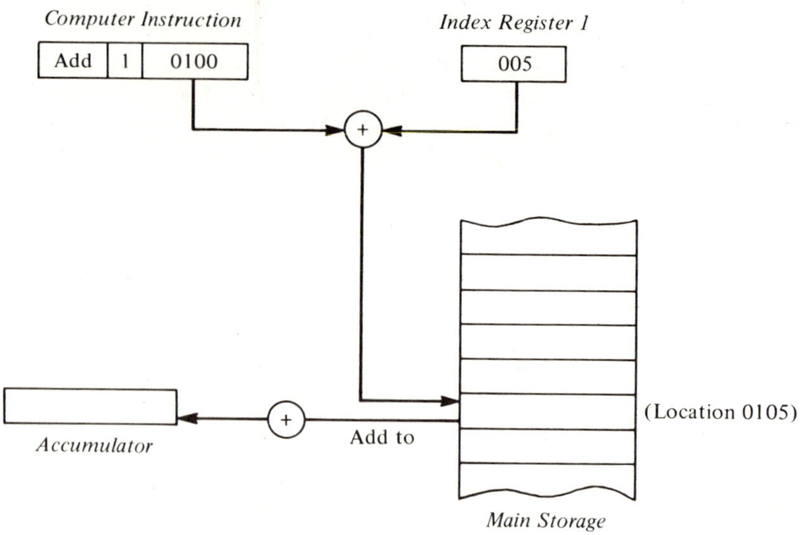

Figure 1.18 Effective addressing.

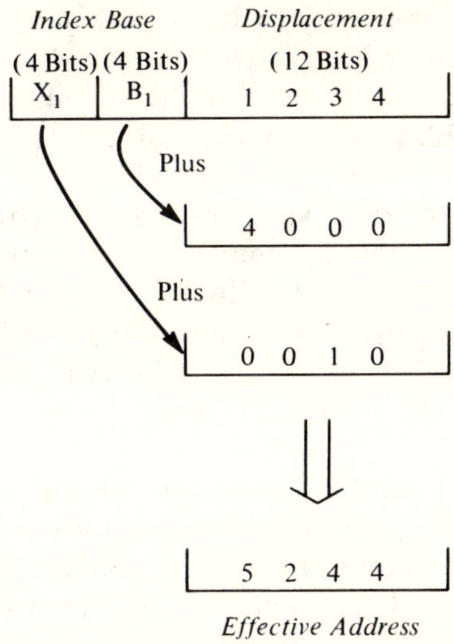

Figure 1.19 Effective addressing in System/370.

tions on index values and provides flexibility in the range of index values that can be used in address calculations.

One of the problems in addressing large amounts of storage is that the size of the address field becomes excessively large to be included in a single computer instruction. The solution to this problem used with System/370 is to structure an effective address into three parts: index, base address, and displacement. Therefore, a single computer instruction need contain only the following information for addressing:

1. the number of the general-purpose register that contains a base address;
2. the number of the general-purpose register that contains an index value; and
3. a displacement field that contains only the difference between a storage location and the base address.

Base/index/displacement addressing is depicted in Figure 1.19; it allows a very large amount of directly addressable main storage to be used without requiring special programming procedures.

Control Storage

The transfer of information within the control unit of a computer can be likened to the transfer of information, under control of a program, within the computer itself. The sequence of operations, performed by the control unit, is considered to be a *microprogram.* In some computers, the control unit is completely hardwired and the specific microfunctions that are executed by it are rarely considered. Other computers, such as the System/370, permit the control unit to be programmed using a series of microinstructions. A meaningful set of microinstructions is termed a microprogram. Instead of performing conditional, arithmetic, or logical operations as ordinary computer instructions do, microinstructions perform control functions within the control unit of the CPU. With an appropriate microprogram, one computer (like the System/370) can be made to function like another computer (like the IBM 1401). The process of making one computer function like another is termed *emulation*.

When a computer operates under control of a microprogram, that microprogram is stored in an area called *control storage*. Control storage comes in two varieties: read-only storage (ROS) and writeable control storage (WCS). Read-only storage is usually provided by the computer manufacturer and cannot be modified by the user. Writeable control storage can be modified under program control or be loaded from the computer operator's console.

Sequence and Control

The state of the computer, at any point in time, can be determined from the contents of local storage and a status word* that is maintained by the control unit. The *status word* contains the following kinds of information:

1. the location of the current instruction in main storage;
2. the storage protection key (mentioned previously);
3. interruption codes;
4. a condition code; and
5. miscellaneous status indicators that are specific to a particular computer.

One of the most important status indicators determines whether the computer is in the supervisor state or the problem state. When a computer program executes in the *supervisor state*, all of the facilities of the computer system are available to that program. Computer operating programs normally execute in the supervisor state. Programs that execute in the *problem state* are limited in function and, as a result, cannot affect the execution of another user's program. The typical business or scientific applications program normally executes in the problem state.

Each time the computer executes an instruction, the address of the

*The status word is called the *program status word* (PSW) in System/370.

current instruction which is maintained in the status word is increased by the size of that instruction. When the control unit needs another instruction, it automatically references the storage address that is specified in the status word. In other words, the computer normally executes instructions that are stored sequentially in main storage. Instructions are executed sequentially until one of two conditions arises:

1. An instruction is executed that alters the sequential order; or
2. an independent event interrupts normal computer processing.

An independent event that interrupts normal computer processing is called an *interruption* and can occur for one of many reasons:

1. A program, in execution, encounters an erroneous or unusual condition;
2. a device external to the central processing unit needs attention;
3. the circuitry of the computer detects a malfunction; or
4. a program executing in the problem state requires services that are available only in the supervisor state.

An interruption is processed automatically by the CPU as follows:

1. The state of the system is switched to the supervisor state (if it is not in the supervisor state already);
2. the computer status word is saved; and
3. control of the computer is switched to a program designed to process interruptions of the type received.

In modern computers, operating programs* rely heavily on the interruption mechanism. The CPU is turned over to a problem program for execution, by the operating program. That problem program executes until an interruption occurs. The operating program is activated by the interruption and performs "housekeeping" instructions and processing appropriate to that event. When the operating program has no more processing to perform, it again dispatches the CPU to a problem program.

Types of Computer Instructions

Computer instructions fall into well-defined categories depending on the functions they perform and the kinds of data they require.

Arithmetic instructions include the fixed-point, floating-point, and decimal operations necessary for performing arithmetic computations

*It is appropriate to mention at this point the difference between operating programs and problem programs. Operating programs (usually called operating systems) are concerned with the operational aspects of the computer system. Problem programs, on the other hand, perform the computer processing for a particular application.

with a computer. Also included in this category are operations for comparing numbers and for converting numbers from one base to another.

Logical instructions perform operations on bytes and bits. Included in this category are operations for data movement, logical comparing, testing, translating, and data editing.

Branching instructions provide the user with a decision-making capability and enable a program to depart from the sequential order of execution. The control point in a program is usually changed in one of three ways: unconditionally, conditionally, and conditionally while modifying the contents of a counter.

Input and output instructions initiate the transfer of information between main storage and external devices. Operations in this category also permit the testing of the status of specific devices and allow control functions to be performed, when required.

Status switching instructions allow the storage keys and the status word to be "loaded" and "stored" under control of an executing program. Operations in this category effectively change the status of the computer between the supervisor and problem states and enable or disable interrupts from taking place.

The number of different instructions in a typical general-purpose computer can easily total in the hundreds. A good rule of thumb, although by no means a standard or design feature, is that more sophisticated computers include instructions for most basic functions that the programmer might want to have performed supplemented by additional instructions that facilitate programming or improve performance. Less sophisticated (and usually less expensive) computers include the most frequently used basic instructions and require that the programmer synthesize sequences of instructions to construct the other basic functions.

1.5 INPUT AND OUTPUT CONTROL

The input and output of information in modern computers is complicated and most computer manufacturers provide programs that function as input/output control systems (IOCS) or data management systems to facilitate the use of different input/output devices. This discussion does not include control systems of this sort; rather, it concerns the physical hardware units and how they function.

An input/output unit is a device for transferring information between the main storage of the computer and appropriate external media for storing information. External devices and their respective media are classified according to the speed with which information can be accessed and the amount of information that can be stored. However, the total process is more complicated, and other hardware units, which perform important functions, are required.

In general, an input/output operation is initiated by a computer instruction that generates a command to an input/output channel. The input/output channel passes the command to a control unit that decodes the command and controls the operation of a specific input or output device. Some devices can be used as an input or an output device—for example, a magnetic tape unit. Other devices serve only as an input device or only as an output device; a card reader is an example of a device that can be used only for input and a card punch can be used only for output. Figure 1.20 depicts a typical input/output configuration including all of the above concepts.

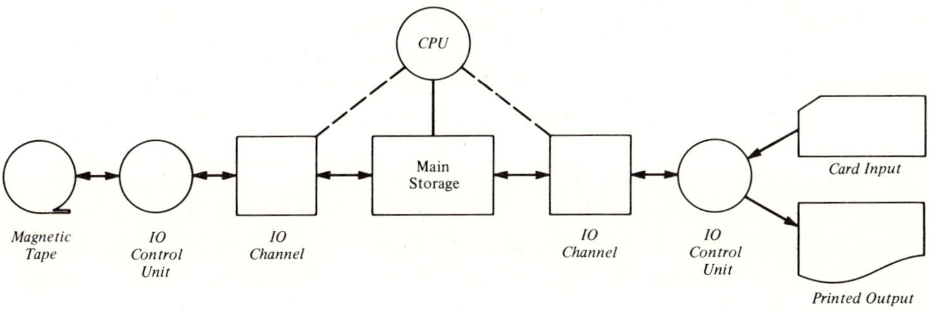

Figure 1.20 Sample input/output subsystem depicting a card reader, printer, and magnetic tape.

Because of the high frequency with which the words "input/output" are used, they are abbreviated here as "IO."

Input/Output Channels

The input/output channels (i.e., IO channels) are more responsible for the high performance of modern computers than any other single piece of equipment. An IO channel is located very close to or is integrated into the central processing unit. It has access to main storage and controls* the function of an IO device or a group of IO devices. Similar to the manner in which the central processing unit operates under the control of a program, the IO channel is also commanded by a program—a *channel program*—that is located in main storage. The steps in a CPU

*The fact that an IO channel performs control functions in addition to transferring data between main storage and IO devices has led some authors to refer to it as a *channel controller*. In IBM terminology, however, a channel controller is a unit that controls IO channels.

program are called instructions; the steps in an IO channel program are called commands. A *channel command* tells an IO channel what operation to perform and the main storage address from which information should be obtained or of where it should be stored. Commands also exist that perform control and sensing functions. A channel program is executed by an IO channel independently of the CPU and can step through channel commands in the same way that the CPU steps through computer instructions. An IO channel uses the "interrupt" philosophy to tell the CPU that an event has occurred. When an IO device control unit signals to the IO channel that an operation has been completed, the IO channel sends an interrupt to the CPU specifying that an IO operation has been completed.

The designers of most computers establish a *standard IO interface*, which refers to the amount of data that can pass between an IO channel and a device attached to it at any point in time. Usually, all devices that are attached to a computer system adhere to the standard IO interface.

Because of the electromechanical nature of IO devices and the use of a standard IO interface, the IO channel operates as a data buffer for incoming and outgoing data. The buffering technique is justified for several reasons: (1) the fairly large difference in data rates between main storage and most IO devices; (2) the difference in the amount of information handled, at any point in time, by main storage (usually 4–8 bytes) and an IO device (usually 1 byte); and (3) the fact that several IO channels and the CPU are competing* for access to main storage, and when a channel finally gains access to storage, it is a good policy to transfer enough data to make the effort worthwhile. An IO channel also can and does perform validity checks on incoming and outgoing data. A typical IO interface is depicted in Figure 1.21.

An IO channel is often referred to as a small hardwired CPU because of the diverse tasks that it can perform. In fact, IO channels for some modern computers contain an appropriate amount of read-only storage (ROS) and operate under microprogram control.

The storage facilities required by an IO channel require, minimally for each IO operation, the following kinds of information: a count, main storage address, the main storage address of the IO command, control and status data, and buffer storage area. This storage combined with functional and logical facilities require a certain amount of overhead in physical equipment. At the same time, the data rates of IO devices vary from 3 million bytes per second (BPS) down to 10 BPS. Therefore, the

*Usually, IO channels are assigned a priority and are serviced by the storage control unit in that sequence when requests for storage access are received at the same time. The CPU is frequently assigned the lowest priority, so the process can be thought of as IO channels "stealing" storage cycles from the CPU—referred to as *cycle stealing*.

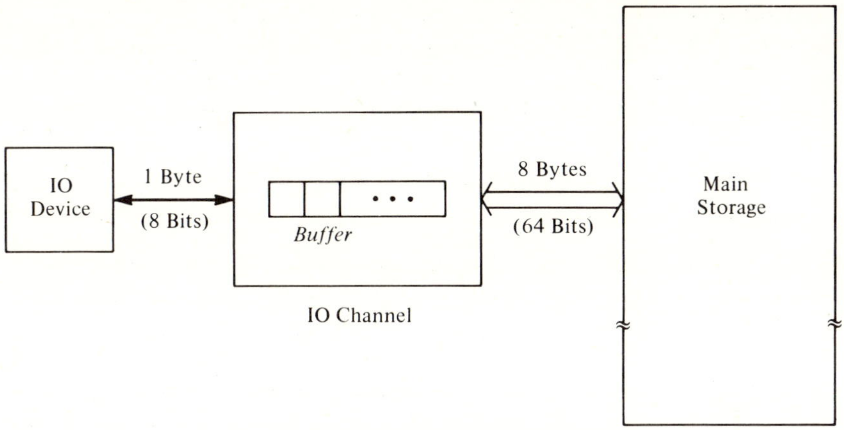

Figure 1.21 Typical IO interface.

economic justification for attaching some classes of IO devices demands that IO channel facilities be shared. In general, logical circuitry in an IO channel is shared and storage facilities (which cost less) are not shared. The portion of an IO channel associated with a specific IO operation is called a *subchannel*, and this is the means by which different types of IO channels are classified. Three kinds of IO channels are identified: selector channel, byte-multiplexer channel, and block-multiplexer channel.

A *selector channel* is intended for attaching high-speed IO devices, such as drum or disk storage. This type of channel contains only one subchannel and can sustain only one data-transfer operation at a time. Once a connection is established between a high-speed device and a selector channel, that connection is maintained until the IO operation has been completed. In other words, the channel is "busy" until that IO operation has been completed.

The *byte multiplexer channel* is intended for attaching multiple low-speed devices and includes multiple subchannels. A byte multiplexer channel can sustain an IO operation on each of its subchannels concurrently. Although a subchannel remains connected to its device for an entire IO operation, it only uses channel facilities during the transfer of a single unit of information, usually taken to be a byte. Thus, many low-speed devices (such as a card reader) can share channel facilities. Some byte multiplexer channels are designed to operate in the *burst* mode for short periods of time to allow medium-speed devices, such as magnetic tape, to be attached. The maximum aggregate data transfer rate of a byte multiplexer channel is governed by logical circuitry and is fixed for a given unit of equipment.

The last type of IO channel is the *block multiplexer channel*; it combines the speed of a selector channel with the interleaved operation of a byte multiplexer channel. The block multiplexer channel is shared by several high-speed devices, operating concurrently, just as the byte multiplexer channel is shared by several low-speed devices. In general, block multiplexer channel facilities are freed during non-data transfer operations (such as a disk seek) so they may be used by another subchannel.

IO Control Units

An IO control unit controls the operation of one or more devices in a given category. Typical kinds of control units are: magnetic tape control units, disk control units, and printer control units. A control unit is frequently integrated into the IO device itself and provides control information to and from an IO device, assigns priorities, and provides status

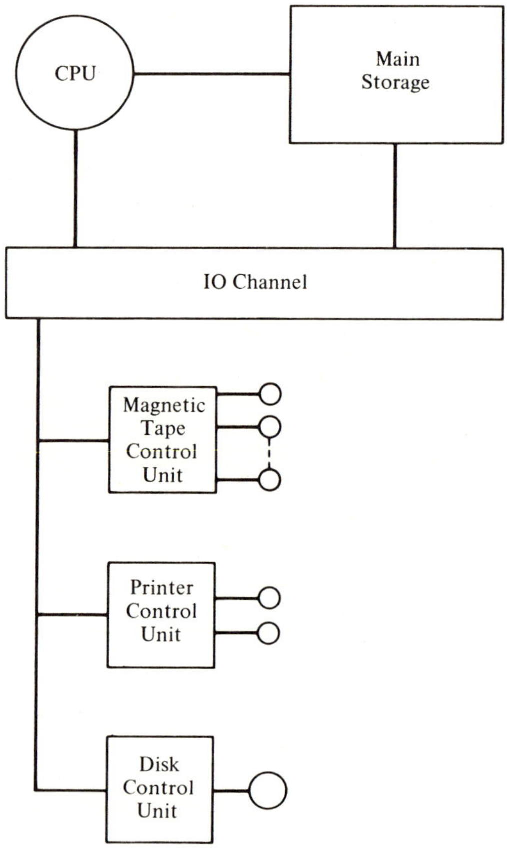

Figure 1.22 Organization of a typical IO subsystem.

information to the IO channel. Organization of a typical IO subsystem is given in Figure 1.22.

Input/Output Devices and the Volume Concept

In a computer, information is stored in main storage on a temporary basis—that is, while that information is being used as instructions or data. External to the computer, information is stored on a medium of some kind, usually on a permanent basis. For example, information stored on a magnetic tape is not destroyed when the power to the computer is turned off. The storage medium should be distinguished, in general, from the IO device that reads or writes the information. Figure 1.23 depicts informa-

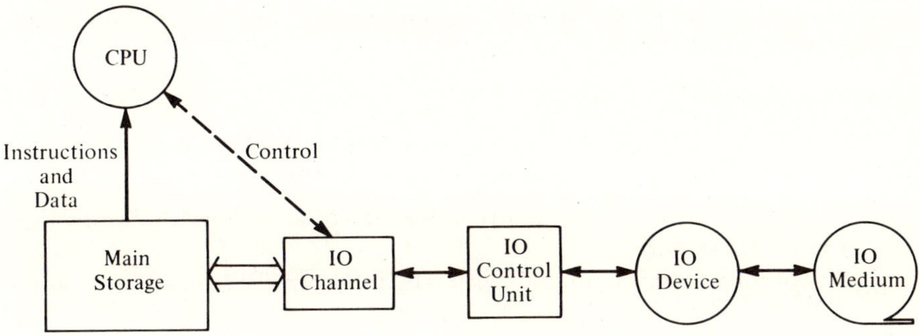

Figure 1.23 Information flow between main storage and an IO medium.

tion flow between main storage and an IO medium, such as magnetic tape. External storage media have names that characterize the functions they serve. When the external medium takes the form of a punched card or printed line, it is regarded as a *unit record* and is used with a *unit record IO device.* For example, printed lines are produced by line printers and punched cards are read by card readers. When the external medium can store several groups of related information, it is referred to as a *volume.* For example, a reel of magnetic tape is frequently called a magnetic tape volume; it is read or written by a magnetic tape device. Disk storage volumes also exist that can be removed from the disk storage device. In any computer system, the number of IO devices is limited by the available equipment. The number of storage volumes is not limited as long as a storage volume can be removed from its IO device.

An IO device is usually classified by whether it is used for mass storage or for input and output. The classification is not exclusive and some devices are used for both purposes.

1.6 MASS STORAGE AND INPUT/OUTPUT DEVICES

Mass storage and input/output devices are usually classified by the media on which the data are recorded. Unit record devices ordinarily pertain to punched cards where each document is a separate transaction such as a set of data, or a source statement from a program. Also included in this category are line printers where each line of printing is a discrete set of characters. Tape devices pertain to magnetic and punched tape where information is recorded serially as a continuous stream. Rotating devices include magnetic disks and magnetic drums where the media are rotated at high speed and recording and reading are performed with electronic read-write heads. The section on terminal devices presents keyboard and cathode ray tube display devices, and the section on miscellaneous devices includes work stations, optical character readers, magnetic card and strip devices, graph plotters, audio response units, and microfilm output facilities.

Unit Record Devices

Unit record devices include punched card readers, card punches, and line printers. Punched cards occur most frequently in two varieties:

1. 80-column cards occasionally referred to as Hollerith cards (see Figure 1.24); and
2. 96-column cards available with IBM System/3 (shown as Figure 1.25).

Punched card readers are electromechanical devices that use optical photocells or sensing brushes to detect the presence or absence of a punch

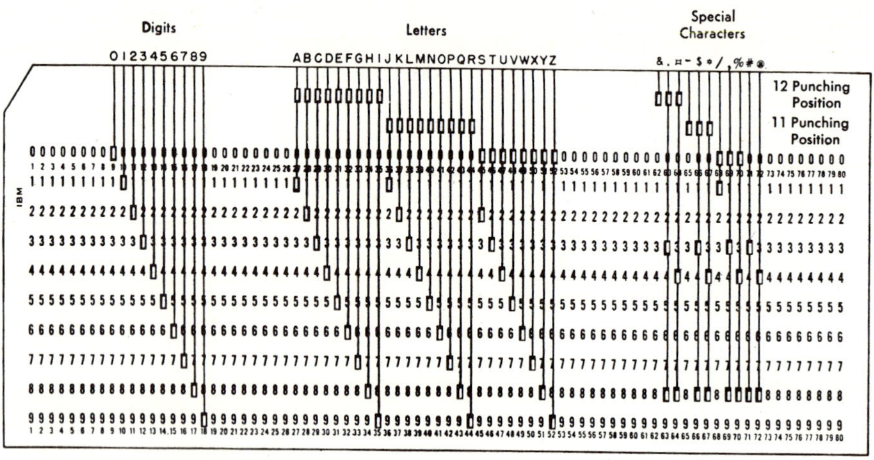

Figure 1.24 80-column card. (Courtesy of IBM Corporation.)

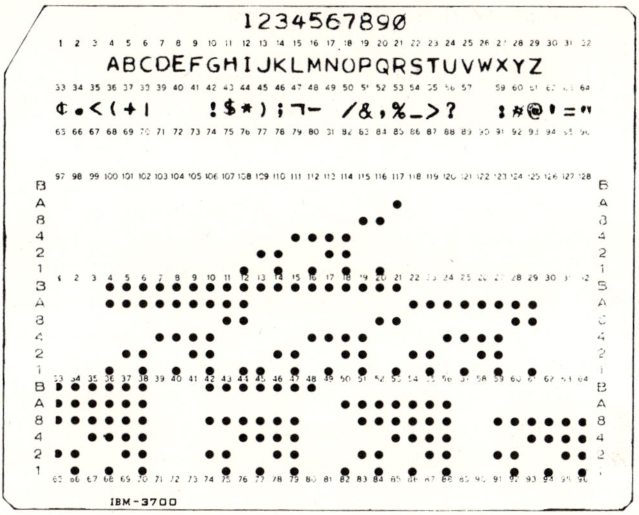

Figure 1.25 96-column card. (Courtesy of IBM Corporation.)

in a particular position on the card. Card punches operate similarly but use mechanical devices to punch holes under control of a computer program or an input/output control device. The speed of card readers ranges from approximately 300 cards per minute to about 1200 cards per minute. Card punches are generally slower and range from approximately 60 cards per minute to about 500 cards per minute.

Line printers print a line of information (usually 120 or 132 characters) at one time by one of two methods:

1. impact printing, and
2. chemical or photographic techniques.

The impact technique is used most frequently because it generally gives better-quality printing—at a loss of line speed. Impact printing uses a type bar, a print wheel, or a print drum and involves impacting the paper (and ribbon) with the printing mechanism or vice versa. Chemical or photographic techniques are generally used in printers with ultra-high line speed but often result in a lower printing quality. The speed of line printers generally ranges from approximately 300 lines per minute to about 2500 lines per minute.

Tape Devices

Tape devices use either magnetic tape or punched tape and provide convenience, low cost, and relatively high speed. The major disadvantage is, of course, that data are stored serially and that access to a particular piece of data often involves searching down the tape until the required information is found.

Punched tape comes in a variety of widths depending upon the number of tracks* recorded. Punch tape readers usually operate at from approximately 250 characters per second to about 1000 characters per second. Tape punches are quite slow with speeds ranging from 50 characters per second to approximately 300 characters per second.

Although magnetic tape is also a serial device, it has some distinct advantages: (1) speed, (2) convenience, (3) capacity, and (4) low cost. Most magnetic tape is either ½ inch or 1 inch wide and is constructed from a plastic-like base coated with iron oxide. The iron oxide is magnetized to indicate the presence of information. Obviously, magnetic tapes differ in length—especially after use. A new reel is approximately 2400 feet in length, costs approximately $20, and can hold significantly more information than $20 worth of punched cards. A 2400-foot reel can hold between one and twenty million characters depending upon the packing density. Table 1.3 gives the data rate for magnetic tape at various forward speeds and at different packing densities. Magnetic tapes are reusable, easy to carry and store, and come in seven-track and nine-track varieties. The choice of seven-track or nine-track is usually dependent upon the internal coding scheme of the main computer.

TABLE 1.3 DATA RATE FOR MAGNETIC TAPE

Tape Speed in		*Density in Bytes Per Inch*		
Inches Per Second	*200*	*556*	*800*	*1600*
36	7,200	20,016	—[a]	—[a]
75	15,000	41,700	60,000	120,000
112.5	22,500	62,550	90,000	180,000
200	—[a]	111,200	160,000	320,000

[a] Not generally available.

Rotating Devices

Rotating devices usually refer to magnetic disk and magnetic drum storage. A magnetic disk unit is a stack of rotating disks in which data are recorded. The number of disks, their capacity, and their removability differ between the various manufacturers. Figure 1.26 gives several views of a disk storage unit. Data are addressed by read-write head number

*A *track* is informally defined as a longitudinal portion of a moving storage medium, such as tape or disk, used for recording information.

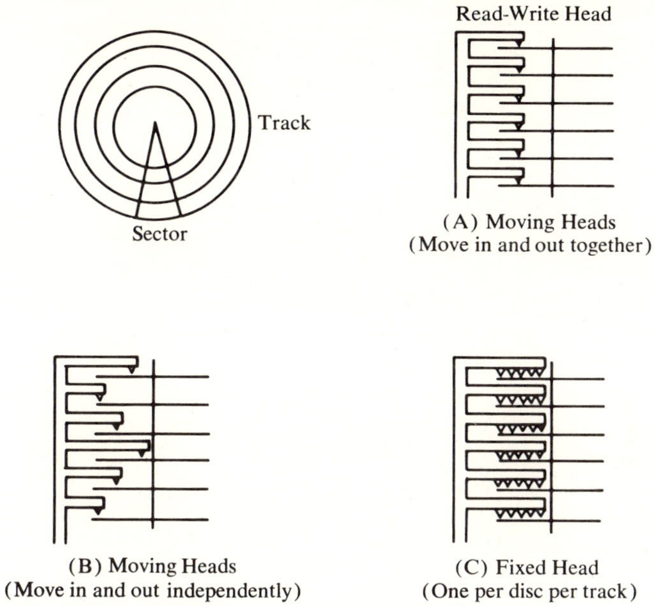

Figure 1.26 Magnetic disk storage (simplified).

and track address. The read-write head can be fixed or moving. A fixed head (view C) eliminates arm movement (since a particular read-write head is selected electronically), and the only delay in access involves rotation time. Moving heads move in and out together (view A) or independently (view B). With a moving head, data access requires that the head be moved to the required track prior to waiting for rotational delay. Magnetic disks are regarded as direct-access devices since information may be located directly instead of serially locating a particular address on the device. Removable disk packs are popular since they serve as both a mass storage and an input/output medium. Disk units without removable disks are generally used for mass storage.

Magnetic drum, as a device type, usually has a storage capacity less than that of magnetic disk and achieves a higher data rate. Magnetic drums are used mainly for mass storage and achieve high data rates because the drum, on which data are recorded, rotates at high speeds and the read-write heads are fixed—one per track (see Figure 1.27). The drum is usually a precision-built cylinder coated with iron oxide, which is magnetized to record data. Magnetic disk and drums are frequently used by an operating system to store programs, such as I/O routines, compilers, etc., which are needed on a demand basis but are too lengthy to reside in main storage permanently.

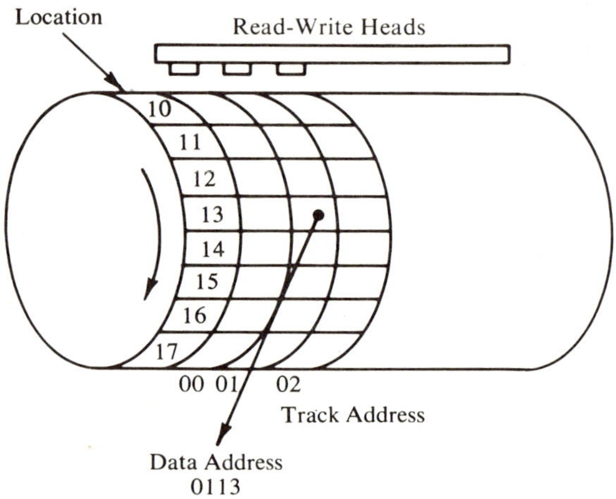

Figure 1.27 Magnetic drum storage.

Although the rotating devices discussed here provide direct-access facilities, they can also be used to store and retrieve data sequentially. Therefore, a sophisticated operating program can provide for considerable generality of use by permitting device types to be interchanged.

Terminal Devices

Terminal devices used with time-sharing systems, data inquiry facilities, and in general remote computing systems, are primarily of two types: keyboard devices and cathode ray tube (CRT) devices. Keyboard devices such as those used with time-sharing systems, are easy to program, and are used extensively for remote input and output. CRT devices generally come in two varieties: character generators and point-to-point displays. Display devices based on the character generator principle usually contain a data buffer so that information is retained on the screen as long as desired. This type of display device, when used for general-purpose computing, also contains a keyboard so that data can be entered, visually inspected, and sent to the computer.

Point-to-point display devices allow a considerable amount of flexibility in the type of information that can be displayed but generally require that the image be refreshed periodically by either the computer or a control device attached to the display unit. Input via a device of this type is usually accomplished with a light pen—a pencil-like device capable of interrupting the instructions of a display control program.

Miscellaneous Input and Output Devices

Several other I/O devices are commercially available to meet the needs of specialized applications. A remote job entry (RJE) *work station* is usually composed of a card reader, card punch, line printer, and optionally a magnetic tape unit, and effectively allows a user to send a job to a computer system from a remote location. Verbal output from a computer can be achieved with an *audio response unit*, which can select a message from an audio drum, and transmit it over a telephone line—all under program control. *Optical readers* can read magnetic characters printed in designated portions of a document (such as a bank check) or can perform a more general analysis using matrix matching, stroke analysis, or curve tracing. *Graph plotters* use pen and ink for drawing smooth curves or point-to-point figures under program control or from magnetic tape using an off-line device. Ultra-high mass storage is achieved with *magnetic cards* and *magnetic strips*. Both devices use iron oxide-coated media, which operate at low speeds, are generally removable, and are capable of storing literally millions of characters on each card or strip. The newest computer output medium is called COM, which is an acronym for *Computer Output Microfilm*. For certain classes of application, microfilm output can incorporate both printed and graphic data and make the information available in one of the well-known forms of microfilm technology, that is, 16 mm film in rolls, 35 mm film, microfiche, or aperture cards (punched cards with microfilm windows).

1.7 MULTISYSTEM ORGANIZATION

Another method that is frequently used to improve computer system performance is to add another computer to the operating environment. The computer is usually added to alleviate input/output problems or to improve reliability. Although at first glance the addition of a computer might appear as a drastic course of action for solving a performance or reliability problem, problems in this area are so acute that the additional equipment is easily justified.

Peripheral Computers

The use of a peripheral computer essentially replaces a potentially low-speed IO device with one of a higher speed. With early systems, and this is partially true today, most input to the system was on punched cards and a substantial amount of the output was to be printed. A nominal rate for card input is between 600 and 1000 80-column cards per minute, and for printed output, it is from 1000 to 1500 120-character lines per minute. These figures amount to an input rate of approximately 1200 characters per second and an output rate of approximately twice that amount or 2400 characters per second. The fact that an average figure for magnetic tape input/output is in the neighborhood of 100,000 characters per second led to the use of a peripheral computer to transfer input cards to tape and output information from magnetic tape to the printer or card punch, as

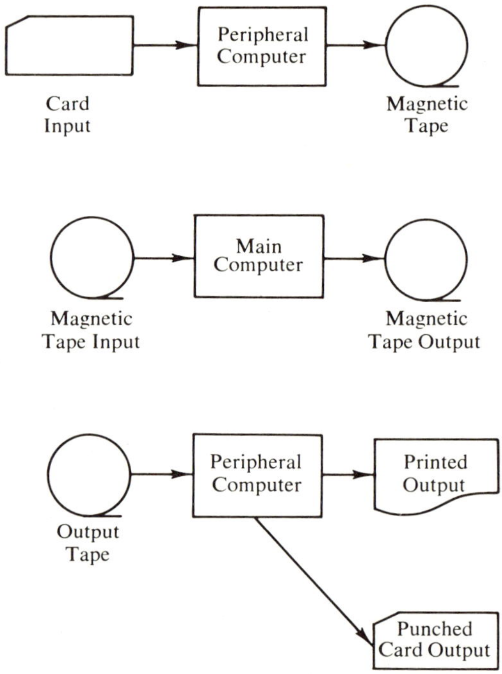

Figure 1.28 Peripheral computers.

shown in Figure 1.28. Thus, both input to and output from the main computer is via magnetic tape. This arrangement more than pays for the use of the peripheral computer, which can additionally be used to perform data editing and error checking.

Satellite Computers

The next step, logically, beyond the peripheral computer is a collection of satellite processors, as shown in Figure 1.29, that are attached to the main computer. Each satellite processor is capable of being programmed and can perform data editing and handle the IO for a given device type. Therefore, a high-speed main computer can use a small computer to control a given IO unit so that data are available and can be disposed of at electronic speeds. In most cases, the satellite computers contain features for interrupting the execution of the main computer and for sharing portions of main storage.

Attached Support Processors

An attached support processor (ASP) combines the facilities of several satellite computers into one high-speed general-purpose computer. An

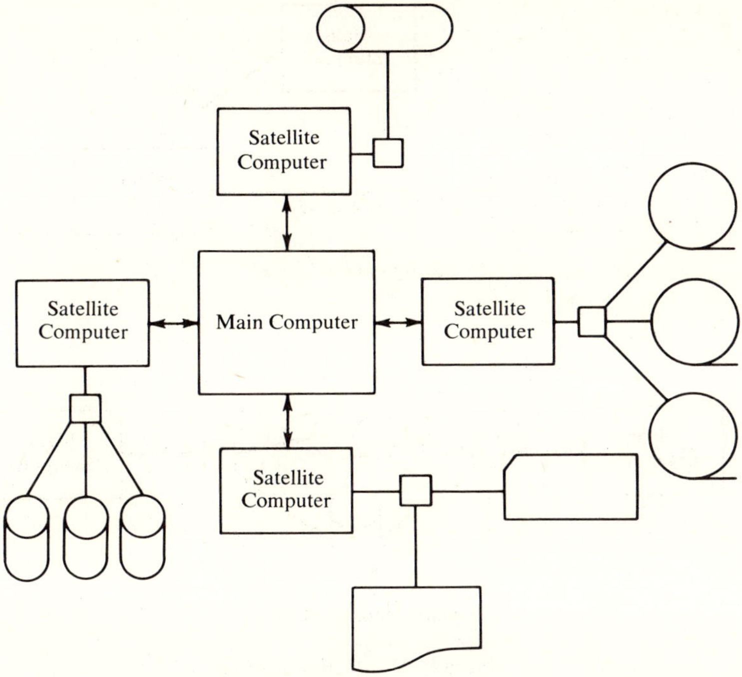

Figure 1.29 Satellite computers.

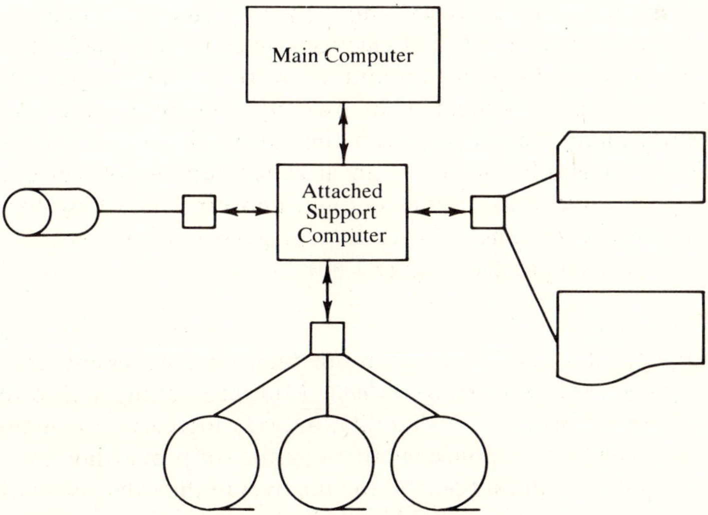

Figure 1.30 Attached support processor.

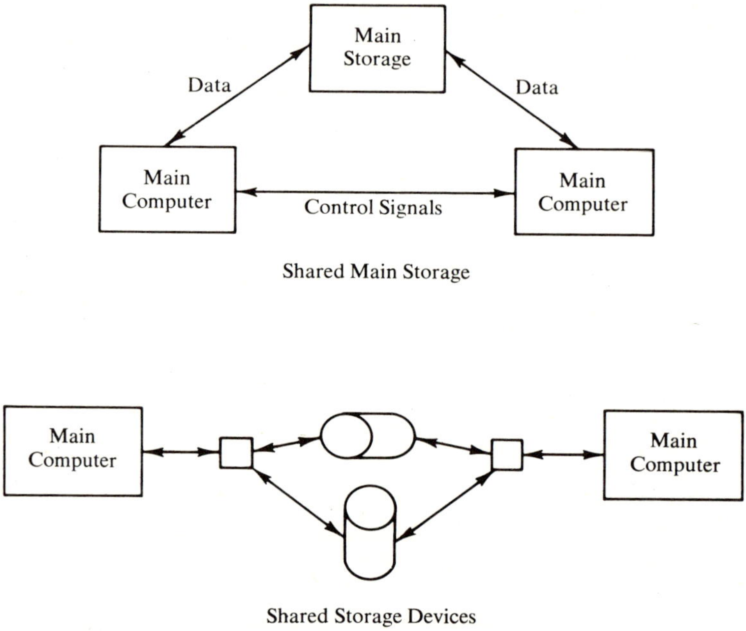

Figure 1.31 Multiprocessing.

attached support computer is usually connected to the main computer in one of two ways: (1) with common access to main storage including inter-system communication features; and (2) with a channel-to-channel adapter permitting a data transfer at electronic speeds. An ASP facility generally relegates a significant amount of work to the support processor since it is a computer system in its own right; in some cases, a support processor has had enough processor time available to process small jobs of its own. Generally, however, an attached support processor handles all low-speed input and output, editing, and error checking for a main high-speed processor and relieves that processor of almost all responsibility for IO processing (see Figure 1.30).

Multiprocessing

A computer system that contains more than one processing unit is generally termed a *multiprocessing system.* Multiprocessing is used for either or both of two reasons: (1) reliability, and (2) increased throughput. In many systems where response is critical, an extra processing unit is made available, under program control, to take over in the event of malfunction in the primary processor. In this case, the processing units must have access to the same storage units and must be able to exchange control signals resulting from a malfunction alert. Some operating systems* also include multiprocessing facilities as a means of increasing work throughput. If the processing units share main storage, then the system control program is also shared and each processor, when looking for work, selects the next task that is ready for execution. If the processing units share direct-access storage devices, then each processor has storage units of its own and selects its next unit of work from an input work queue—stored on the shared direct-access storage device. Both configurations are depicted in Figure 1.31.

1.8 SUMMARY

A computer system is a complex combination of different hardware components: a central processing unit, main storage, input/output data channels, and input/output control units and devices. The central processing unit controls the operation of the computer and performs arithmetic and logical functions. Main storage is directly addressable by the central processing unit and is used to hold the instructions and data that are being used by it. An IO data channel can access main storage independently of the central processing unit and is used for data transfer operations—allowing the central processing unit to continue its normal processing. Input/output control units and devices take a variety of forms and are used as auxiliary storage or as a means of entering or retrieving data from the computer.

Two or more computers can also be operated together to improve performance or system reliability. The computers may operate independently (from a hardware point of view) or be connected via main storage or via direct-access storage devices.

REFERENCES

1. Brooks, F.P., Jr., and K.E. Iverson, "Automatic Data Processing: System/360 Edition," John Wiley & Sons, Inc., New York, 1969.
2. Davis, G.B., "Computer Data Processing," McGraw-Hill Book Co., New York, 1969.
3. Flores, I., "Computer Organization," Prentice-Hall, Inc., Englewood Cliffs, N.J., 1969.
4. Katzan, H., Jr., "APL Programming and Computer Techniques," Van Nostrand Reinhold Co., New York, 1970.

*An *operating system* has been referred to previously as an operating program. In general, an operating system is a collection of programs concerned with the operability of the computer system. The subject is presented in Chapter 2.

5. "The structure of System/360," *IBM Systems Journal*, **3**(2), Part I, Outline of the logical structure, G.A. Blaauw and F.P. Brooks, Jr.; Part II, System implementation, W.Y. Stevens; Part III, Processing unit design considerations, G.M. Amdahl; Part IV, Channel design considerations, A. Padegs; Part V, Multisystem organization, G.A. Blaauw.
6. "Introduction to IBM Data Processing Systems" (Student Text), Form C20-1684, IBM Corporation, White Plains, 1968.

2 PROGRAMMING SYSTEMS AND LANGUAGES

2.1 INTRODUCTION

The concept of a computer program was introduced in Chapter 1 as a means for directing the computer to perform a well-defined sequence of operations. The subject is amplified in this chapter through a discussion of algorithms and programs, programming languages, operating systems, information management, and remote computing. As with many other subjects, the complexity of these topics is dependent upon how deeply one wants to study them. A level of knowledge consistent with the remainder of the book is presented here.

Although a computer program is indeed nothing more than a series of computer instructions, it differs from another computer program in the function it performs and the method by which it was constructed. In a general sense, programs can be placed in the following categories:

1. Applications-oriented programs that solve a problem, process a given set of data, or provide information.
2. Programs that process other computer programs, as input.
3. Programs that control the operation of a computer system and provide facilities for using it.
4. Programs that perform decision and control functions.

It necessarily follows that the effectiveness of a computer system is dependent upon the programs available for using it.

Although programs vary in scope and complexity, their basic structure is derived from that of an algorithm—a mathematical concept known in ancient times. The concept of an algorithm is presented as a general introduction to the nature of computer programs. Also included here is a discussion of program structure, some comments on the need for programming language, and some basic information on compilers, assemblers, and interpreters.

The next section on the structure of programming languages is intended to give the reader, with a background in programming, a more comprehensive view of this important area of computer science. The material is concerned, primarily, with the means by which programs are constructed and can be skipped without loss of continuity.

The remainder of the chapter covers how a computer system is used and presents the following topics: operating system principles, information management, and remote computing. These programming systems facilitate the processing of a program in the same way that a programming language facilitates its construction.

Collectively, programming systems and languages are known as *software* and provide a logical interface between the user and the computer system. The computer system, termed the *hardware*, and the software operate cooperatively. Hardware features enhance the functional capability of the software and the software facilitates the use of sophisticated hardware features.

2.2 ALGORITHMS AND PROGRAMS

One of the concepts fundamental to computing is that of an algorithm, defined informally as follows:

> An *algorithm* is a list of instructions specifying a sequence of operations that will give the answer to any problem of a given type.

Thus, the notion of an algorithm is particularly appropriate for computing problems in which most computer processes that need be performed can be constructed from elementary arithmetic and logical operations.

The Nature of an Algorithm

Generally speaking, an algorithm is a sequence of steps leading to the solution of a given problem; however, one feature distinguishes it from an ordinary procedure or list of instructions. The distinguishing feature is that an algorithm is designed to operate on data that are not known beforehand. In fact, the input of data may be a part of the algorithm itself. As an example, consider the familiar *Euclidean algorithm* that is stated as follows:

Given two positive integers a and b, find their greatest common divisor.

There are, of course, as many different problems of this type as there are different pairs of positive integers a and b. Any of the problems can be solved by constructing a descending sequence of numbers, the first of which is the larger of the two numbers and the second the smaller. The third number is the remainder from dividing the first by the second. The fourth number is the remainder from dividing the second by the third, etc. When one of the divisions leaves no remainder, the divisor in the last division is then the required number. Another example is the square root algorithm that computes the square root r of a number x, where $x \geq 0$ and ϵ is a very small value:

Step	*Instruction*
1	Set r equal to 1.
2	Compute $r = r + \frac{1}{2}\left(\frac{x}{r} - r\right)$.
3	If $\lvert (r^2 - x) \rvert < \epsilon$, then r is the desired result; otherwise, return to step (2) and continue.

The preceding algorithm applies not only to a single value but to all positive values of x.

From these examples, it can be noted that the number of actual instructions that must be executed in solving a particular problem is not known beforehand and is dependent upon the input data; in the first case, a and b, and in the second case, x. The number is discovered only during the course of computation. Thus, an algorithm is conveniently characterized by two properties:

The deterministic nature of an algorithm. An algorithm must be given in the form of a finite list of instructions giving the exact procedure to be followed at each step of the calculation. The calculation does not depend on a specific calculator; it is a deterministic process which can be repeated successfully at any time and by a wide range of computing devices.

The generality of an algorithm. An algorithm is a single list of instructions defining a calculation which may be carried out on any initial data and which, in each case, gives an appropriate result. In other words, an algorithm tells how to solve not just one particular problem, but a whole class of similar problems.

The design of modern computing machines parallels the algorithmic nature of most applications. The computer operates under control of a series of instructions which are stored in high-speed internal storage, along with data, and are interpreted and executed by the circuitry of the machine. The instructions are usually primitive in nature, each being composed essentially of an operation and one or more operands or modifiers, and exist in a form chosen for the representation of data.* Machine instructions which exist in this form are said to be in *machine language* since they are numerically coded and directly executable by a specific computer.

The Concept of a Program

A computer program† is similar in concept to an algorithm or to a sequence of machine language instructions; it is defined as follows:

> A *program* is a meaningful sequence of statements, possessing an implicit or explicit order of execution, and specifying a computer-oriented representation of an algorithmic process.

A statement, in turn, is a string of symbols from a given *alphabet*, composed of letters, digits, and special characters. The form of each statement adheres to a set of rules (*syntax*), and implies an operational meaning (*semantics*). Collectively, the alphabet, syntax, and semantics are termed a *language*. Thus, a machine language instruction, synthesized from the alphabet of internal machine codes, adhering to a primitive syntax of operation codes, operands, and modifiers, and possessing an operational meaning determined by the circuitry of the machine, satisfies the definition of a statement even though the set of basic operations is not directly suited to the execution of commonly needed procedures, and the representation of operands, that is, numeric addresses, affords little mnemonic advantage.

The Need for Programming Languages

Since machine languages, in general, are not suitable for human use, it is necessary and feasible to define languages which are and then translate programs written in these languages to machine language for subsequent execution on a computer, or to interpretively execute the programs without going through a translation phase.

Languages of this sort are often termed *programming languages* and come in a variety of forms. The most primitive form of programming

*A computer instruction or a data item is usually stored as a sequence of binary digits. Exceptions do exist and some computers use a decimal or binary coded decimal internal form.

†Usually referred to simply as a *program*.

languages is closely akin to machine language except that operations, operands, and modifiers are replaced by symbolic equivalents. A language of this type is called *assembler language*, a simple example of which follows:

```
              .
              .
              .
GROSS         L        3,QUAN
              M        2,PRICE
              A        3,TAX
              ST       3,TOTAMT
              .
              .
              .
```

Although assembler language negates the principal disadvantage of machine language (i.e., the necessity of manipulating internal machine codes), it is obvious that basic machine operations (or their symbolic equivalents) are not convenient for representing most algorithmic processes.

A *procedure-oriented language* is a form of programming language that is related, in a sense, to a class of programs under consideration. Procedure-oriented languages are usually classed as to whether they are scientifically oriented or commercially oriented or whether they are amenable to applications programming or to a form of systems programming. The following statements

```
SUM=SUM+A(I)*Y**2
MOVE NAME TO REPORT-FIELD.
```

are examples of the FORTRAN and COBOL languages, respectively, and are typical of the general form of most programming languages.

Although programming languages differ widely in scope, form, and content, the various statements can be grouped into five well-defined classes that perform distinct basic functions. The classes of statements are: data manipulation, program control, input and output, declarative, and subprogram.

Data manipulation statements perform the calculations, data movement, list processing, or string editing required by a particular application. As a result of data manipulation, computation is performed and/or a data variable is replaced.

Program control statements provide a facility for altering the sequential flow of execution in a program. Control statements are divided into four categories: unconditional branches, conditional statements, looping, and execution control. Statements in the last category halt or terminate program execution or supply the computer with compile-time information.

Input and output statements are the facilities with which a program communicates with the outside world. A variety of device types is usually supported and sets of data can be organized in any of several ways.

Declarative statements specify problem and execution-control data, establish storage requirements, define file types, inform the compiler of hardware configurations, and specify the manner in which execution-time conditions are processed.

Subprogram statements permit a program to be structured into functionally distinct and efficient subprograms. Function or subroutine type procedures can be defined by the programmer or retrieved from a personal or installation-based library of programs.

The structure of programming languages is discussed in more detail in Section 2.3.

Program Structure

In its simplest form, an executable program is composed of a collection of machine instructions and data (whether it be initial data, intermediate values, or intermediate results) stored in contiguous locations in computer storage. However, very few programs are actually executed in this form. The reason is that common ordinary functions, such as the trigonometric sine or the square root, need to be used, and it would not be feasible, from an efficiency standpoint, for each programmer to prepare his own version. This leads, generally, to the notion of a subprogram, a concept which permits the execution of identical kinds of computation with different data.

Thus, most executable programs are composed of a *main program* and a collection of subprograms, where a *subprogram* is defined informally as a segment of coding that is prepared in a general fashion for use at multiple points in a program.

Subprograms exist in two forms: functions and subroutines. A *function* has an explicit result and assumes a value as a constituent of a mathematical expression. The trigonometric functions (SIN, COS, TAN), the square root (SQRT), and the absolute value (ABS) are common examples of functions. A *subroutine* does not have an explicit result and is usually invoked by a special statement in the programming language.* As described below, a subroutine is classed as a closed subprogram. A function, on the other hand, can be an open or closed subprogram.

In some cases, the number of machine instructions required to invoke a subprogram is not justified by time and space savings. For these cases, it is convenient simply to insert the necessary instructions directly into the

*The most familiar example is the CALL statement used in COBOL, FORTRAN, and PL/I.

machine language program at each place where it is used. A subprogram of this type is called an *open* subprogram and is contrasted to a *closed* subprogram for which only one copy exists per program and standard linkage is made to it each time it is referenced.* The two types are depicted as follows:

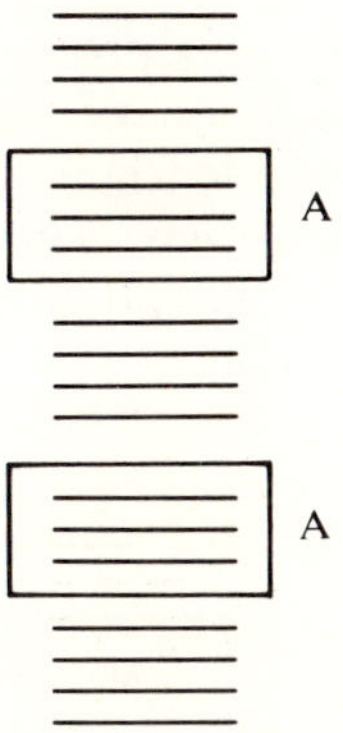

Open Subprogram

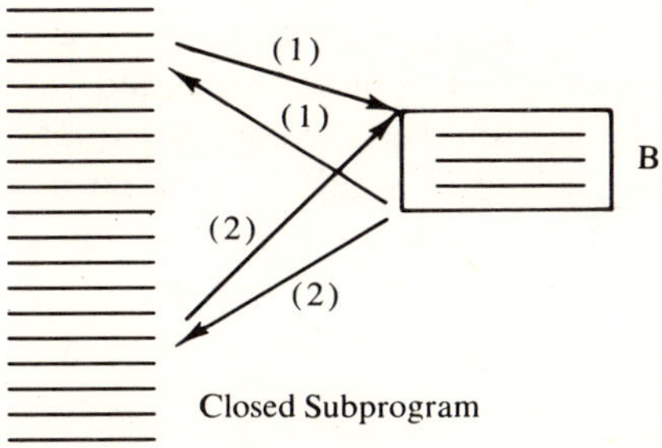

Closed Subprogram

Metaprograms

Clearly, a computer can only execute a program in machine language but as mentioned previously, that form is inconvenient for human use. Therefore, most programs are written in a programming language and a translation to machine language is required. Much of the detail associated with programming is effectively subordinated to a program, termed a metaprogram, that performs the translation from a programming language to machine language. More formally, a *metaprogram* is a computer program that operates on programs as data. If the output of a metaprogram is also a program, then the metaprogram is known as a *translator*. Translators usually come in two principal forms: assemblers and compilers. An *assembler* is used to translate a program written in assembler language to machine language. A *compiler* is used to translate a program written in a procedure-oriented language (such as FORTRAN or COBOL) to machine language, although in some cases, the output of the compiler is an assembler language program that must also be passed through the assembler.

An *interpreter* is a special form of metaprogram from which no program is produced as output. The execution of an interpreter usually proceeds as follows: Each statement in the programming language is first translated to an internal intermediate language, is then *interpreted* in

*Other common names for open and closed subprograms are *in-line* and *out-of-line*, respectively.

that language, and is finally executed—usually by prewritten subroutines. Only the results of the executed statement are retained. Moreover, the statements in a program are selected for processing by the interpreter in a sequence determined by the execution of preceding statements, whereas in a compiler or assembler, all of the statements are processed before any of them is executed.

Special terminology applies to a program before it is processed by a metaprogram and after it is translated to machine language form. The program as written by the programmer, in assembler language or a procedure-oriented language is termed a *source program*. The machine language output from an assembler or a compiler is called an *object program*. Metaprogram terminology is depicted in Figure 2.1.

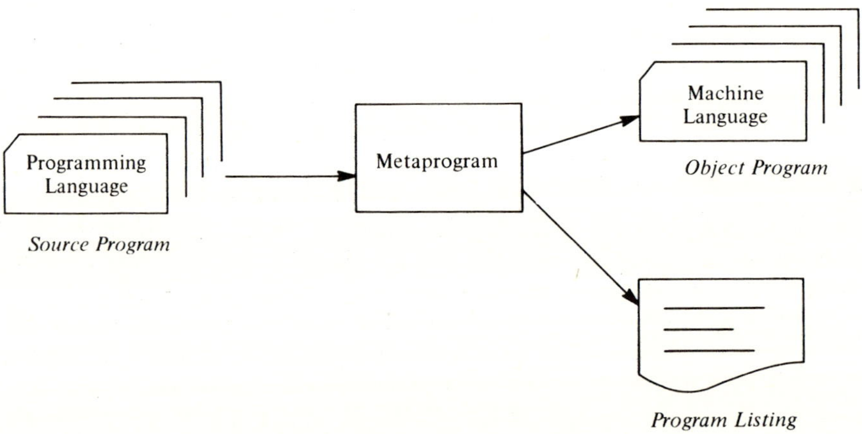

Figure 2.1 Metaprogram terminology.

2.3 THE STRUCTURE OF PROGRAMMING LANGUAGES*

Throughout the short history of computers, the study of programming languages has been one of the most popular topics. This is true for a variety of reasons. First, programming languages are the key link between man and the computer and are obviously of prime importance. Second, the user spends a significant amount of time and energy using his programming language and wants it to be as concise and as appropriate to his application as possible. Lastly, it is desirable to have the programming language independent of a particular model of computer, so that the user can change computers without reprogramming and programs can be exchanged between installations, yet powerful enough to take good

*This section may be skipped without loss of continuity.

advantage of the facilities inherent in the computing system. This last reason has contributed to the widespread acceptance of machine independent programming languages, such as FORTRAN and COBOL, which are oriented towards a particular class of users, and multipurpose languages, such as PL/I, which is designed to satisfy the needs of the broad spectrum of computer applications.

Frequently Used Procedure-Oriented Languages

In subsequent parts of this section, reference is made to several of the most frequently used programming languages. Although detailed knowledge of these languages is not necessary, a casual familiarty is useful for understanding the implications of some of the examples.

COBOL (*CO*mmon *B*usiness *O*riented *L*anguage) is a programming language intended for data processing applications that involve relatively large amounts of data. The language was intended to be English-like to increase readability and facilitate programming; it was also designed to be machine independent so that programs could be easily interchanged among computer installations with different kinds of equipment. The COBOL project was initiated by the Department of Defense in 1959, monitored by the CODASYL (*CO*nference on *DA*ta *SY*stems *L*anguages) committee, and heavily supported by business and the government since then.

FORTRAN (IBM Mathematical *FOR*mula *TRAN*slating System) was originally developed by IBM in the years 1954–1957 to facilitate the preparation of mathematical programs for execution on a computer. Although FORTRAN is still primarily a scientifically oriented language, it is used for a variety of applications and has achieved national standardization and international acceptance.

PL/I (*P*rogramming *L*anguage/I) was designed by IBM in conjunction with the SHARE* FORTRAN project and developed by IBM as a multipurpose programming language. In general, PL/I combines the most useful facilities of ALGOL,† COBOL, and FORTRAN and is particularly useful for applications that span traditional language boundaries. PL/I is also an appropriate replacement for each of these languages and is suitable for real-time and systems programming.

The remainder of this section on the structure of programming languages uses concepts from these three languages. Sammet[6] gives an excellent survey of the history and fundamentals of programming languages.

*SHARE is an IBM user's group.

†ALGOL is an acronym for Algorithmic Language—an internationally used language for describing algorithmic processes.

Data Structure

Computers are designed and developed to operate on data, and a fundamental knowledge of data and the ways that they can be organized is essential for developing a firm foundation in the structure of programming languages. Most readers are immediately cognizant of at least three kinds of data: numeric data, logical data, and descriptive data. Numeric data are ordinarily used in arithmetic calculations and assume a variety of familiar forms. Logical data can assume the values *true* or *false* and are used with the logical operators. The representation of logical data in the computer frequently varies between programming systems. Descriptive data are usually formed from the characters in the alphabet and are stored as strings of characters.* The operations available on character data are usually limited to movement, comparison, pattern matching, and alteration.† Numeric, logical, and descriptive data are used to represent values to be processed by a program and are classed as *problem data.* Unfortunately, the various kinds of problem data are classified differently in different programming languages so terminology also differs. Thus a knowledge of basic concepts is essential for a thorough understanding of the structure of programming languages. Some programming languages allow *program control data* which are used by the programmer to control the execution of his program. Familiar examples of program control data are label data (such as statement numbers or statement labels) and pointer data (i.e., machine addresses) that are used with list processing applications. The characteristics that distinguish one kind of data from another are termed *attributes.* An obvious attribute is whether the data are numeric, logical, or descriptive. Other attributes pertain to the size of the data and how they are stored in the computer.

In everyday arithmetic, one deals with the decimal digits 0 through 9 and optionally a decimal point and an algebraic sign. Arithmetic operations are performed by using digit by digit operations on the numbers and by applying well-defined rules for signs and decimal points. A number of this type is termed a *decimal number* or a *fixed-point* number (see Chapter 1) since the exact position of the decimal point is explicitly stated. Thus, a fixed-point number x is represented by an expression of the form:

$$x = n + 0.d_1d_2d_3\ldots$$

where n is a whole number and each d_i is a decimal digit. For example, .123, 340, 0.00000789, −19374, and 38.791 are all valid fixed-point numbers. An *integer* is a fixed-point number with no fractional part; it is used

*In a sense, numeric data can also be interpreted as being descriptive. However, that meaning is not intended in this discussion.

†For a discussion of string operations, see Katzan,[2] p. 31.

as a distinct data type in some programming systems since arithmetic operations on integer values can be performed efficiently and in a straightforward manner. Two important attributes of fixed-point data are their size (i.e., *precision*) and the location of the decimal point.

Although fixed-point notation is satisfactory for representing some numerical values, it is not convenient for representing (and storing in the computer, as well) very large or very small values. It also poses potential problems in computer storage when the number of decimal places in a datum is not known in advance. In situations such as these, scientists frequently use *scientific* or *exponential notation*, which consists of a number times a power of ten. For example, a million is commonly written as 1×10^6 and .00000123 is written as 1.23×10^{-6}. Computer input is restricted to linear sequences of characters so that an exponent is denoted by the letter *E* followed by a power of ten. Thus, the previous examples would be entered as 1*E*6 and 1.23*E*−6, respectively. A common practice for storing an exponential number in computer storage is to maintain a fixed size *fraction* (six, seven, or eight digits, for example) and a smaller *exponent* (two or three digits), which is also fixed-size. The above examples could be represented in computer storage as:

+	71	100000

+	59	123000

Here, an implied decimal point is assumed to be placed immediately to the left of the leftmost digit of the fraction and the exponent is biased by adding a positive base value (64 here) to eliminate the need for carrying two signs. This convention for storing exponential values is commonly referred to as *floating-point* notation, as discussed in Chapter 1, and that terminology is also used to denote an exponential number written with the letter *E* to express a power of ten (e.g., 1.23*E* 6). When performing arithmetic operations on floating-point numbers, the circuitry of the computer makes whatever adjustments are necessary. The most significant attribute of floating-point data is precision—precision of the exponent and of the fraction.

Complex numbers are permitted in some programming languages and require two components—one for the real part and one for the imaginary part. Although the real and imaginary parts of a complex number can be either fixed-point or floating-point, they are usually not mixed (i.e., one part cannot be fixed and the other floating). In at least one programming language (namely FORTRAN), a floating-point number is given the type REAL and the components of a complex number (which is of type COMPLEX) are stored as floating-point values. Other languages (such as PL/I) allow more flexibility in this regard so that the parts of a complex number can be stored in either fixed-point or floating-point form. Obviously, the most significant attribute of complex data is whether the real and imaginary components are stored as fixed-point or as floating-point numbers. It follows that fixed or floating components may have attributes of their own.

The range of logical values includes only the values *true* and *false*, permitting a great deal of latitude in how those values are stored and written by the programmer. The FORTRAN user writes .TRUE. and .FALSE. as logical constants and these values are stored as implementation-defined data items. In PL/I, on the other hand, logical constants are stored as bit strings (to be covered next) that can be used as operands in arithmetic operations. COBOL does not provide any means of storing a logical value but allows comparison and logical operations as part of conditional statements.

Descriptive data are usually regarded as *string* data and are stored as strings of characters in most programming systems. When written as a constant value, a string is usually enclosed in delimiters, such as quote marks, and is called a *literal.* The convention of using delimiters is necessary since any character in the alphabet of the language is permitted in a string and a means must be provided to distinguish between descriptive data and a valid construction in the language. PL/I also allows a string to be of type BIT, with permissible characters being limited to 0 and 1. However, a series of bits may result from a comparison or logical operation and may also represent a fixed-point number. Thus, in PL/I to cite a single example, a meaningful correspondence is made between different types of data. The most important attribute of a string datum is its length in terms of characters or bits.

Variables and Identifiers

The practice of giving a name to a quantity (or an unknown quantity) is basic to the study of algebra and essential for higher mathematics and computer programming. In general, the concept has enabled basic procedures to be developed that exist independently of the particular data being used.

In computer programming, a name is given to a data item or to a location in computer storage. That name is termed a *variable*, although to be precise, a variable always requires two constituents: a name and a data item or what amounts to the same thing, a name and a location in storage. After a variable has been assigned a value, then it can be used in other statements. Consider the following statements from the FORTRAN language:

```
A = 14      (1)
B = 3       (2)
```

```
C=A*B        (3)
```

Statements (1) and (2) assign values to A and B, respectively. After statements (1) and (2) have been executed, then statement (3) can effectively compute A*B and assign the result to C. If statements (1) and (2) did not exist or were not executed, then statement (3) would be invalid. A variable always assumes the attributes of the data that it represents. The assignment of attributes may be made explicitly by the programmer or implicitly by the programming language.

It is frequently desirable to name other constructs in programming languages besides data items or storage locations. A series of characters that name a constituent of a programming language is termed an *identifier.* The rules for forming an identifier vary between languages but, in general, an identifier begins with a letter and is followed optionally by one or more letters or digits. Thus, the following examples are valid identifiers:

A1	DO
ELSE	X
TZVK4	OVERFLOW
DECLARE	SQRT
K12345	END

The uses of identifiers in programming languages can be grouped into several categories which exist independently of a particular programming language. They are presented here for reference:*

Data names
Data file names
Statement labels
Entry point names
Keywords

A *keyword* is of particular concern since it is part of a programming language and carries a meaning beyond that of an ordinary name. Keywords are grouped into six categories: (1) statement identifiers, (2) attributes, (3) separating keywords, (4) built-in function names, (5) option names, and (6) condition names. A short description along with a familiar example is given for each category of keyword. In each case, the programming language used for the example is given and the keyword under discussion is underlined.

A *statement identifier* indicates a type of statement and is placed at the beginning of that statement (reading from left to right); e.g.,

<u>DO</u> 10 I=1,10 (FORTRAN)

*Reference 8 contains a complete description of the manner in which identifiers are used.

```
READ A-FILE AT END GO TO E-PAR.     (COBOL)
GOTO LOOP1;                          (PL/I)
```

An *attribute* specifies the properties of a program element (usually data), e.g.,

```
DECLARE (CNT,DEL1) FIXED;                      (PL/I)
02 ACCTNO, SIZE IS 6, CLASS IS NUMERIC.(COBOL)
```

A *separating keyword* augments the meaning of a statement or separates distinct program elements; e.g.,

```
ASSIGN 525 TO N                 (FORTRAN)
DO I=1 BY 2 TO 13;                 (PL/I)
ADD PAY, OVTIME GIVING GROSS.     (COBOL)
```

A *built-in function* name represents a name recognized by the compiler and identifies a function supplied by the programming system; e.g.,

```
X=SQRT (A**2-1)              (FORTRAN)
PUT LIST (FLOOR(ABS(X)));       (PL/I)
```

An *option name* is recognized by the compiler and effects the execution of a statement; e.g.,

```
DIVIDE WEEKS INTO GROSS ROUNDED. (COBOL)
PUT EDIT (TITLE) (A) PAGE;         (PL/I)
MASTER, PAYREC=NEWREC, BY NAME;    (PL/I)
```

A *condition name* specifies an event for which special action must be taken; e.g.,

```
WRITE OLDREC INVALID KEY GOTO ERRPAR. (COBOL)
ON SIZE GOTO ABEND;                     (PL/I)
```

Collectively, the keywords of a programming language along with its syntax and semantics distinguish it from other programming languages. In some languages, the keywords are *reserved* which means that they cannot be used as other identifiers.

Data Organization

A single item of data, such as a height, weight, or distance, which can assume one of the forms given earlier, is known as a *scalar*. A variable associated with a scalar value is termed a *scalar variable*. It is often convenient to group data with similar characteristics—not only with respect to the type of data (i.e., fixed, floating, etc.) but also on the basis of what the data mean to the user. Lists and tables are everyday examples of data aggregates that are used for descriptive and analytic purposes.

In computer programming, an aggregate of data with the same attributes is termed an *array*. The most elementary form of array is a linear sequence of data items commonly called a *vector*; similarly, a two-dimensional or rectangular collection of elements is termed a *matrix*. The concept is easily extended to *n*-dimensional aggregates—hence the name array. Analogous to mathematical notation, which treats vectors and matrices as single entities, only the array itself is given a name, termed an *array variable*. A distinct element of an array is selected by giving its relative position among the other elements. Thus in the matrix

$$A = \begin{pmatrix} {}^{-}7 & 3 & 9 & 6 \\ 5 & 1 & 4 & 3 \\ - & - & - & - \end{pmatrix}$$

the element located at the junction of the second row and the third column has the value 4 and is usually denoted symbolically in mathematics by A_2^3 or $A_{2,3}$. Since computer input is restricted to a linear sequence of characters, the indices 2 and 3 in the preceding example are enclosed in parentheses or brackets, following the array variable name, and separated by commas. Thus $A(2,3)=4$ and $A(1,4)=6$. A quantity used to select an element of an array is called a *subscript* and can take the form of a constant, a variable, or an expression; in each case, the accepted practice is to reduce its value to an integer before the selection of an element of an array takes place.

Consider the array A represented symbolically as follows:

$$A = \begin{pmatrix} a_{-1,1} & a_{-1,2} & a_{-1,3} \\ a_{0,1} & a_{0,2} & a_{0,3} \\ a_{1,1} & a_{1,2} & a_{1,3} \\ a_{2,1} & a_{2,2} & a_{2,3} \end{pmatrix}$$

It has several important properties. The first is the number of dimensions, of which it has two: a row dimension and a column dimension. Each dimension is further characterized by a bounds and an extent. The *bounds* of a dimension are the lowest and highest indices that apply to that dimension and determine which elements are selected. The *extent* is the number of elements in a dimension, regardless of how they are referenced. In array A, for example, the row bounds are $(-1{:}2)$ and the column bounds are $(1{:}3)$. The row extent is 4 while the column extent is 3.

It is customary to store an array in contiguous locations in computer storage, and that convention permits an array to be treated as a single entity and facilitates the selection (by indexing) of successive elements of that array. Figure 2.2 depicts two common methods for storing the ele-

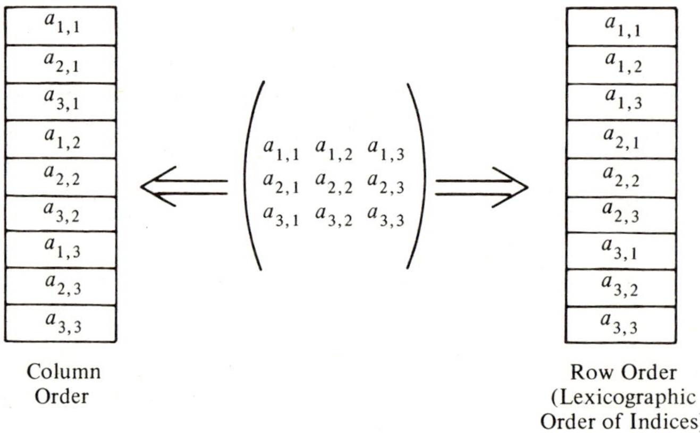

Figure 2.2 Two established conventions for storing a matrix in contiguous locations of computer storage.

ments of a matrix: in column order and in row order. Row order, also called lexicographic order, is more natural for human use* and is used most frequently. The concepts are easily extended to arrays of higher dimension.

Data with different attributes can be collected into an aggregate called a *structure*. A structure is hierarchical in the sense that it can contain elements that are also structures. The following PL/I example depicts a simple structure:

```
DECLARE 1 A,
          2 B FIXED,
          2 C,
            3 D FLOAT,
            3 E (10,10) FIXED,
          2 F  CHAR (10);
```

In other words, each level in the hierarchy may be another structure complete with its own hierarchical structure. Eventually, the lowest levels of hierarchy must represent scalar values. Structures are used most frequently in data processing applications where the structure is the repre-

*See Knuth,[4] p. 296.

sentation in storage of a data record from an input/output file. The same data names are often used within different structures: e.g., in PL/I

```
DECLARE 1 MASTER,              DECLARE 1 UPDATE,
          2 NAME,                        2 NAME,
            3 FIRST...,                    3 FIRST...,
            3 MI...,                       3 MI...,
            3 LAST...,                     3 LAST...,
          2 ADDRESS,                     2 ADDRESS,
            3 STREET...,                   3 STREET...,
            3 CITY...,                     3 CITY...,
            3 STATE...,                    3 STATE...,
            3 ZIP...;                      3 ZIP...;
```

Thus, when referencing the item ADDRESS in the structure MASTER, it must be distinguished from the item with the same name in the structure named UPDATE. The distinction is achieved with a *qualified name*, written in PL/I as

MASTER.ADDRESS (PL/I)

and in COBOL as

ADDRESS IN MASTER (COBOL)

or

ADDRESS OF MASTER (COBOL)

Structures are also permitted in COBOL but are defined in a slightly different fashion.

Operators and Expressions

By its very nature, the use of a computer implies the manipulation of data using well-defined operations, ordered in a meaningful sequence. In specifying these operations in a programming language, the notation of a particular class of applications is usually selected. Of interest here is the mathematical notation used in arithmetic statements.

An elementary* operation such as addition is commonly denoted by its equivalent mathematical symbol, as is subtraction. Other operator symbols differ from ordinary usage; for example, multiplication is denoted by *, division by /, and exponentiation by **. Even though some operator symbols differ from common usage, the manner in which they

*Elementary in the sense that the operation is *usually* not constructed from more primitive operations. Exponentiation (or the power function as it is sometimes called) is an obvious exception, since few if any computers have a single built-in operation that performs that function. However, it is usually classed as an elementary operation because of its frequent use in mathematical work.

are used does not. Addition, for example, requires two operands and is written with the operator separating the operands (i.e., $x+y$). An operator of this type is called a *dyadic* or *binary* operator because of the number of operands. Multiplication, division, and subtraction are other familiar examples of a dyadic operator. It is also possible to define an operator with one operand that is written with the operator symbol preceding the operand. An operator of this type is classed as a *monadic* or *unary* operator. The monadic form of minus, for example, changes the sign of its operand, so that the expression $-X$ is defined as $0-X$. If A is equal to 5, then $-A$ produces the value -5. The result is cumulative so that $--A$ is equal to A. Monadic and dyadic operators are also referred to as *prefix* and *infix operators*, respectively.

In mathematical notation, several operators can be combined in the same expression (such as $a \times x + b$) to specify a series of calculations. The concept is included in most programming languages because of its obvious usefulness in denoting complex sequences of calculations in a notation familiar to the user. The order in which operations are executed is of particular interest. For example, the statement

```
Y=A*X+B                (FORTRAN)
```

implies a sequence of machine operations expressed somewhat as follows:

```
L  5,A
M  4,X
A  5,B
ST 5,Y
```

This or a similar interpretation for the statement is assumed regardless of whether actual machine code is produced by a compiler or the statement is interpretively executed by an interpreter. The key point involves the rationale used for assigning a meaning to an arithmetic statement. In general, either of two approaches is taken: (1) A priority is assigned to the operators and an operator is executed before one of lesser priority; or (2) the operators in an expression are executed in a strict left-to-right or right-to-left sequence, without regard to priority of operators. Thus if A=3, X=5, and B=2 in the expression

```
A*X-B
```

then using a right-to-left convention produces a result of 9, whereas a priority scheme with the priority of multiplication exceeding that of subtraction produces a result of 13. The COBOL, FORTRAN, and PL/I languages use a hierarchy among operators, defined as follows:

Operator	*Hierarchy*
**	Highest
*,/	↓
+, −	Lowest

The use of parentheses is a universally accepted means of departing from the established convention for the execution of operators. Parentheses indicate grouping such that expressions within parentheses are executed before the expressions of which they are a constituent part. Thus, if X=2, then the expression

X*(X+2)+1

evaluates to the value 9. The concept obviously extends to as many levels as necessary so that X*(X*(X+3)+3)+1 evaluates to 27 if X=2 and ((((A)))) is equivalent to A.

Data Manipulation

Data manipulation statements perform the calculations, data movement, list processing, or string editing required by a particular application. As a result of a data manipulation statement, the value of a data variable is replaced. The general form of a data manipulation statement, often called the *assignment statement* is:

$$v=e$$

(where e is an expression and v is a variable) which is interpreted to mean: Replace the value of v with the result of e. The assignment statement is usually written without a statement identifier as depicted in the following FORTRAN example:

```
Y=A*B**2+C
```

In commercial computing, data manipulation normally incorporates data movement and a limited amount of arithmetic computation. The following statements, written in COBOL, are illustrative of commercial computing:

```
MOVE RESULT TO ANSWER.
ADD PAY, GROSS GIVING TOTAL.
```

Program Control

Program control statements are the mechanism by which sequential execution is altered in programs. Control statements are divided into four categories: (1) unconditional branches; (2) conditional branches and conditional statement execution; (3) looping; and (4) execution control.

Unconditional branches alter sequential execution and indicate the statement to be executed next, either singly or multiply as the result of some computation. In most languages, this statement takes the form of the GOTO, as shown in the following FORTRAN examples (where statements are labeled by statement numbers):

```
GOTO 25
GOTO(10,20,30),I
```

where in the second statement, control is transferred to statement 10, 20, or 30, depending upon whether I contains 1, 2, or 3.

In other languages such as COBOL and PL/I, paragraphs or statements may be labeled by names, as depicted in the following COBOL examples:

```
GOTO PAR-ONE.
GOTO P1,P2,P3 DEPENDING ON I.
```

Similar to FORTRAN, control is transferred to paragraphs P1, P2, or P3, depending upon I, in the latter statement. In PL/I, variables can have the attribute LABEL, so they may contain label values instead of data values. For example (in PL/I),

```
GOTO SWITCH;
```

would transfer program control to the statement whose label is contained in the variable SWITCH. In general, this facility provides the programmer with a great amount of flexibility, since the contents of label variables can be modified with the standard assignment statement.

Conditional statements allow the programmer to change the sequence of execution or to execute a given statement on a conditional basis. This feature can be used for iterative procedures, for providing a means of processing exceptional cases, or for making basic decisions during the course of program execution. The conditional element can be based on either a propositional or arithmetic expression; e.g. (in FORTRAN):

```
IF(A+1) 10,20,30
IF(A*B.GT.X)X=X+1
```

In the first statement, program control goes to statements 10, 20, or 30, if the expression A+1 is less than zero, equal to zero, or greater than zero, respectively. In the second case, the statement X=X+1 is executed only if the logical expression has the value *true*. COBOL provides a slightly extended capability with a *condition name facility*, in addition to a logical if statement (first example):

```
IF AGE IS GREATER THAN 400 MOVE 99 TO AGE.
IF MALE NEXT SENTENCE OTHERWISE GOTO FEMALE-PAR.
```

In the second example, the condition name MALE is associated with a specific value of an appropriate variable. If the variable contains the specific value, then the condition name MALE has the value *true*. PL/I, perhaps, combines the best of both languages with an IF statement of the form:

IF <expression> THEN <group> ELSE <group>

where *expression* can be a logical or a scalar expression. If it is a scalar expression, it is converted to a bit string and interpreted as being *true* if any bit is one. The element *group* may be a statement, a DO group, or a begin block.

The ability of a computer program to repeat the same operations with different data, called *looping*, is a powerful tool which greatly reduces programming effort and the size of programs, as well. In general, a loop has the following elements: (1) an indexing or induction variable; (2) a range of statements to be executed; and (3) indexing parameters or a conditional expression which controls the number of iterations. (In any given application, however, any one of the above elements may not be required.) In writing a loop, two components are required: (1) the *loop head* gives the *mode* of execution, the induction variable, and the indexing or control parameters; and (2) the *loop body* gives the range of statements to be executed iteratively. During the machine processing of a loop, one of three modes of iteration is implicitly selected from the information in the loop head. Either the loop body is executed a specified number of times; or it is executed until a specific condition is met; or it is executed as the induction variable assumes a given set of values. In the last case, the loop may be terminated when the list of values is exhausted or when a predetermined condition is met. Clearly, the list of values may be listed explicitly or given as a range. The next examples demonstrate these concepts:

<u>FORTRAN</u>

```
      DO 100 I=1,10
      .
      .
      .
100   _____
```

<u>COBOL</u>

```
PERFORM LOOP-ONE VARYING I FROM 1 BY 1 UNTIL I IS
   GREATER THAN 10.
PERFORM B-BLOCK THRU E-BLOCK 13 TIMES.
```

PL/I

```
LOOP: DO WHILE(A<B);
        .
        .
        .
      END LOOP;
```

The FORTRAN example contains a loop head and a loop body, and the mode of iteration permits the induction variable I to assume a set of values, given as a range. Two COBOL examples are given, and in both cases, only a loop head is provided. The first example specifies a loop where the induction variable assumes a set of values which is terminated by a predetermined condition. In the second COBOL example, a loop is performed a given number of times. In the PL/I example, a loop head and a loop body are written, and the loop body is executed while a specified condition is satisfied.

Execution control statements halt or terminate program execution or supply the compiler with compile-time information. Execution control statements, in general, vary from language to language, with the STOP and END statements being the most common forms, and between different operating systems.

Input and Output

Input and output statements are the facilities with which programs communicate with the outside world. The outside world may be a card deck supplied by the user on the system input stream, a printed page, or an intermediate storage device such as a tape or disk. Two modes of input and output are usually available in higher level languages: formatted and unformatted. *Formatted output* goes through an editing procedure which converts the data from the internal representation of the machine to an external form required by a particular application. *Formatted input* reverses the process. With *unformatted input/output*, the data are stored externally in a manner which is closely akin to the form in which they are found internally. Consider the following FORTRAN examples:

```
READ(N,9000)(A(I),I=1,20)
WRITE(10)A,B,(C(J),J=1,5)
```

In the first statement, a formatted record is read from input unit N, utilizing a format denoted by the numeral 9000. In the second statement, an unformatted record is written on output unit 10. In COBOL, the programmer need not be concerned with the formatting problem, and any required conversions are made during the course of performing the desired computation; for example,

READ CHANGE-FILE INTO UPDATE-RECORD,AT END GOTO EOF.

WRITE SAVER.

Clearly, the mode of input and output in COBOL is determined either by the compiler or by the operating system under which the COBOL programs are to be run. PL/I provides the advantages of both FORTRAN and COBOL. Consider, for example, the following PL/I statements:

```
PUT EDIT(X,Y) (X(3), F(12,5), X(7), E(30,15));
READ FILE(PERSONNEL-FILE)SET(PTR);
```

The first statement involves stream* input/output and puts the variables X and Y in formatted form in the system output stream. The second statement reads a record from the file named PERSONNEL-FILE and sets the pointer variable PTR to its location in computer storage.

Specification Statements

Specification statements declare problem and execution-control data, file types, establish storage requirements, inform the compiler of expected execution-time conditions (relating to machine configurations, etc.), and specify how exception-type conditions should be handled.

Data and storage declaration may be *static* or *dynamic*, as required. Static declarations are effective at load time. Dynamic declarations are effective at execution time and are explicitly invoked or implicitly specified. Problem data declaration may specify the base, scale, mode, or precision of *arithmetic data* and the mode and length of string data, as well as initial values for both. Execution-control data declarations may specify *label data*, *event data*, and the manner in which storage should be allocated. In general, *file types* are denoted implicitly, although most programming languages, which are used for commercial applications, have facilities for declaring them (and associated records) explicitly. *Environment* declarations extend the compatibility of programming languages among different machine types and may be used to specify run-time system configurations, as well. *Exceptional-condition* specifications may be handled on either a specific or a general basis. That is, all occurrences of a given exception (e.g., a floating-point overflow) may be processed in the same way, or facilities may be available to handle each occurrence on an individual statement basis. A complete set of examples,

*With *stream-oriented input/output*, the respective unit is considered to be a continuous stream of data items, in character form, to be assigned from the input stream to variables or from variables to the output stream. It is contrasted to *record input/output*, where the input or output exists in the form of physically separate records.

in this category, would be quite lengthy and beyond the intent of this introduction. Some problem data declarations are included, however, to give the reader an intuitive notion of how declarations are made in the various languages:

FORTRAN

```
INTEGER A/10/,MTX(100,10)
REAL MAT1(10,10,10)
COMMON MAT1
```

COBOL

```
01 EMPLOYEE-RECORD, CLASS IS ALPHANUMERIC, USAGE
   IS DISPLAY.
        02 NAME, SIZE IS 30 CHARACTERS.
        02 BADGE, SIZE IS 4, CLASS IS NUMERIC.
            03 LOCATION, SIZE 2.
            03 DEPT, SIZE 2.
   02 SALARY, SIZE IS 12, PICTURE IS $,$$$,$$$.99.
```

PL/I

```
DECLARE ALPHA CHAR(20), SWITCH BIT(1),(X REAL,
Y COMPLEX)
          FLOAT BINARY, TOT BINARY FIXED (17,2),
               CNT DECIMAL FIXED(8);
          DECLARE 1 FORMAT 1 BASED (PTR),
                  2 FORMAT CHARACTER (1),
                  2 PAY-NUMBER CHARACTER (7),
                  2 WAGES FIXED DECIMAL (5,2);
```

Subprograms

The definition of a subprogram is composed of two parts, a subprogram head and a subprogram body. A *subprogram head* names the subprogram, denotes its attributes, and specifies its parameters. The parameters indicate which variables are to be replaced when the subprogram is invoked. The *subprogram body* gives the statements to be executed when the subprogram is used, and usually all statements which are ordinarily available in the programming language are permitted to be used when a subprogram is being developed.

When invoking a subprogram, the programmer specifies what arguments are to replace the dummy parameters given in the subprogram definition. During actual processing of an open subprogram, the machine set up. During the execution of a closed subprogram, the parameters are language instructions are executed directly, since no parameters need be replaced by the given arguments, and the statements are executed as if they were one of a kind.

Facilities for defining and using subprograms differ between programming languages, although most languages provide the CALL statement to invoke a subroutine subprogram. As with the previous class of statements, several examples are provided to clarify the concepts. A FUNCTION definition in FORTRAN would look somewhat as follows:

```
      FUNCTION AVER (X,N)
      REAL X(N)
      SUM=0.0
      DO 10 I=1,N
   10 SUM=SUM+X(I)
      AVER=SUM/FLOAT(N)
      RETURN
      END
```

It would be invoked by the term AVER(*a*,*n*) in an arithmetic expression. Similarly, the subprogram head of a COBOL subroutine definition might appear somewhat as follows:*

```
U1. ENTER LINKAGE-MODE.
    ENTRY 'GETREC' USING NUMBER, ADDRESS, COUNT.
U2. ENTER COBOL.
```

and the subprogram body would follow accordingly. Subprogram facilities provided in PL/I are similar in concept to those provided in FORTRAN, although the syntactic appearance seems to be quite different. Both types of subprograms are available and are declared by the same subprogram definition statement PROCEDURE. They differ, however, in the manner in which control is returned to the calling program. A function-type subprogram returns an explicit result with the RETURN (*expression*), while the subroutine subprogram returns an implied result with the RETURN statement without an operand. As an example of both types combined, consider the following random number generator which is entered as a subroutine to set the starting numbers and entered as a function for obtaining a random number:

```
SETRAND: PROCEDURE(M,N)
         DECLARE(GENNUM, RANDNUM) FIXED STATIC;
         GENNUM=M; RANDNUM=N;
         RETURN;
```

*Implementors of the COBOL language are given considerable freedom in implementing the ENTER verb. The sample given is perhaps typical of the many versions which exist.

```
RAND:    ENTRY:
         RANDNUM=GENNUM*RANDNUM;
         RETURN(RANDNUM);
         END;
```

The subprogram would be invoked for initialization and for obtaining a random number by statements such as:

```
CALL SETRAND(I,J);
      .
      .
      .
ALPHA=RAND;
```

In the first case, it is used as a subroutine; in the second, as a function.

Other Topics in Programming Languages

A wealth of other topics exists in the area of programming languages. *Block structure* refers to the process of grouping statements for control purposes and to establish the scope of a name. *Local* and *global variables* concern the program blocks in which a variable has meaning. *Macro facilities* are useful for program editing and for including, in a program, prepared program statements. Additional topics might include asynchronous processing, interrupt processing, data communications facilities, and dynamic storage allocation. The reader is referred to the references for information on these topics.

2.4 OPERATING SYSTEM PRINCIPLES

In general, computer systems are used in three ways: in a basic programming environment, with an operating system, and via remoting computing facilities. The first two methods are discussed here. Remote computing is discussed later.

Basic programming involves running each program step separately, as shown in Figure 2.3 and as listed in the following procedures:

1. The user prepares his program in a programming language and has the information punched into cards or recorded on magnetic or punched tape.
2. A compiler program, which can translate a program written in a programming language to one in machine language, is loaded into the computer.
3. The compiler program reads the program, prepared by the user, as data and produces a machine language program.
4. The user's machine language program is loaded into the computer; the program reads the user's data and produces results as output.

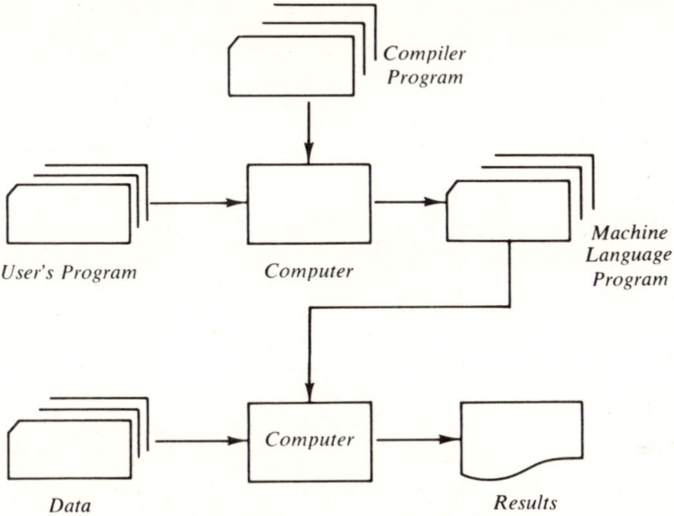

Figure 2.3 Basic programming environment.

The operations are usually distinct and require an appropriate amount of manual intervention between one step and the next. The steps are essentially repeated for each user. The second method (Figure 2.4) uses a computer program, called an *operating system*, to reduce setup time between jobs and to minimize operator intervention. The steps, present in basic programming, also exist in an operating environment monitored by an operating system. The major difference is that sequencing between jobs is automatic and that jobs are submitted to the operating system as a batch. The last topic is treated in more detail in the following paragraphs.

Batch Processing

The term *batch processing* originated with early operating systems and refers to the practice of collecting a batch of jobs and submitting them to the computer on an input tape. Similarly, output for the entire batch of jobs was collected on an output tape. A peripheral computer, as discussed in Chapter 1, was used for the card-to-tape operation and for the processing of the output tape.

The input tape was accessed by the operating system and the problem programs, and when one job terminated, the operating system readied the next job for execution. The early batch environment can be characterized in several ways. First, when a job was given control of the processing unit, it had complete control until its work was finished. Next, IO units

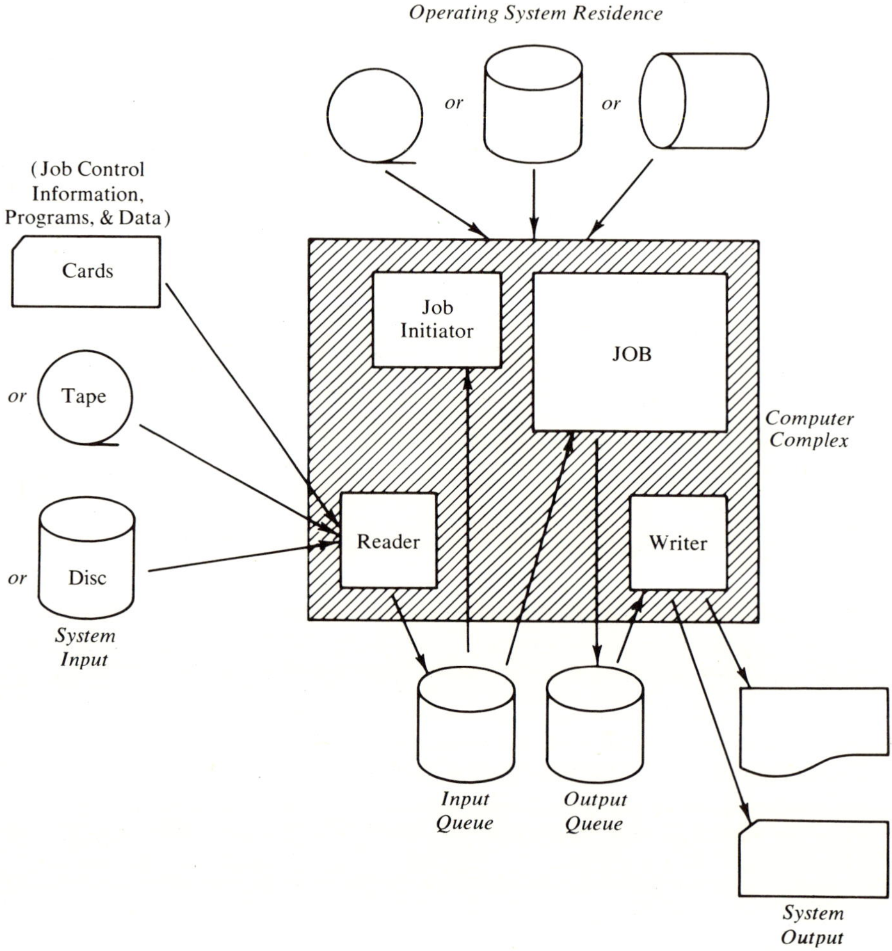

Figure 2.4 Operating system environment.

were addressed physically so that when a user wanted to change an IO device or device type, he had to recompile (or reassemble) his program. Last, programs to perform input and output were either coded in assembler language or provided with a programming language, such as FORTRAN.

The invention of the data channel (see Chapter 1) changed the situation considerably. Most importantly, it awakened an interest in operating systems and encouraged research and development personnel to explore ways of using the IO-compute overlap available with those devices. This research was the forerunner of the modern operating systems, and as a result of it, three basic components of an operating system were recognized:

1. *Input/output systems*, which provide a software interface between programs and external IO devices.
2. *Processing programs*, such as compilers, assemblers, and problem programs, which process data and produce results.
3. *Supervisory systems*, which provide a logical interface between the hardware system and the remainder of the software system.

The new interest in operating systems had three happy consequences:

1. IO procedures were generalized so that they now exist on a system-wide basis.
2. The programmer is now able to code his program without having to commit himself to a particular IO unit. In other words, he is able to specify a device symbolically at compile time and postpone making an actual device assignment until run time.
3. It was recognized that the natural waits (i.e., for IO, etc.) embedded in most programs could be used effectively to run other jobs in the machine.

Consequences (1) and (2) led to what is now known as data management. The last consequence led to multiprogramming and time-sharing systems.

In most operating systems, a minimum operational facility is provided, regardless of the number of user jobs that can reside in the system at one time:

1. The ability to process jobs sequentially and pass automatically to the next job when the first is completed.
2. The facility for controlling system input and output concurrently with the processing of the primary job. This involves the reading of jobs into the system and stacking them up on direct-access storage for subsequent processing, and the printing and punching of system output, which is similarly stacked up in direct-access storage.

Job Control

When a computer program is run in an operating system environment, the following information must be available before computer processing can begin:

1. Job control information.
2. Input/output requirements.
3. Program(s).

Job control information is usually presented on control cards which are interpreted by the operating system and provide the following information: job identification, priorities, and passwords; a specification of input/output requirements; and requests to have specific processing programs executed. Two types of data exist: problem data and source programs. Source programs are data to the language processors; for example, a FORTRAN or COBOL compiler. Problem data usually follow a request to have a problem program executed and exist in a form determined by the particular application. Depending upon the stage of program development, the job control information provided to the operating system may also contain debugging commands and request the services of "service programs" provided by the operating system. Figure 2.5 con-

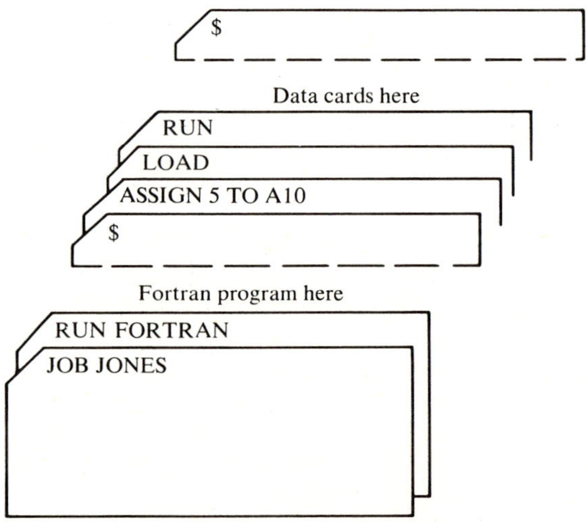

Figure 2.5 Sample deck setup.

tains a sample deck setup.* The various types of control cards are of particular interest. The JOB card establishes the programs and data as a unit of work to the operating system. The RUN card specifies that a particular processing program is to be executed. The $ card denotes end-of-data and is used to indicate the last card of a particular type. The ASSIGN card assigns a physical IO device to a symbolic name specified in the program. The LOAD card initiates loading of the machine language programs into main storage and readies them for execution. The second RUN card causes the user's programs to be executed. Lastly, the

*The control cards presented do not necessarily correspond to any existing operating system. The intent here is to describe representative functions that are available with an operating system.

user's program reads data from the job stream until the final $ card is read.

Normally, many users will be contending for the use of the computer system; it is the function of the operating system to utilize the job control information to recognize priorities and maintain job schedules in accordance with installation guidelines.

*Control Programs**

The input/output and supervisory systems, mentioned previously, were the forerunners of what are now regarded as control programs. They are responsible for the overall functioning of the computer system and have well-defined objectives, that is:

1. To maximize the use of the system's resources.
2. To provide for the continuous operation of the system.
3. To establish and maintain job priorities.
4. To insure the integrity of individual jobs.

The control programs which satisfy these needs are classed into three categories—system management, job management, and data management. First, the functions performed by the system in response to a job are introduced.

The system first reads the entire job (i.e., job control information, programs, and data) into main storage and places it on external storage as an input job stream; it then initiates the job as a unit of work to the operating system. This involves creating an initial program structure and forming a *job control block*, which will contain execution-control data and identify the job to the operating system. This function is accomplished by the *system management*† control program which also performs the following job-oriented functions for each job on a system-wide basis.

1. Schedules the job for execution on either a priority or a sequential basis.
2. Performs actual input/output for all jobs.
3. Processes normal and abnormal job terminations.
4. Allocates main storage.
5. Controls the printing and punching of output files by peripheral devices.

Other functions are oriented toward a particular job. *Job management* routines interpret job control information, execute service requests, and

*Control programs were mentioned in Chapter 1 under the name computer operating programs—which in fact they are.

†System management functions are referred to as *task management* in some operating systems—for example, OS/360.

monitor the execution of processing programs. *Data management* routines initiate input and output for the processing programs, maintain catalogs and libraries, and manage storage buffers.*

The three types of control programs have structural properties which, perhaps, are as significant as their functions. *System management* routines provide a logical interface between the hardware and the remainder of the software system. *Job management* routines provide a logical interface between processing problems and control programs. *Data management* routines provide a software interface between processing programs and external storage.

Most operating systems are interrupt-driven in the sense that the computing system processes a given unit of work until one of two events occurs: (1) It requires a system management function; or (2) a system management function is required for some other reason on a demand basis. In either case, the unit of work is interrupted and control is passed to a system management routine to interrogate the interruption. These interruptions are termed hardware interruptions in that they are initiated from an IO device, the processing unit, a machine instruction, or an external electronic device such as a timer or the computer console. System management's basic function is to respond to these interruptions by classifying them as to type and by initiating appropriate routines to process each. In so doing, system management maintains control over system facilities. The system facilities include the processing unit(s), main storage, and input/output devices. System management routines have several important characteristics which enable them to perform effectively the functions listed above:

1. They reside permanently in main storage.
2. They are not directly addressable by processing programs.
3. They execute in the supervisor state.†
4. Only one active copy of each exists in the system.

Job management's prime function is to monitor the execution of a job. Although job management routines, like data management routines, are considered control programs, they do not necessarily reside permanently in main storage. When system management gives control to a job, it normally returns where execution was last terminated. If a program interruption is pending, however, control is passed to a subsystem of job management called the *job monitor*. This is what is generally meant by a *software interruption*. The job monitor interrogates the program in-

*A storage buffer is an area of main storage set aside for use by data management to increase the efficiency of IO operations.

†The supervisor state is discussed in Chapter 1. Ordinarily, only control programs are allowed to execute in this state.

terruption condition and passes control to one of its own diagnostic routines or a routine provided by the user. A major portion of job management is concerned with job control information. Usually, job management contains a job control subsystem which reads the input job stream, interprets control cards, and calls appropriate routines to process them. Generally, a processing routine exists for each type of control card, although in some cases, data management routines are used to perform a major portion of the requested operation. The last major function of job management is to handle job terminations which may occur on a normal or abnormal basis.

Data management routines provide input/output support for processing programs and job management routines. They are grouped into four classes:

1. *Access routines* manage the transfer of data between an IO device and main storage.
2. *Catalog service routines* manage a system catalog so that data files may be referenced by name.
3. *Device management routines* control the allocation of physical IO devices to a job.
4. *External storage management routines* determine the manner in which space on direct-access volumes is allocated to the users of the system.

Although data management is concerned with input and output, it does none itself; but rather, it passes program control to a system management routine to have the operation performed.

The next section, on the architecture of operating systems, is concerned with the various types of systems. Basically, they all contain system, job, and data management routines but differ, for the most part, in how the overall system is organized.

Operating Systems Architecture

Operating systems architecture refers to the overall design of hardware and software components and their operational effectiveness as a whole. To be effective, however, an operating system must not only comprise the collection of hardware and software modules, but must also be designed in light of the programs and data which the system processes, and the people it serves. Early operating systems increased system performance by simplifying the operations side of the system. Current operating systems additionally attempt to maximize the use of hardware resources while maintaining a high level of work throughput or providing a certain level of terminal response. A multitude of programmer services is usually provided as well.

A *multiprogramming system* is an operating system designed to maintain a high level of work throughput while maximizing the use of hardware resources. As each job enters the system, an internal priority, which is a function of external priority and arrival sequence, is developed. This internal priority is used for processor scheduling. During multiprogramming operation, the program with the highest internal priority runs until a natural wait is encountered. While this wait is being serviced, processor control is turned over to the program with the next-highest priority until the first program's wait is satisfied, at which time processor control is returned to the high-priority program, regardless if the second program can still make use of the system. The first job has, in a sense, demanded control of the system. The concept is usually extended to several levels and is termed the *level of multiprogramming*.

One of the problems frequently faced by installation management involves running two different operating systems, each of which requires a dedicated but identical machine. A *hypervisor* is a control program that, along with a special hardware feature, permits two operating systems to share a common computing system. A relatively small hypervisor control program is required which interfaces the two systems. Although only one processor is involved, a hardware prefix register divides storage into two logically separate memories, each of which is utilized by an operating system. Input/output channels and devices are dedicated to one or the other operating system and use the hardware prefix register to know to which half of storage to go. All interruptions are indirectly routed to a *common interruption routine* which decides which operating system should receive the most recent interruption. Processor control is then passed to the hypervisor control program for dispatching. The hypervisor control program loads the prefix register and usually dispatches processor control to the operating system which received the last interruption. Alternate dispatching rules are to give one operating system priority over another or to give one operating system control of the processor after a fixed number of interruptions have been received by the other side. Hypervisors are particularly useful when it is necessary to run an emulator and an operating system at the same time. Under System/370, emulation facilities are available through a combination of hardware and software features that are analogous to the hypervisor concept. System/370 permits other computers *and* other operating systems to be emulated.

Although *time sharing* is used in a variety of contexts, it most frequently refers to the allocation of hardware resources to several users in a time-dependent fashion. More specifically, a *time-sharing system* concurrently supports multiple remote users engaging in a series of interactions with the system to develop or debug a program, run a program, or obtain information from the system. The basic philosophy behind time sharing is to give the remote user the operational advantages of having a machine to himself by using his *think*, *reaction*, or IO time to run other programs. Operation of a time-sharing system is summarized as follows:*

> Time-shared operation of a computer system permits the allocation of both space and time on a temporary and dynamically changing basis. Several user programs can reside in computer storage at one time while many others reside temporarily on auxiliary storage such as disk or drum. Computer control is turned over to a resident program for a scheduled time interval or until the program reaches a delay point (such as an IO operation), depending upon the priority structure and control algorithm. At this time, processor control is turned over to another program. A nonactive program may continue to reside in computer storage or may be moved to auxiliary storage, to make room for other programs, and subsequently be reloaded when its next turn for machine use occurs.

2.5 INFORMATION MANAGEMENT

A basic knowledge of information management is essential for an understanding of data management processes in a computer system. The following discussion is not exhaustive but does provide the reader with important terminology.

Storage Technology

It is necessary to distinguish between units of storage and units of data. Units of storage are essentially dependent upon hardware facilities, whereas units of data are formed from a combination of software programs and a user's application. In main storage, the basic unit of addressable storage is the 8-bit byte. The basic unit of secondary storage is a sector on disk or the information between gaps on tape or address markers on disk. The basic unit on secondary storage is a *volume*, such as a reel of magnetic tape or a disk pack.

Units of data are normally associated with units of storage but are given different names whenever necessary. In main storage, a useful unit of storage is termed a *field*, which can take the form of fixed or floating point numbers, a packed decimal number, or a series of bytes. A group of related fields is called a *logical record*. A unit of interchange between main storage and secondary storage is a *block*, which can be composed of one or more logical records. In secondary storage, a block corresponds to a physical record; in fact, the term block is frequently used interchange-

*See reference 2, p. 190.

ably with physical record. A series of consecutive blocks in secondary storage is known as an *extent*. The manner in which physical storage facilities are used determines the effectiveness of a data management system.

Data Organization

In data management applications, the user groups logical records into a *file*, as depicted in Figure 2.6. To an operating system, a named file is

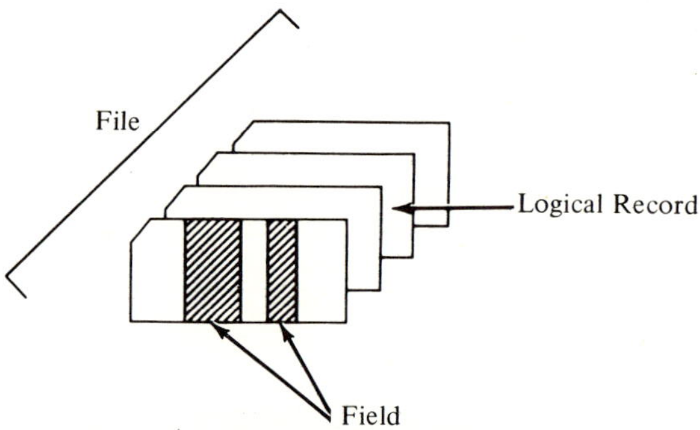

Figure 2.6 User data units.

termed a *data set* that is stored in secondary storage in one or more extents. Thus, by definition, a file need not necessarily be stored as consecutive blocks and may reside on one or more volumes. Data names are frequently grouped to form a *catalog* maintained by the operating system. The catalog entry for a data set contains control information allowing the data set to be referenced by name alone.

Clearly, a data set is a collection of blocks in which logical records* are stored. Data set organization is depicted in Figure 2.7. Records can be blocked according to one of four formats: fixed-length records, variable-length records, undefined-length records, and spanned records. The size of a *fixed-length record* is constant for all records in a file. Figure 2.8 shows blocked and unblocked fixed-length records. The *variable-length record* type allows variable-length blocks of records, as well as variable-length logical records. The block length (L) included as part of the block and precedes the data. Similarly, the record length (l) is included as part of the logical record and also precedes the data. Figure 2.9 depicts this type of format. The *undefined-length record* type is provided to allow the processing of files that do not meet the requirements of the preceding types. As shown in Figure 2.10, each block is treated as a record by the

*Logical records are often referred to as *data records*.

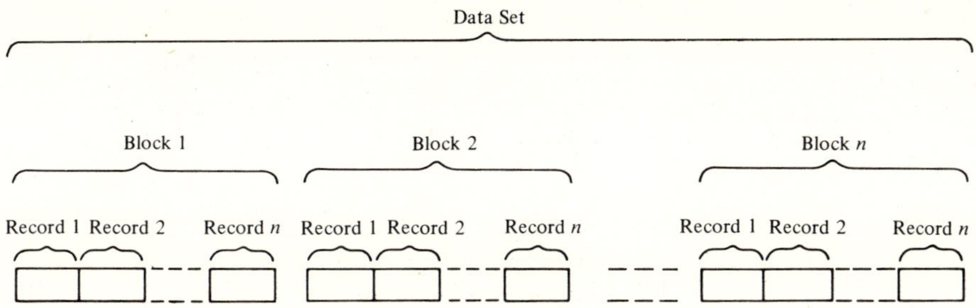

Figure 2.7 Data set organization.

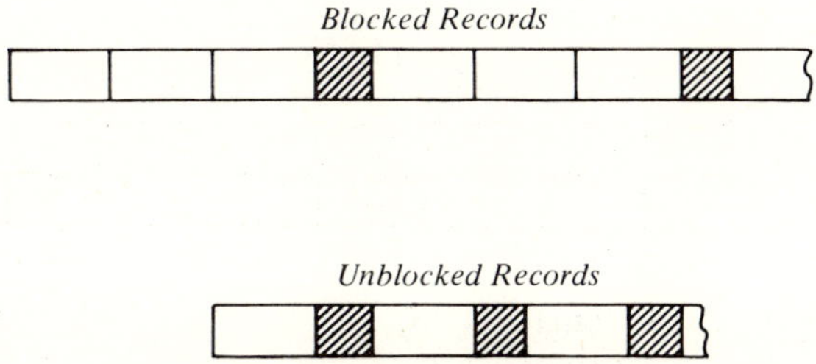

Figure 2.8 Fixed-length records.

data management routines and any unblocking must be programmed by the user. The use of a *spanned record* permits a logical record to span one or more blocks and is frequently used when the size of a data buffer is fixed or limited for some reason (Figure 2.11).

The technique of blocking logical records for input or output is usually transparent to the programmer who uses macros in assembler language or statements in a procedure-oriented language to program his input and output operations. Blocking and unblocking are performed by data management routines that perform those functions on a system-wide basis.

Access and Data Set Organization

The structure of information within a data set is usually determined by a particular application or by installation guidelines. *Data set organization* refers to established conventions for the arrangement of information in a data set. Three basic types exist and are supplied with most operating systems:

1. *Sequential.* This type of data organization is characterized by the fact that records are written and retrieved in physical rather than logical sequence. This type of organization is normally used for

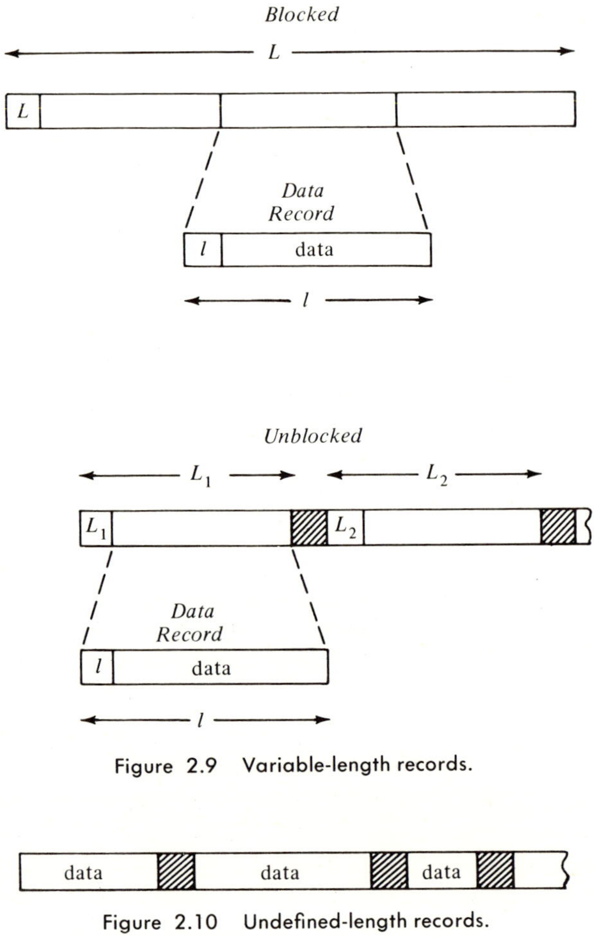

Figure 2.9 Variable-length records.

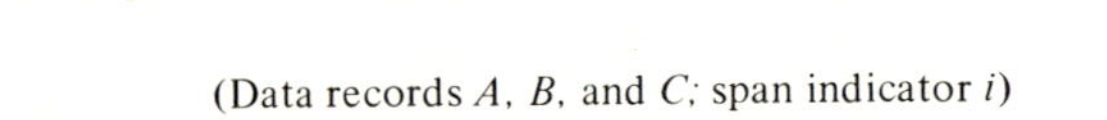

Figure 2.10 Undefined-length records.

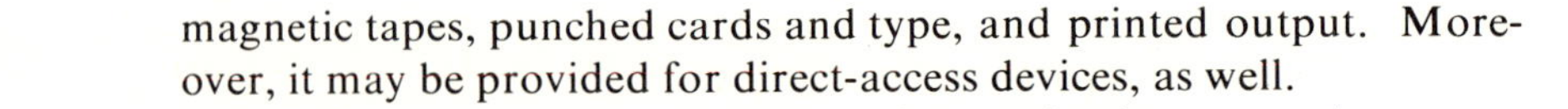

(Data records A, B, and C; span indicator i)

Figure 2.11 Spanned records.

magnetic tapes, punched cards and type, and printed output. Moreover, it may be provided for direct-access devices, as well.

2. *Indexed Sequential.* In this type of organization, records are arranged in collating sequence, according to a key field that is part of every record. This organization is normally used with direct-access devices and permits direct as well as sequential access to any record.

3. *Direct.* Records within data sets on direct-access devices may be retrieved directly if their physical locations are known. Direct organization provides for this type of processing.

Each method has advantages of its own. Sequential organization is particularly appropriate for data sets with long blocks that are accessed sequentially. Indexed sequential organization permits records to be inserted and deleted without rewriting the entire data set. Direct organization is appropriate for applications where information is accessed in a nonsequential order and where the physical location of a record is known.

Different techniques are normally available to the user for transferring data between main storage and an input/output device. These are termed access methods, which are available through macro instructions recognized by the assembler system. The techniques are classified by their treatment of buffering* and input/output synchronization with processing. The two techniques are named basic access and queued access and are defined as follows:

1. *Basic access.* An access method in which each input/output macro instruction causes a corresponding machine operation to be executed.
2. *Queued access.* An access method in which the transfer of data between the program and input/output devices is automatically synchronized, eliminating delays for input/output operations.

In discussing information management, several important topics have been omitted. Some of the most obvious omissions are: catalog structure, organization of information on direct-access devices, buffering techniques, and input/output programming. The reader is directed to Flores[1] for more information on these subjects.

2.6 REMOTE COMPUTING

Remote computing involves use of the computer from a remote location using telecommunications facilities—such as ordinary telephone lines. Usually, a remote computing application requires appropriate operating system control programs to manage the message handling in addition to user-written programs pertinent to the application. In other cases, such as time sharing, the operating system control program itself is designed to operate in a remote computing environment.

Applications

In most remote computing applications, a terminal device in the user's work area is used to transfer information between the remote location and

**Buffering* is generally regarded as a technique used to compensate for a difference in the rate of flow of information or the time occurrence of events when transferring information from one device to another.

the computer. The terminal device can take the form of a keyboard driven device; a graphic CRT-like device; a data entry device; an output device such as an audio response unit; or a general-purpose work station including a magnetic tape unit or a card reader and a line printer. Applications range from simple data entry systems to utility-class computing facilities where the resources of the system are shared among the users.

Data collection is an application in which data are received from a remote location by the main computer and stored for later processing. *Message switching* is an application where information is received from one remote terminal and sent to one or more other remote terminals. *Remote job processing* allows the user to enter a batch job into a computing system for processing and to receive the results later in time—all from a remote location. *Time sharing* is a mode of operation in which a number of users concurrently use a central computer to solve a problem or develop a program. In time sharing, the users may enter into a conversation with the computer to enter or receive information on a demand basis. The conversational mode is frequently used for computer aided instruction. *Inquiry and transaction* applications allow large data files to be updated or interrogated from a remote location. The terminal device for this application may be one of the devices mentioned previously or one that is specially designed for the given application.

Message Control Programs

By definition, a *message* is a unit of information that is transferred between a remote location and the central computer. A *message control program* is usually provided with an operating system and permits a user's program (called a processing program) to use the data communications facilities of the computer. In a sense, a message control program is the interface between the remote terminals and the message processing programs. When *queued access* is used, the message control program maintains storage buffers and receives and transmits messages in conjunction with normal computer processing. When *basic access* is used, a message processing program has direct control over the time when messages are transmitted and received. Figure 2.12 depicts a simple diagram of message processing.

Message Processing Programs

Message processing programs are written by the user and are required for most data collection, message switching, and inquiry and transaction applications. In many cases, data management packages that perform these functions are available commercially. Time sharing and remote job processing facilities are usually provided as part of an operating system control program.

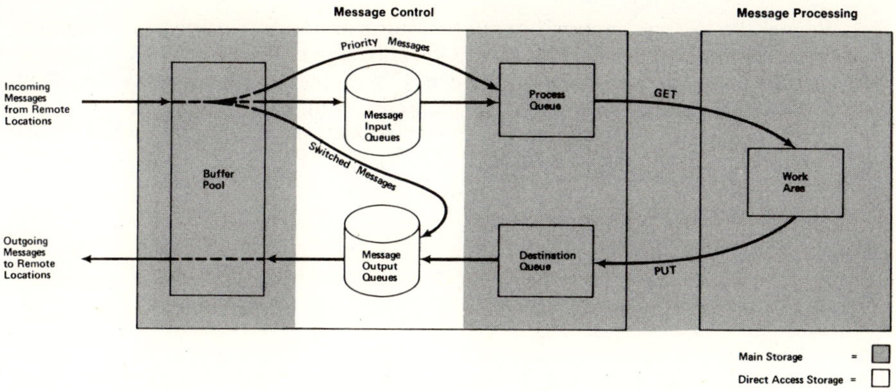

Figure 2.12 Message processing. (Courtesy of IBM Corporation.)

2.6 SUMMARY

The notion of an algorithm is a key concept in mathematics and characterizes many computer applications. A computer program is similar in concept to an algorithm and is usually defined in a programming language. Programming languages are of particular interest since they are the primary means of man-computer communications. An operating system controls the operation of a computing system and is the interface between a program and the computer hardware. Computers are designed to process information, and the means of storing that information in main storage and on secondary storage devices is of particular interest. Several methods are usually available with an operating system for organizing and accessing data. Lastly, remote computing is now an accepted mode of operation for many computer installations and requires a unique combination of control programs and processing programs.

REFERENCES

1. Flores, I., "Data Structure and Management," Prentice-Hall Inc., Englewood Cliffs, N.J., 1970.
2. Katzan, H., Jr., "Advanced Programming: Programming and Operating Systems," Van Nostrand Reinhold Co., New York, 1970.
3. Katzan, H., Jr., "Operating systems architecture," *Proceedings of the Spring Joint Computer Conference* (1970).
4. Knuth, D.E., "The Art of Computer Programming," Vol. 1, "Fundamental Algorithms," Addison-Wesley Publishing Co., Reading, Mass., 1968.
5. Rosen, S. (ed.), "Programming Systems and Languages," McGraw-Hill Book Co., New York, 1967.
6. Sammet, J.E., "Programming Languages: History and Fundamentals," Prentice-Hall Inc., Englewood Cliffs, N.J., 1969.

7. Wegner, P., "Programming Languages, Information Structures, and Machine Organization," McGraw-Hill Book Co., New York, 1968.
8. "PL/I Language Specifications," Form GY 33-6003, IBM United Kingdom Laboratories Ltd., Hursley Park, Winchester, Hampshire, England, 1969.
9. "IBM System/360 Operating System Introduction," Form C28-6534, IBM Corporation, Poughkeepsie, N.Y., 1969.

PART TWO: THE STRUCTURE OF SYSTEM/370

3 SYSTEM/370 ARCHITECTURE

3.1 BASIC SYSTEM STRUCTURE

The IBM* family of System/370 computers is a logical outgrowth of and an extension to the IBM System/360 family of computers. The design philosophy with both families of computers is to have a computer architecture that appears essentially the same to the user—regardless of the relative price/performance index of a particular model. Thus, an installation is provided with a growth path without reprogramming and the capability to exchange programs between systems that would ordinarily not be available with independently designed and constructed computers. From the user's point of view, therefore, the System/370 can be regarded as a single machine with the differences between models being a function of engineering implementation. The modular design of System/370 makes the computer appropriate for a wide range of applications: scientific, business, real time—to name only a few. Functional units such as input/output channels and devices can be added to the system to meet the needs of a particular application.

The discussion of System/370 given here is intended to be neither a definitive treatment of that computer nor an exhaustive presentation of the capabilities of the computer. It is intended to serve as a general introduction for the general reader—that is, a professional with an interest in

*IBM is a registered trademark of the International Business Machines Corporation with corporate headquarters in Armonk, New York, U.S.A.

the subject matter but not necessarily possessing any particular background.

For a definitive treatment of System/370, IBM reference manuals should be consulted. Specific references are given whenever appropriate.

System Organization

A System/370 model is composed of five different types of functional units: storage, a central processing unit, input/output channels, control units, and input/output devices. As depicted in Figure 3.1, the input/output units are attached to input/output channels through control units. Although the operation of the entire system is controlled by the central processing unit, it shares access to storage with the input/output channels, allowing input/output and computing to overlap in time to some degree. As with most modern computers, instructions and data are held in storage for use by the central processing unit. Information can be stored on a permanent or temporary basis with a complete range of input/output and mass storage devices, including tape, cards, and direct-access storage units.

Data Representation and Addressing

The basic unit of addressable main storage in System/370 is the 8-bit byte, which can represent one character, two decimal digits, or eight binary bits. Bytes may be processed separately or be grouped to form words or variable-length fields. Different-sized words are permitted. A *half word* is composed of two consecutive bytes and is the basic building block of instructions; fixed-point arithmetic is also permitted on half words. A *word* is composed of four consecutive bytes (32 bits) and can be used for fixed-point and floating-point arithmetic. Floating-point arithmetic is also available with *double words* (8 bytes or 64 bits) and is extended on some models of System/370 to *extended-precision words* (16 bytes or 128 bits).

Storage addresses within the computer are represented as binary integers starting at zero and the location in main storage of any field or group of bytes is specified by the address of its leftmost byte.

Character information is conveniently represented as 8-bit units of information allowing 2^8 (or 256) possible characters. System/370 uses the Extended Binary Coded Decimal Interchange Code (EBCDIC) depicted in Figure 3.2 with the bits being numbered as follows in any byte:

```
Byte
+-----------------+
|        A        |
| 1 1 0 0 0 0 0 1 |
+-----------------+
  0             7
```

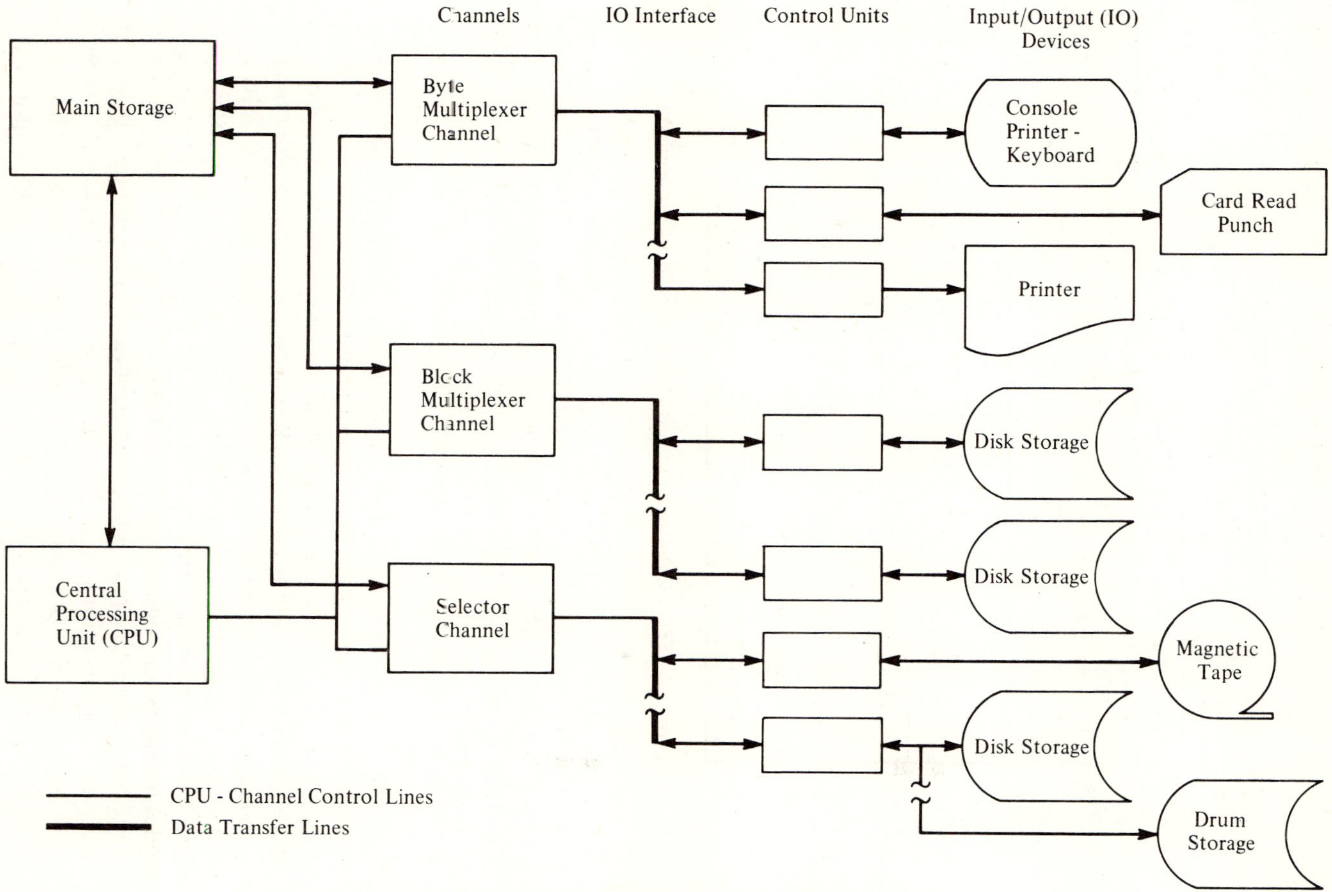

Figure 3.1 System/370 organization. (Courtesy of IBM Corporation.)

EBCDIC Bit Order
0 1 2 3 4 5 6 7

Bit Positions 0123 \ Bit Positions 4567	0000	0001	0010	0011	0100	0101	0110	0111	1000	1001	1010	1011	1100	1101	1110	1111
0000																
0001																
0010																
0011																
0100	Blank										¢	.	<	(	+	|
0101	&										!	$	*	)	;	¬
0110	-	/										,	%	_	>	?
0111											:	#	@	'	=	"
1000		a	b	c	d	e	f	g	h	i						
1001		j	k	l	m	n	o	p	q	r						
1010			s	t	u	v	w	x	y	z						
1111																
1100		A	B	C	D	E	F	G	H	I						
1101		J	K	L	M	N	O	P	Q	R						
1110			S	T	U	V	W	X	Y	Z						
1111	0	1	2	3	4	5	6	7	8	9						

Figure 3.2 EBCDIC character codes. (Courtesy of IBM Corporation.)

The value of the contents of a byte location is also conveniently denoted by two hexadecimal digits—each requiring four bits. Thus, the letter A given above can be denoted by the hexadecimal number C1 and an unedited dump of main storage displays the contents of each byte location as a pair of hexadecimal (called "hex") digits.

Data Formats

Numeric data may be stored in any of four formats: zoned decimal, packed decimal, fixed-point binary, and floating-point binary. Moreover, computer instructions are available for conversion between zoned decimal and packed decimal and between packed decimal and fixed-point binary.

Zoned decimal number format is available for use with EBCDIC input and output and permits a sign overpunch in the low order position of the field. Zoned decimal format is depicted in Figure 3.3; permissible bit codes for digits and signs are given in Table 3.1.

Packed decimal format allows efficient use of computer storage for commercial applications and permits arithmetic computation without conversion to a fixed-point or a floating-point representation. The packed decimal format is depicted in Figure 3.4. A variable field length is per-

TABLE 3.1 BIT CODES FOR DIGITS AND SIGNS

Digit	*Code*	*Sign*	*Code*	
0	0000	+	1010	(ASCII)[a]
1	0001	−	1011	(ASCII)
2	0010	+	1100	(EBCDIC)
3	0011	−	1101	(EBCDIC)
4	0100	+	1110	
5	0101	+	1111	
6	0110			
7	0111			
8	1000			
9	1001			

[a] The ASCII (American Standard Code for Information Interchange) mode is discontinued in System/370.

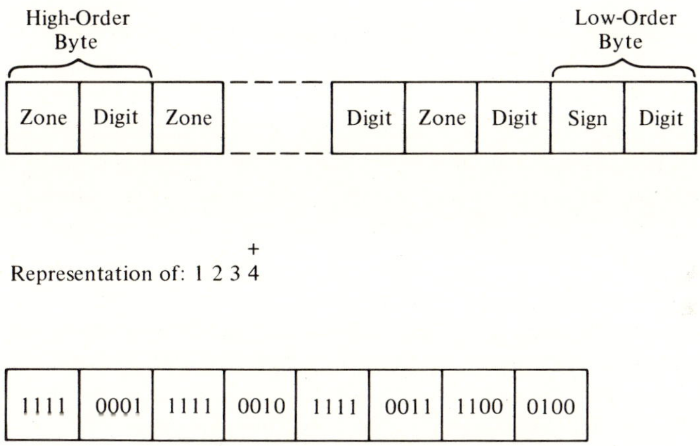

Figure 3.3 Zoned decimal number format.

mitted up to 16 bytes, which is equivalent to 31 digits and a sign. The numbers are treated as signed integers and a negative integer is carried in true form. (The digit and sign codes are given in Table 3.1.)

Fixed-point binary numbers can be represented as half words (2 bytes) and full words (4 bytes), as depicted in Figure 3.5. The format allows 15 and 31 bits of precision, respectively. If the sign bit is 0, the number is positive. If the sign bit is 1, the number is regarded as a negative integer stored in 2s complement form.

The architecture of System/370 includes three formats for floating-

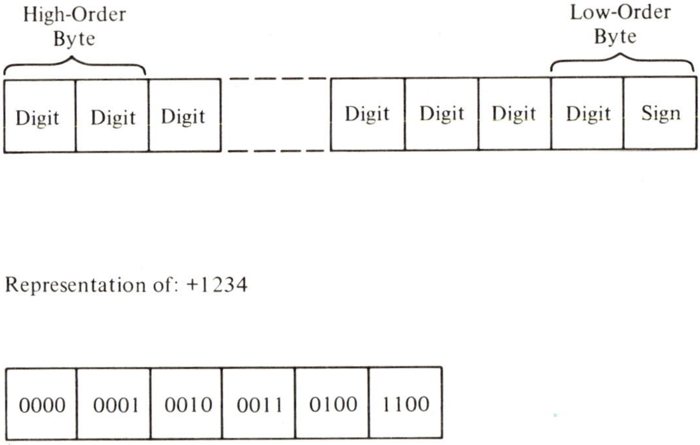

Figure 3.4 Packed decimal number format.

point binary data: short, long, and extended. All formats are depicted in Figure 3.6. The short form uses a full word and is equivalent to seven decimal places of precision. The long form uses a double word and provides 17 decimal places of precision. The extended form is considered later. The fraction of a floating-point number is regarded as hexadecimal digits with the radix point immediately to the left of the high-order digit of the fraction. The exponent portion of the number represents a power of 16, in excess 64 form, that should be considered as a multiplier of the fraction. The exponent provides a range of -64 through $+63$ which permits decimal numbers to be represented in the range of 10^{-78} to 10^{75}. A negative number is carried in true form where a 0 sign represents plus and 1 denotes minus. A normalized fraction has a nonzero high-order *hexadecimal* digit. The practice of regarding the exponent as a power of 16 allows a relatively large range of values to be represented with a relatively short (only 7 bits) exponent. An extended-precision floating-point number consists of two long-precision floating-point numbers, called the high-order and low-order parts. The fraction of the low-order part is considered an extension to the fraction of the high-order part. The high-order part carries the true exponent and the true sign. The exponent of the low-order part is always 14 less than the exponent of the high-order part. An extended-precision floating number can be used to carry approximately 34 decimal places of accuracy.

Local Storage

Local storage in System/370 includes 16 general registers and 4 floating-point registers. (See Figure 3.7.) Each *general register* has a capacity of a full word (32 bits) and can be used for arithmetic and logical operations

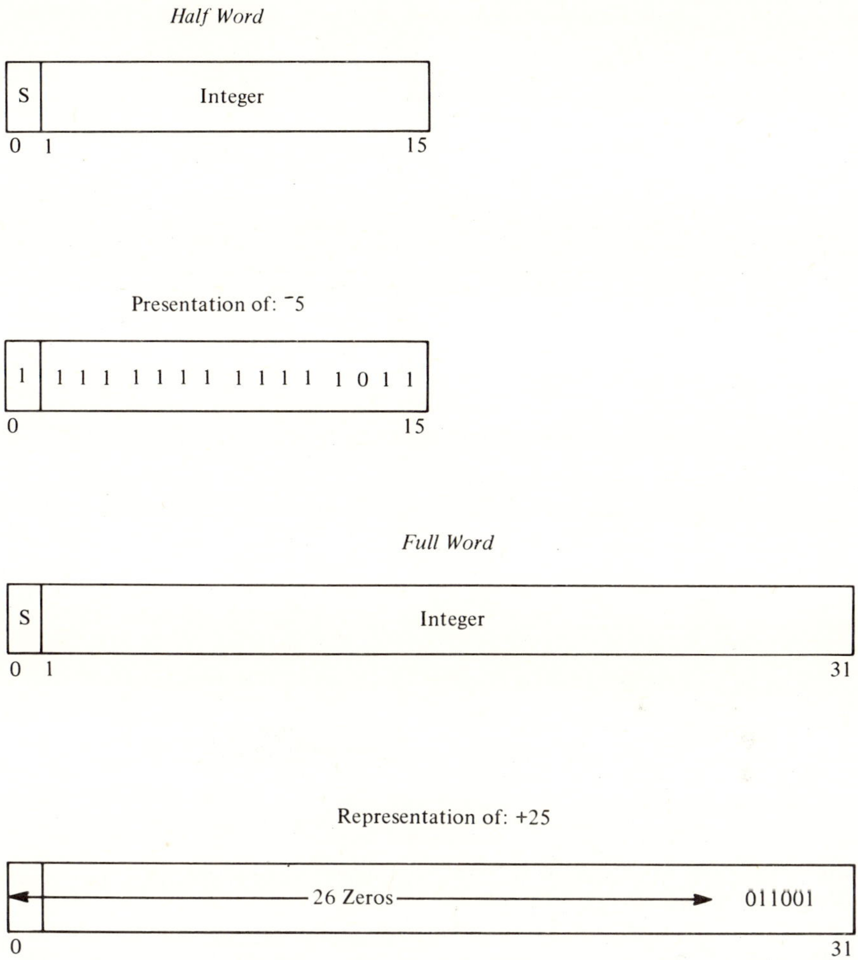

Figure 3.5 Fixed-point binary number format.

and in address arithmetic and addressing. The general registers* are numbered 0 through 15 and are identified by a 4-bit R field in a computer instruction. The floating-point registers are used for floating-point operations and are identified by the numbers 0, 2, 4, and 6. Each floating-point register is a double word (64 bits) in length and can hold either a short, long, or extended precision floating-point number. In the last case, the high-order and low-order parts must occupy adjacent registers, that is, registers 0,2 or registers 4,6. Any computer instruction that uses a local

*General registers are also called General-Purpose Registers (GPRs).

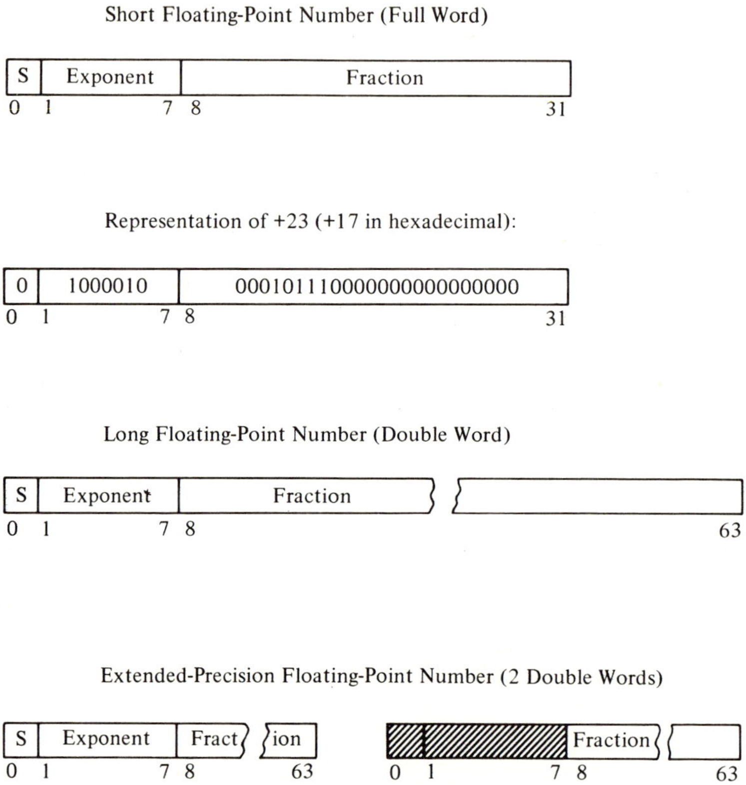

Figure 3.6 Floating-point number formats.

storage register contains an R field that specifies the number of the register to be used in the specified operation.

Instruction Formats

In System/370, computer instructions use five different formats that are generally related to the amount of information necessary to specify a given operation. The length of an instruction format can be one, two, or three half words, as summarized in Figure 3.8. The five formats are denoted by the codes: RR, RX, RS, SI, and SS. RR denotes a register-to-register operation; RX denotes a register and indexed storage operation; RS denotes a register and storage operation; SI denotes a storage and an immediate operand* operation; and SS denotes a storage-to-storage operation. The components of a computer instruction are denoted by letters,

*The term immediate operand refers to a data value that is held in the instruction itself.

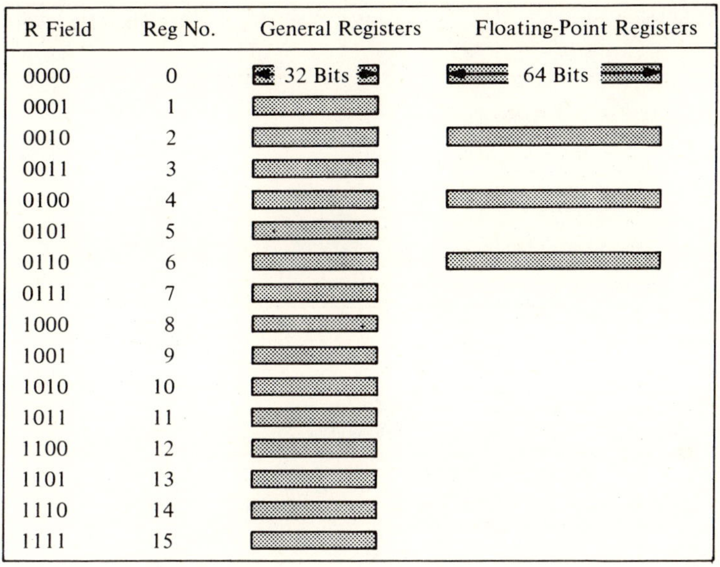

Figure 3.7 Local storage in System/370. (Courtesy of IBM Corporation.)

such as R for register and B for base. When instructions are described, the letters are subscripted to denote the manner in which the operands participate in the instruction. Computer instructions are discussed further in this chapter under *Processing Unit Functions*.

System Operation

System/370 operates by fetching instructions from main storage, decoding them, and initiating their execution by an appropriate functional unit. A general schematic of central processing unit (CPU) operation is given as Figure 3.9. It is seen from that diagram that floating-point arithmetic operations use the 4 floating-point registers, and the 16 general registers are used for fixed-point arithmetic operations and for address arithmetic. The execution of instructions proceeds sequentially until either a branch instruction is executed or an interrupt is received by the CPU; in either case, sequential execution is suspended and execution proceeds by fetching the next instruction from a specified location in main storage.

Although input/output (IO) operations are initiated by the CPU, IO transfer and control proceeds asynchronously under control of commands and orders. A *command* controls the operation of an IO channel and specifies a main storage address and a byte count for a data transfer operation or control information for a control operation. An *order* is par-

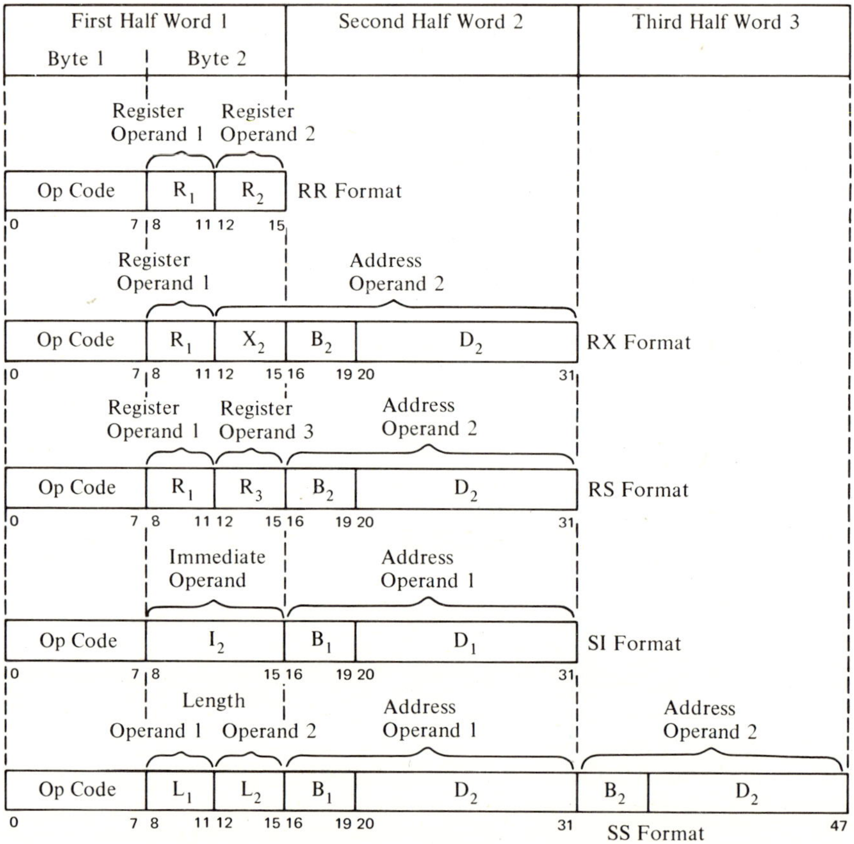

Figure 3.8 Instruction formats. (Courtesy of IBM Corporation.)

ticular to a particular IO control unit or device and specifies functions such as rewinding a tape unit or skipping a line on a printer. The relationship of IO instructions, commands, and orders is given in Figure 3.10.

The entire computer system runs under the direction of a collection of programs called an *operating system*, as introduced in Chapter 2. The operating system effectively manages computer system resources and schedules programs for execution. The question is, "How do the programs of the operating system get started?" The answer is that they are stored in machine-readable form on a mass storage or IO device. The computer operator's console contains a rotary dial that indicates the appropriate device and a LOAD (Initial Program Load) button. The operator positions the dial and pushes the LOAD button. The IPL operation

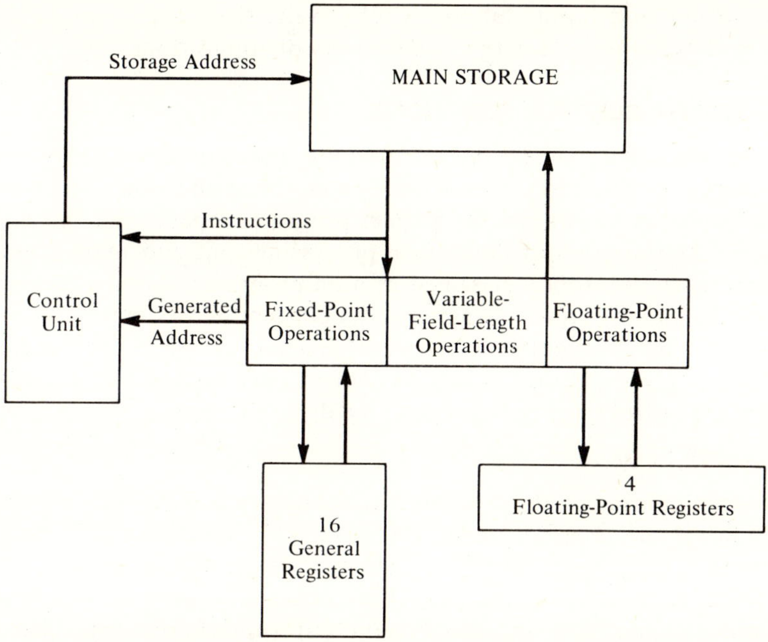

Figure 3.9 Central processing unit operation. (Courtesy of IBM Corporation.)

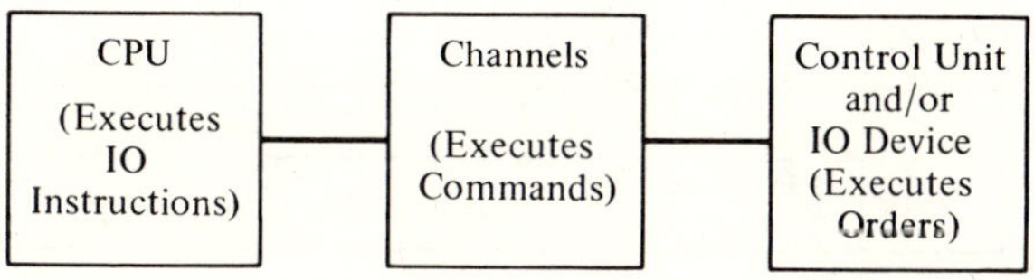

Figure 3.10 Relationship of IO instructions, commands, and orders.

initiates a series of machine functions that reads a small number of computer instructions from the specified device and transfers control to them. The instructions then read into main storage other programs of the operating system.

Outline of System/370 Structure

The basic structure of System/370 has been given. There is considerably more to be covered including system control functions, storage design and addressing, processing unit functions, branching and control, channel organization, and input/output. Collectively, these topics indicate how System/370 can be used with a wide variety of applications.

3.2 SYSTEM CONTROL FUNCTIONS

System/370 satisfies the need for a computer that can supervise itself without manual intervention over a wide range of applications. The design of the computer allows several distinct programs, operating concurrently, to share the resources of the central processing unit and main storage—an operating philosophy classified as multiprogramming or as time sharing. Similarly, the input/output channel concept allows input and output to proceed independently of program execution. All of the preceding facilities imply a certain amount of control over system operation; however, that control must be managed on a dynamic basis.

Program Status Word

Operating control of the System/370 computer is inherent in a double word called the *program status word* (PSW). Whenever a System/370 computer is operating, there is a current PSW held in a register internal to the central processing unit. The PSW denotes the state of the computer by indicating the following information: interruptions that can occur, program states, condition and mask bits, interruption codes, and the current instruction address. Thus, the process of storing the current PSW would preserve the state of the system at that point in time for further inspection.

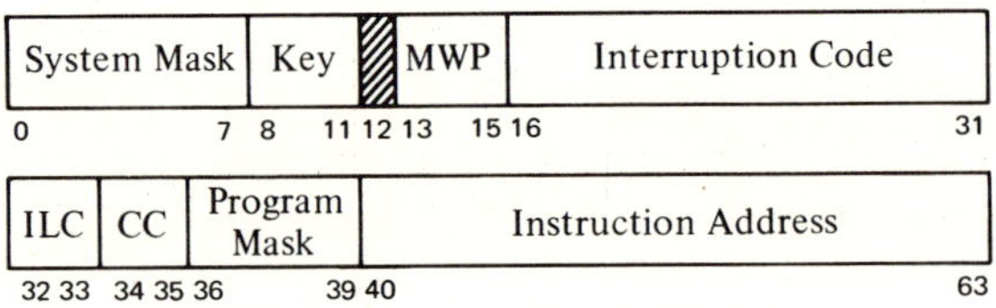

0-7	System mask	14	Wait state (W)
0	Channel 0 mask	15	Problem state (P)
1	Channel 1 mask	16-31	Interruption code
2	Channel 2 mask	32-33	Instruction length code (ILC)
3	Channel 3 mask	34-35	Condition code (CC)
4	Channel 4 mask	36-39	Program mask
5	Channel 5 mask	36	Fixed-point overflow mask
6	Channel 6 mask	37	Decimal overflow mask
7	External mask	38	Exponent underflow mask
8-11	Protection key	39	Significance mask
12	Not used	40-63	Instruction address
13	Machine-check mask (M)		

Figure 3.11 Program status word format.

Moreover, by loading a new PSW, the state of the system is changed. The PSW format is given in Figure 3.11. The fields in the PSW are described in subsequent paragraphs.

Control Registers

The design structure of System/370 provides for sixteen 32-bit control registers that augment the PSW in controlling the operation of the computer. The registers are not a part of addressable storage but can be loaded and stored by appropriate computer instructions that are executable in the supervisor state. Only five of the control registers (0, 2, 8, 14, and 15) are currently used with the remainder being reserved for further expansion. Moreover, not all bit positions may be relevant to a given model of the computer. The information stored in the control registers is listed in Table 3.2.

TABLE 3.2 CONTENTS OF CONTROL REGISTERS

Word	*Bits*	*Name of Field*	*Function*	*Value after System Reset*
0	0	Block multiplex mode	Block multiplexing control	0
0	24	Timer mask	Extended external masking	1
0	25	Interrupt key mask	Extended external masking	1
0	26	External signal mask	Extended external masking	1
2	0–31	Channel masks	Extended IO masking	1
8	16–31	Monitor masks	Monitoring	0
14	0	Hard stop mode	Machine check handling	1
14	1	Synchronous MCEL[a] mask	Machine check handling	1
14	2	IO extended logout	Machine check handling	0
14	4	Recovery report mask	Machine check handling	0
14	5	Configuration report mask	Machine check handling	0
14	6	External damage report mask	Machine check handling	1
14	7	Warning mask	Machine check handling	0
14	8	Asynchronous MCEL mask	Machine check handling	0
14	9	Asychronous fixed log mask	Machine check handling	0
15	8–31	MCEL pointer	Machine check handling	512

[a] Machine Check Extended Logout.

Program States

The execution of a program is affected by the states that determine the overall CPU status. Four distinct alternatives are possible: Problem/Supervisor state, Wait/Running state, Masked/Interruptable state, and the Stopped/Operating state.

The CPU is in the supervisor state when bit 15 of the PSW is zero. In this state, all computer instructions are valid—including IO instructions, protection instructions, and status changing instructions. IO, protection, and status changing instructions are classed as privileged instructions. When bit 15 of the PSW is one, the CPU is in the *problem state*, in which only nonprivileged instructions can be executed. The problem state is normally used for the execution of user programs. Bit 15 of the PSW is changed by executing a privileged computer instruction that loads a new PSW.

The *wait state* is usually entered when awaiting an interruption by loading a new PSW with bit 14 set to one. In the wait state, no instructions are processed but the timer continues to run. When bit 14 of the PSW is set to zero, the processing of instructions proceeds in the normal manner.

When the CPU can be interrupted for a particular interruption, that interruption is said to be *enabled* and a mask bit in either the PSW or one of the control registers is set to one. When the mask bit is zero, the interrupt will not occur and the interruption is said to be *masked off* or *disabled.* Interruptions are covered in the next section; however, not all interruptions can be masked off. The status of mask bits can be changed by loading a new PSW, loading a control register, or by executing one of two privileged instructions—SET SYSTEM MASK and SET PROGRAM MASK—that modify mask bits in the PSW.

The CPU can also be in either the stopped or the operating state. In the *stopped state*, instructions are not executed and interruptions cannot take place; in the *operating state*, the system is either waiting or running, as determined by the wait state bit, and interruptions can take place. The stopped and operating states can be entered only by manual intervention at the system control panel or by a machine malfunction.

Interruption

The interruption system permits the System/370 to respond to external conditions, to requests for system monitoring or service, and to error conditions on a dynamic basis. As a result of an interruption, the CPU can change state and normal execution proceeds from a specified location. By setting an appropriate bit in the PSW or a control register, an interruption can be enabled or disabled (i.e., masked off). A disabled interruption may be ignored by the CPU or be left pending, depending upon the type of interruption. A pending interruption is taken when that type of interruption is enabled. An interruption takes place after the execution of one instruction is finished and before the execution of a new instruction is started. Moreover, an interruption is accepted even if it is enabled for a single instruction execution.

Five types of interruption are possible: input/output, program, supervisor call, external, and machine check. Associated with each type of interruption are two fixed locations in main storage—each of which can hold a double word. In the first double word, the CPU automatically stores the current PSW at the instant of interruption; that double word is called the *old PSW*. The second double word is called the *new PSW* and the CPU automatically makes that double word the current PSW. The process of switching PSWs is depicted in Figure 3.12. The instruction

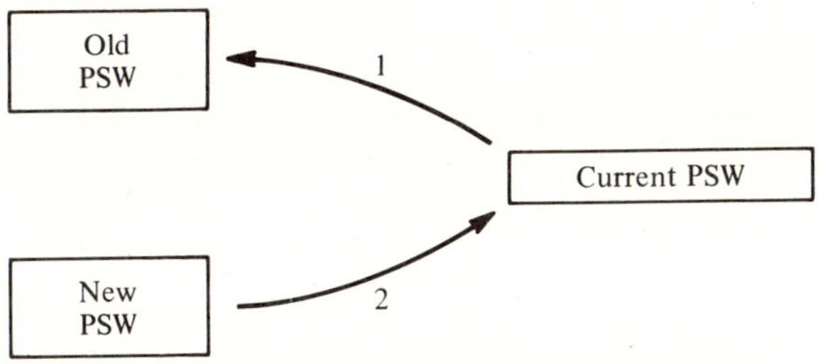

Figure 3.12 PSW switching after an interruption.

address field of the new PSW would naturally contain the address of the first instruction of a sequence of instructions designed to process that type of interruption. Clearly, the state of the CPU at the time of interruption is stored in the old PSW location for subsequent inspection. Table 3.3 lists the old and new PSW locations for the five types of interruptions. Bits 16–31 of the old PSW contain an *interruption code* that specifies the cause or source of the interruption. The interruption code differs among the five types of interruption.

TABLE 3.3 FIXED MAIN STORAGE LOCATIONS FOR OLD AND NEW PSWs FOR THE FIVE SYSTEM/370 INTERRUPTIONS

Type of Interruption	*Old PSW Location*	*New PSW Location*
External	24	88
Supervisor call	32	96
Program	40	104
Machine check	48	112
Input/output	56	120

An *input/output interruption* signals to the CPU that an IO channel is free, that a specific channel or control unit activity has been completed, or that a special condition has arisen. The address of the IO channel and control unit associated with the interruption are stored in bits 16–31 of the old PSW. Additional information on the nature of the interruption is saved in a *channel status word** that is stored when the interruption is

*For a description of the channel status word (CSW), see Chapter 4.

accepted by the CPU. IO interruptions can be masked off with bits 0–6 of the PSW and with control register 2. Channels numbered 0–5 are controlled by channel mask bits 0–5 in the PSW. IO masking for channels 6–11 (if implemented) are controlled by corresponding bits in control register 2, which are effective when channel mask bit 6 of the PSW is set.

A *program interruption* arises from an improper specification of computer facilities, an illegal use of an instruction or data, or a request for system monitoring. Sixteen possible conditions are listed in Table 3.4; the interruption code is placed in bits 16–31 of the PSW. Of these 16 conditions, 4 can be ignored by setting the respective bit in the PSW (bits 36–39).* The other program interruptions cannot be masked off. The system monitoring feature is also implemented through the program interruption system. It is described in a subsequent section.

The major purpose of the *supervisor call interruption* is to provide a means of switching from the problem state to the supervisor state. The supervisor call interruption is initiated by a supervisor call instruction (SVC) in a problem program and bits 8–15 of that half word instruction become bits 24–31 in the interruption code of the old PSW. Thus, information may be passed between the calling program and a supervisor program.

The *external interruption* allows the CPU to respond to the timer, an interrupt key on the operators console, or to one of six signal-in lines to the CPU. The signal-in lines may be part of a *direct control* feature that allows inter-CPU communications. The cause of an external interruption is identified by bits 24–31 of the old PSW; the interruption code bits are listed in Table 3.5. External interruptions are controlled by bit 7 of the PSW and an appropriate bit in control register 0. When bit 7 of the PSW and also bits 24, 25, or 26 of control register 0 are set to one, then timer, interrupt key, and external signal interruptions, respectively, are enabled. An interruption that is masked off is left pending. Bit 7 of the PSW must be set to one before any external interruption can occur.

A *machine check interruption* (MCI) results from a system malfunction and is classified as either hard or soft. A hard MCI is caused by a nonrecoverable machine error and results in an immediate termination of CPU activity and a logout of machine status if PSW bit 13 is set to one. A soft MCI is caused by a recoverable error and results in normal interruption processing. Both types of interruptions may be held pending. The circuitry of System/370 provides for error checking and correction (ECC) related to single bit storage error. Other types of errors are detected but not corrected automatically by the circuitry. Machine check

*Four conditions that can be ignored are fixed-point overflow, decimal overflow, exponent underflow, and significance. These conditions are listed in Figure 3.11.

TABLE 3.4 INTERRUPTION CODE FOR PROGRAM INTERRUPTION

	Interruption Code (bits 24–31 of old PSW)	*Program Interruption Cause*
1	00000001	Operation
2	00000010	Privileged operation
3	00000011	Execute
4	00000100	Protection
5	00000101	Addressing
6	00000110	Specification
7	00000111	Data
8	00001000	Fixed-point overflow
9	00001001	Fixed-point divide
10	00001010	Decimal overflow
11	00001011	Decimal divide
12	00001100	Exponent overflow
13	00001101	Exponent underflow
14	00001110	Significance
15	00001111	Floating-point divide
	10000000	Monitoring

TABLE 3.5 INTERRUPTION CODES AND MASK BITS FOR EXTERNAL INTERRUPTIONS

Interruption Code Bit (old PSW)	*Cause of Interruption*	*Mask Bit*	*Bit in Control Register 0*
24	Timer	7	24
25	Interrupt key	7	25
26	External signal 2	7	26
27	External signal 3	7	26
28	External signal 4	7	26
29	External signal 5	7	26
30	External signal 6	7	26
31	External signal 7	7	26

interruptions are controlled by PSW bit 13 in conjunction with control register 14. Machine check conditions governed by control register 14 are listed in Table 3.2. When a machine check interruption is taken by the CPU, a machine check interruption code (MCIC) of 8 bytes is stored in fixed location 232 and the new PSW is fetched from location 112. The MCIC identifies the cause of the machine check interruption and the interruption code field in the PSW is set to zero. Extended machine check information, including failing-storage address, region codes, and the contents of local and control registers, is stored in permanent storage locations. Machine check processing is necessarily model-dependent and differs in the amount of permanent storage required. The minimum amount of permanent storage required for machine check processing is

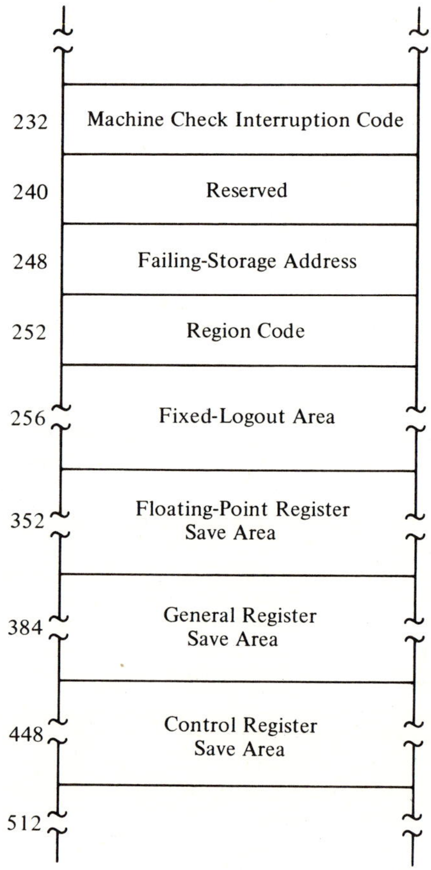

Figure 3.13 Permanent storage required for machine check processing. (Courtesy of IBM Corporation.)

given in Figure 3.13. Also, if machine check extended logout (MCEL) bits are set in control register 14, then additional model-dependent information on the status of the CPU is stored in a location specified in control register 15 (Figure 3.14). Machine check processing is discussed further with respect to specific models of System/370.

A priority is defined among interruptions for the case when more than one interruption request occurs during the execution of a single instruction. The machine check interruption has the highest priority and inhibits

Control Register 15

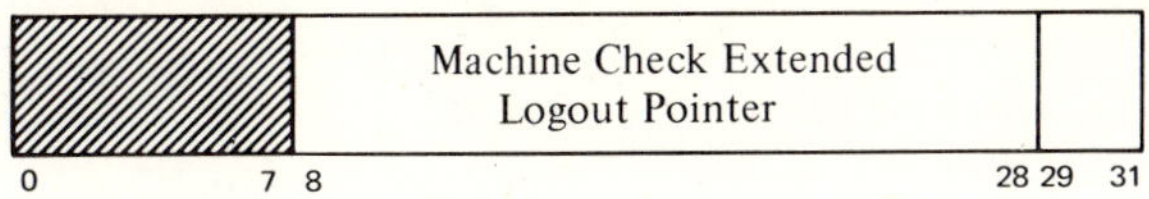

Figure 3.14 Machine check extended logout pointer.

other interruptions. When no machine check occurs, the program or supervisor call interruptions are taken first, followed by the external interruption, and lastly by the IO interruption. The CPU responds to multiple interruptions by performing the PSW switching for the first interruption taken. Then, before a single instruction execution, the next interruption is taken. The process continues until no more interruptions exist; the execution of instructions is initiated with the PSW fetched last. Thus, the interruptions are serviced in reverse to the order in which they were taken.*

When an interruption is taken, the instruction address field of the old PSW contains the address of the next instruction that would have been executed if the interruption had not occurred. Bits 32 and 33 of the old PSW contain an instruction length code (ILC) that indicates the length in half words of the last instruction that was interpreted by the CPU. The ILC is valid for program and supervisor call interruptions and is unpredictable for the other types of interruption. In high-performance models of System/370, the instruction length code is invalid for certain kinds of program interruptions. This event, called an *imprecise interruption*, is caused by the overlapping of instruction unit and execution unit operations.

Condition Code

The PSW contains a 2-bit field called the *condition code* (CC) that is set by the majority of arithmetic and logical operations. The two bits provide four settings: 0, 1, 2, and 3. The meaning of the various settings is determined by the operation that sets it. For example, a fixed-point add operation generates the following conditions:

Condition Code	*Result*
0	Sum is zero
1	Sum is less than zero
2	Sum is greater than zero
3	Overflow

*That is, unless masking occurs during the switching of PSWs.

Similarly, a floating point compare operation would yield one of these conditions:

Condition Code	*Result*
0	Operands are equal
1	First operand is low
2	First operand is high
3	Undefined

The condition code is stored as part of the old PSW and a new condition code is loaded with a new PSW in status switching or with the set program mask instruction. During normal program execution, the condition code is used by the branch instruction to alter the normal sequential execution of instructions.

Monitoring

The high-performance nature of the System/370 and its suitability for use in multiprogramming and time-sharing environments have created a need for a feature that provides a means of selectively recording information during the execution of the system. The *monitor call* instruction is available that designates one of sixteen monitoring classes and initiates a program interruption when executed by the CPU. A program is monitored by inserting monitor call instructions at selected locations in that program. The program interruption generated by the monitor call is usually serviced by a monitoring routine that records a monitor code supplied with the instruction.

The monitor call instruction is of the storage immediate type (SI) and provides a *monitor class* (bits 12–15) and a *monitor code* (base + displacement). The instruction operates in conjunction with mask bits 16–31 of control register 8. The mask bits, in ascending order, correspond to monitor classes 0–15. The mask bit for a monitor class denotes that events of that type are being monitored at that point in time. Several mask bits may be set at one time. When a monitor call instruction is executed by the CPU, the mask bit in control register 8 specified by the monitor class field in the instruction is inspected. If the mask bit is zero, no program interruption is initiated. If the mask bit is one, a program interruption is taken and the following steps take place:

1. The interruption code (See Table 3.4) is placed in the old PSW.
2. The monitor class number is placed in byte location 149 of main storage (location 148 is set to zero).
3. The monitor code (base + displacement) is placed in locations 157–159 of main storage (location 156 is set to zero).

It follows that once monitor call instructions are inserted in a program, the program interruption corresponding to a given monitor class can be enabled or disabled by altering the appropriate bit in control register 8. Within each of the sixteen monitor classes, 2^{24} (corresponding to the 24-bit effective address) distinct monitor codes can be used.

System Timers

Each model of the System/370 family of computers includes an interval timer and a time-of-day clock. The *interval timer* is maintained in fixed location 80 in main storage and has a resolution of 3.33 milliseconds. It occupies a 32-bit word (4 bytes); however, only bits 0–23 are used corresponding to a full cycle of 15.5 hours. The timer is counted down at a rate of 60 cycles per second and generates an external interruption (if not masked off) when its value goes from positive to negative. The interval timer is frequently used to measure elapsed time over short intervals. Location 80 may be referenced by a nonprivileged computer instruction provided that that area is not storage protected.

The *time-of-day clock* is an internal double word binary counter that provides an accurate measure of elapsed time, independent of system activity. The double word is essentially a fixed-point number of double precision with bits numbered from 0 to 63. The resolution of the clock is one microsecond, achieved by adding a one in bit position 51 each microsecond. The cycle of the clock is approximately 142 years. A privileged instruction, set clock, permits the contents of the clock to be set; however, the set clock instruction is operational only when the clock security switch on the operator intervention panel is positioned accordingly. A nonprivileged instruction, store clock, allows the current value of the clock to be placed in main storage. It is stored as an 8-byte field; zeros are provided for bits 52–63, which are not updated by the clock.

System Control Panel

The switches, keys, and lights necessary for operating a System/370 computer are placed on the system control panel. Physical implementation of the system control panel varies between different models of System/370. In general, the three main functions provided are: the ability to reset the system; a means of manually storing and displaying information in main storage, in registers, and in the PSW; and initial program load (IPL) facilities.

The *system reset* function resets the CPU, channels, and IO system so that processing can be initiated without the occurrence of machine checks. All pending interruptions are eliminated, the parity of internal registers is corrected, and all status indicators are reset to zero.

The *store and display* function allows the CPU to be stopped and permits the storing and displaying of information in main storage and the internal registers. The procedure may require that dials, switches, and lights be used or may involve a CRT display unit, depending upon the model of System/370 used. After manual intervention has been completed, normal instruction execution can be initiated.

Initial program loading (IPL) involves selecting an input device with the load-unit switches and then pressing the load key on the control panel. Pressing the load key causes a system reset, performs several internal functions, and initiates a read of 24 bytes from the selected device into storage locations 0–23. The CPU uses the double word stored in location 0 as the new PSW and initiates execution under control of that PSW. The double word read into location 8 is used as the channel command word for a subsequent IO operation. The IPL sequence is normally used to invoke an operating system control program.

3.3 STORAGE DESIGN AND ADDRESSING

The main storage facilities of the System/370 are designed to support high-performance computing over a broad spectrum of applications. This section covers a variety of topics related to the function and use of main storage.

Performance Factors

The performance of a main storage unit is dependent upon several important factors: capacity, access widths, cycle time, and degree of interleaving. Performance is also affected by parity and error checking, storage protection, address generation, and addressing; however, these are treated as distinct topics.

Main storage *capacity* of System/370 ranges from 96K (98,304) bytes to 3072K (3,145, 728) bytes depending, in part, upon the model of the CPU. Implementation of main storage is also model-dependent and varies between discrete ferrite cores and monolithic technology. *Access width* refers to the amount of information that is transferred between main storage and the CPU with each access. The width is particularly important for operations that allow variable-length and double word operands since a given instruction may require more than one access to storage. The access width is model-dependent and ranges from 4 to 16 bytes. *Cycle time* refers, in general, to the time that storage is busy after a reference is made to it. Cycle time is related to the performance index of a given model; in addition, it is effectively reduced further with a buffer storage system (see Chapter 1) implemented on Models 155 and 165. Storage is also *interleaved* with some models of System/370 allowing storage accesses to be overlapped, in time, depending upon the sequence of references required by a given program. Performance factors are discussed further with respect to a specific model of System/370.

Parity and ECC

Data are transferred between main storage and the CPU and within the CPU in multiples of 8-bits; in other words, one or more bytes are transferred. CPU registers, buffers, and data transfers carry a ninth *parity* bit along with each byte. Odd parity is maintained and a machine check is generated whenever a parity error cannot be corrected.

Error checking and correction (ECC) refers to a storage facility that associates an ECC code with a group of bytes called an *ECC block*. ECC permits single bit errors to be automatically corrected. The number of bytes in an ECC block and the method of implementation is model-dependent.

Storage Protection

The storage protection facility in System/370 protects against unauthorized access to specified storage blocks. As described in Chapter 1, a 5-bit storage key is provided with each 2048 bytes of main storage. A protection key field occupies bits 8–11 of the PSW and bits 0–3 of the channel address word (see Chapter 4). The protection key must match the storage key of a storage block before that block can be accessed by either the CPU or an IO channel. Depending upon the setting of the fetch bit in the storage key (i.e., the fifth bit), a storage block is protected against a storage operation or against storage *and* fetch operations. Access is also permitted if the protection key is zero. The storage protection system operates independently of the various states of the CPU. Two privileged instructions, set storage key and insert storage key, allow the storage key for a specified 2048-byte storage block to be changed or inspected, respectively. Thus, a program executing in the supervisor state can reference any storage block by first inspecting its storage key and then by setting the protection key in the current PSW accordingly.

Address Generation

The System/370 uses a base/displacement addressing scheme that allows relative addressing within a 4096-byte block of main storage. Three fields in a computer instruction pertain to main storage addressing: a base register specification (B), an index register specification (X), and a displacement (D). Register specifications denote one of the 16 general registers and are 4 bits in length. The displacement is 12 bits long and allows relative addressing of up to 4095 bytes beyond the base address. Many System/370 instructions designate an index register that is also used in address generation. An effective main storage address is calculated by adding the contents of the base register, the contents of the index register (if used), and the displacement field—as depicted in Figure 3.15. Address

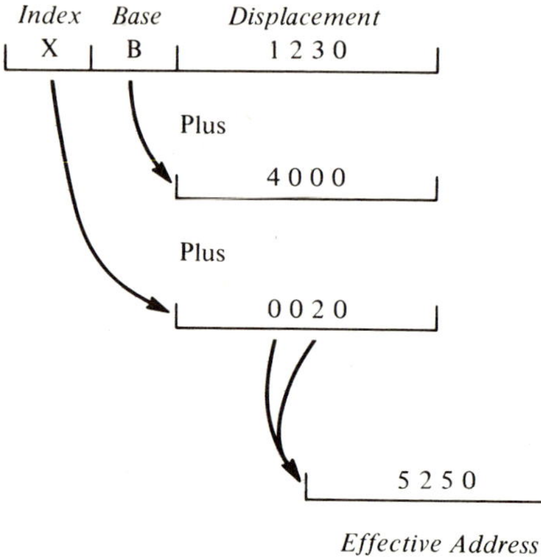

Figure 3.15 Address generation.

arithmetic uses the low-order 24 bits of the specified registers. A zero base or index field in an instruction denotes that a zero value is to be used in computing the effective address, regardless of the contents of general register 0. When supported by appropriate software, base/displacement addressing facilitates the addressing of a very large storage and the implementation of shared programs and dynamic program relocation.

Boundary Alignment

One of the design factors that contributed to the good performance of the System/360 computers was that fixed-length fields, such as half words, words, and double words, had to be located in main storage on an *integral boundary* for that unit of information. An integral boundary for a given word requires that its storage address be a multiple of the word length in bytes. For example, a word (4 bytes) had to be located in main storage so that its address was a multiple of the number 4. Boundary alignment works in conjunction with *access width* to insure that unneeded storage fetches are not made. Figure 3.16 gives integral boundaries for half words, words, and double words. Subsequently, a byte-oriented operand feature became available with System/360 that eliminated the boundary alignment restriction for operands of non-privileged instructions.

The byte-oriented operand feature is *standard* with any model of System/370. However, performance degradation can be expected over the same program using boundary alignment. The byte-operand feature does not apply to computer instructions and CCWs (see Chapter 4), which must be located on half word boundaries, and to the operands of privi-

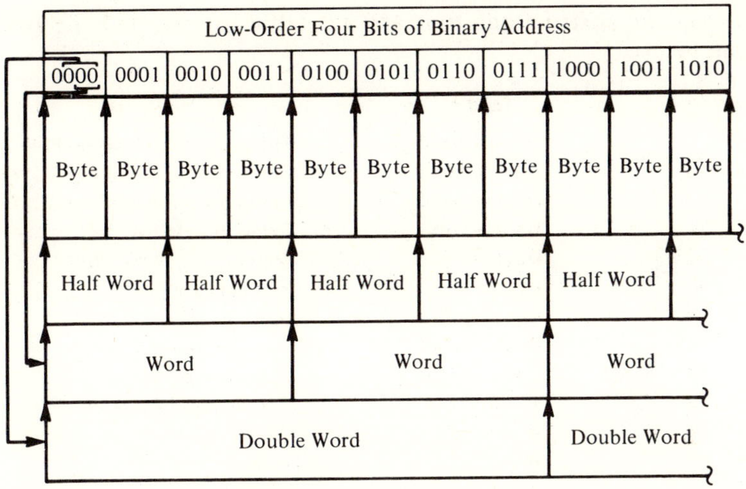

Figure 3.16 Integral boundaries for half words, words, and double words. (Courtesy of IBM Corporation.)

leged instructions, which must satisfy the boundary alignment requirement.

Variable-length operands may be located on byte boundaries.

Permanent Storage Assignments

Many system control functions utilize fixed storage areas, located in the lower portion of main storage. Byte positions 0–127 are System/370 model-independent and compatible with System/360 models except for the ASCII bit (bit 12) of the PSW. The fixed logout area extends from byte position 232 to position 511; it is also model-independent. In general, positions 128–167 are unused* and positions 168–231 vary slightly between models. The CPU extended logout begins in byte position 512 and varies in length from 192 bytes in the model 145 to 1000 bytes in the model 165. A figure giving the complete permanent storage assignments would be inappropriate here. Byte positions 0–127, however, are given in Figure 3.17 and Figure 3.13 shows the fixed logout area. Model-dependent storage assignments are given with the description of that model.

3.4 PROCESSING UNIT FUNCTIONS

The power of a computer is reflected in the instruction repertoire that can be used to construct programs. System/370 includes considerable variety

*The monitor call instruction uses locations 148–149 and locations 156–159.

in the types of instructions that are available for use and the operands that can be used.

Address	*Length*	*Purpose*
0	Double word	Initial program loading PSW
8	Double word	Initial program loading CCW1
16	Double word	Initial program loading CCW2
24	Double word	External old PSW
32	Double word	Supervisor call old PSW
40	Double word	Program old PSW
48	Double word	Machine check old PSW
56	Double word	Input/output old PSW
64	Double word	Channel status word
72	Word	Channel address word
76	Word	Unused
80	Word	Timer
84	Word	Unused
88	Double word	External new PSW
96	Double word	Supervisor call new PSW
104	Double word	Program new PSW
112	Double word	Machine check new PSW
120	Double word	Input/output new PSW

Figure 3.17 Permanent main storage assignments for byte positions 0–127. The fixed logout area is given as Figure 3.13. Model-dependent information is given with the description of that model. (Courtesy of IBM Corporation.)

Instruction Sets

Computer instructions, in System/370, are generally classed as follows:

Fixed-point binary arithmetic and logic
Floating-point
Decimal
Protection

Within each class, instructions are identified by the functions they perform. *Fixed-point binary arithmetic and logic instructions* include the basic instruction sets necessary for using the System/370. Also included in this class are the IO, branching, and control instructions. *Floating-point instructions*, used primarily in scientific operations, permit calculations on data with a wide range of magnitude. *Decimal instructions* are used primarily in commercial applications and permit arithmetic operations without conversion to a form of binary notation. Editing instructions also fall into this class. *Protection instructions* are used with the storage protection facility of main storage. Figure 3.18 describes the System/370 instruction sets. The fixed-point binary arithmetic and logic instructions

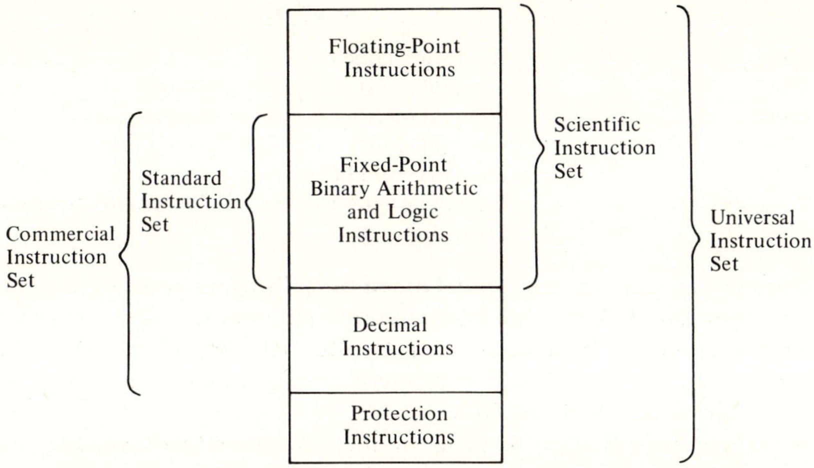

Figure 3.18 System/370 instruction sets. (Courtesy of IBM Corporation.)

are classed as the *standard instruction set.* The standard instruction set and the floating-point instructions comprise the *scientific instruction set*. The *commercial instruction set* includes the standard instruction set and the decimal instructions. The *universal instruction set* is formed when the protection instructions are combined with the standard, commercial, and scientific instruction sets.

Input and output instructions are discussed in the next chapter on channel organization and input/output.

Instruction Codes and Formats

An operand of a computer instruction can assume one of three forms: a register number, a main storage address, or an immediate value contained in the instruction itself. The instruction format types are listed for reference.

Bit Positions 0–1 of Operation Code	*Length (in half words)*	*Designation*	*Explanation*
00	1	RR	Register to register
01	2	RX	Register to indexed storage
10	2	RS	Register to storage
10	2	SI	Storage and immediate operand
11	3	SS	Storage to storage

The fields that participate in an instruction are of fixed length and are also designated by capital letters for convenience.

Field Length	*Designation*	*Meaning*
8 bits	OP	Operation code
4 bits	R	General register used in operation
4 bits	X	General register used as in *index register*
4 bits	B	General register used as a *base* register
12 bits	D	Displacement field
4 or 8 bits	L	Length designation for variable length operation
8 bits	I	Immediate value

Operation codes are represented mnemonically as a series of meaningful letters, for example L denotes load, and that mnemonic is also used as the assembler language machine operation code. All instructions generate a program interrupt condition if improperly specified and many instructions set the condition code in the PSW.

No information is given on programming, on assembler language, or on the use of a higher-level language. Appropriate IBM reference manuals should be consulted; however, machine and assembler language formats are given in Figure 3.19 to facilitate further study.

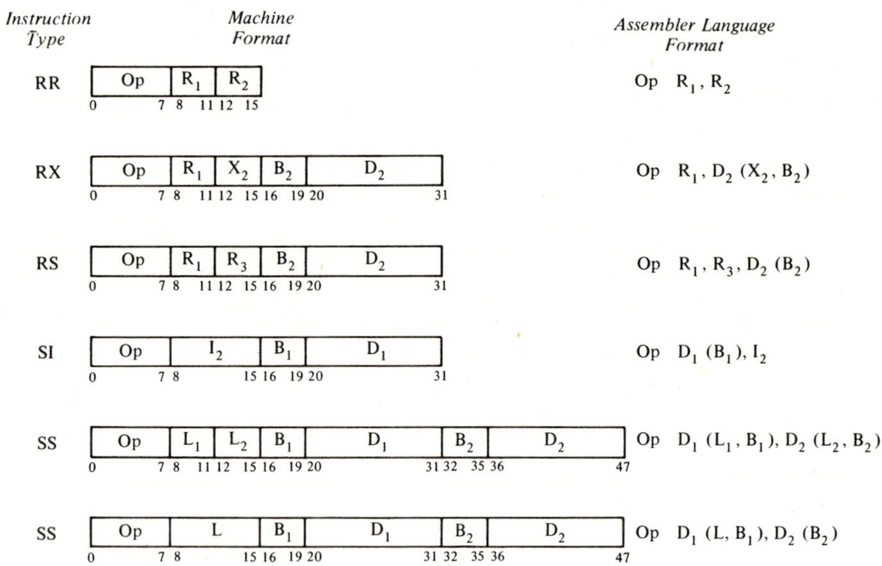

Figure 3.19 Machine and assembler language formats.

Fixed-Point Arithmetic

Fixed-point binary arithmetic is performed in the general registers and is defined as words and half words. Some multiply, divide, and shifting operands use a pair of adjacent general registers (i.e., 63 bits plus a sign)

TABLE 3.6 FIXED-POINT ARITHMETIC INSTRUCTIONS

Name	*Mnemonic*	*Type*		*Exceptions*
Load	LR	RR		
Load	L	RX		P,A,S
Load half word	LH	RX		P,A,S
Load and test	LTR	RR	C	
Load complement	LCR	RR	C	IF
Load positive	LPR	RR	C	IF
Load negative	LNR	RR	C	
Load multiple	LM	RS		P,A,S
Add	AR	RR	C	IF
Add	A	RX	C	P,A,S, IF
Add half word	AH	RX	C	P,A,S, IF
Add logical	ALR	RR	C	
Add logical	AL	RX	C	P,A,S
Subtract	SR	RR	C	IF
Subtract	S	RX	C	P,A,S, IF
Subtract half word	SH	RX	C	P,A,S, IF
Subtract logical	SLR	RR	C	
Subtract logical	SL	RX	C	P,A,S
Compare	CR	RR	C	
Compare	C	RX	C	P,A,S
Compare half word	CH	RX	C	P,A,S
Multiply	MR	RR		S
Multiply	M	RX		P,A,S
Multiply half word	MH	RX		P,A,S
Divide	DR	RR		S, IK
Divide	D	RX		P,A,S, IK
Convert to binary	CVB	RX		P,A,S,D,IK
Convert to decimal	CVD	RX		P,A,S
Store	ST	RX		P,A,S
Store half word	STH	RX		P,A,S
Store multiple	STM	RS		P,A,S
Shift left single	SLA	RS	C	IF
Shift right single	SRA	RS	C	
Shift left double	SLDA	RS	C	S, IF
Shift right double	SRDA	RS	C	S

Notes

- A Addressing exception
- C Condition code is set
- D Data exception
- IF Fixed-point overflow exception
- IK Fixed-point divide exception
- P Protection exception
- S Specification exception

and are addressed by the leftmost register which must be identified by an even number. Negative numbers are represented in 2s complement form and a half word occupies the right half of a general register. When a half word is loaded into a general register, the leftmost digit is extended to occupy the left half of that register.

Table 3.6 lists the fixed-point arithmetic instructions and indicates those that set the condition code and the program interruptions that can occur.

Two instructions, convert-to-binary (CVB) and convert-to-decimal (CVD), perform conversion between packed decimal format and fixed-point binary format. As described in the next section, they are key links in the data processing cycle.

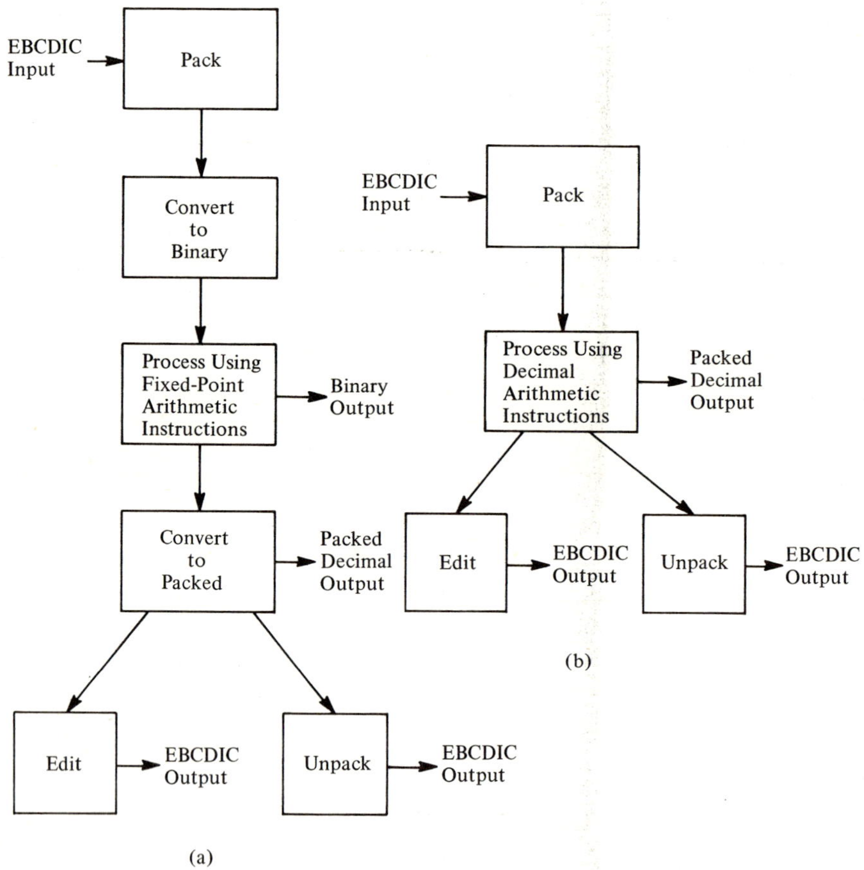

Figure 3.20 Typical arithmetic data processing cycle. (a) Binary arithmetic. (b) Decimal arithmetic.

Decimal Arithmetic

Decimal arithmetic instructions operate on packed decimal data and utilize operands retained in main storage. Operands can maintain a precision of up to 31 digits plus a sign. Figure 3.20 depicts a typical arithmetic data processing cycle. Input data are in EBCDIC* form. They are first converted from zoned decimal format to packed decimal format with the pack instruction (PACK). Calculations can be made in decimal arithmetic or in fixed-point arithmetic after a conversion to binary. Lastly, output can be recorded in three forms: binary, decimal, or EBCDIC. In the last case, packed decimal data must be converted to zoned decimal with the unpack instruction (UNPK) or be edited with the edit instruction (ED) before output in EBCDIC form.

Decimal arithmetic values are carried in true form. Table 3.7 lists the decimal arithmetic instructions, condition code information, and program interruptions.

TABLE 3.7 DECIMAL ARITHMETIC INSTRUCTIONS

Name	*Mnemonic*	*Type*	*Exceptions*
Add decimal	AP	SS T,C	P,A, D,DF
Subtact decimal	SP	SS T,C	P,A, D,DF
Zero and add	ZAP	SS T,C	P,A, D,DF
Compare decimal	CP	SS T,C	P,A, D
Multiply decimal	MP	SS T	P,A,S,D
Divide decimal	DP	SS T	P,A,S,D,DK
Pack	PACK	SS	P,A
Unpack	UNPK	SS	P,A
Move with offset	MVO	SS	P,A
Shift and round decimal	SRP	SS T,C	P,A, D,DF

Notes

A	Addressing exception
C	Condition code is set
D	Data exception
DF	Decimal-overflow exception
DK	Decimal-divide exception
P	Protection exception
S	Specification exception
T	Decimal feature

Floating-Point Arithmetic

Floating-point arithmetic is performed in the floating-point registers and is defined on short, long, and extended precision floating-point numbers.

*Extended Binary Coded Decimal Interchange Code.

A floating-point number is said to be normalized if the leftmost hexadecimal digit of the fraction is nonzero. The practice of representing the exponent as a power of 16 increases the range of possible values and decreases the number of left shifts required for normalization. Unnormalized arithmetic is also permitted. Table 3.8 lists thc floating-point arithmetic instructions.

Extended precision instructions use either the (0,2) pair or the (4,6) pair of floating-point registers. Instructions are also available for conversion from extended to long formats and from long to short formats and for rounding the result. Extended precision and rounding instructions are listed in Table 3.9.

TABLE 3.8 FLOATING-POINT ARITHMETIC INSTRUCTIONS

Name	*Mnemonic*	*Type*	*Exceptions*
Load (long)	LDR	RR F	S
Load (long)	LD	RX F	P,A,S
Load (short)	LER	RR F	S
Load (short)	LE	RX F	P,A,S
Load and test (long)	LTDR	RR F,C	S
Load and test (short)	LTER	RR F,C	S
Load complement (long)	LCDR	RR F,C	S
Load complement (short)	LCER	RR F,C	S
Load positive (long)	LPDR	RR F,C	S
Load positive (short)	LPER	RR F,C	S
Load negative (long)	LNDR	RR F,C	S
Load negative (short)	LNER	RR F,C	S
Add normalized (long)	ADR	RR F,C	S,U,E,LS
Add normalized (long)	AD	RX F,C	P,A,S,U,E,LS
Add normalized (short)	AER	RR F,C	S,U,E,LS
Add normalized (short)	AE	RX F,C	P,A,S,U,E,LS
Add unnormalized (long)	AWR	RR F,C	S, E,LS
Add unnormalized (long)	AW	RX F,C	P,A,S, E,LS
Add unnormalized (short)	AUR	RR F,C	S, E,LS
Add unnormalized (short)	AU	RX F,C	P,A,S, E,LS
Subtract normalized (long)	SDR	RR F,C	S,U,E,LS
Subtract normalized (long)	SD	RX F,C	P,A,S,U,E,LS
Subtract normalized (short)	SER	RR F,C	S,U,E,LS
Subtract normalized (short)	SE	RX F,C	P,A,S,U,E,LS
Subtract unnormalized (long)	SWR	RR F,C	S, E,LS
Subtract unnormalized (long)	SW	RX F,C	P,A,S, E,LS
Subtract unnormalized (short)	SUR	RR F,C	S, E,LS
Subtract unnormalized (short)	SU	RX F,C	P,A,S, E,LS
Compare (long)	CDR	RR F,C	S
Compare (long)	CD	RX F,C	P,A,S
Compare (short)	CER	RR F,C	S
Compare (short)	CE	RX F,C	P,A,S
Halve (long)	HDR	RR F	S,U

TABLE 3.8 (continued)

Name	*Mnemonic*	*Type*	*Exceptions*
Halve (short)	HER	RR F	S,U
Multiply (long)	MDR	RR F	S,U,E
Multiply (long)	MD	RX F	P,A,S,U,E
Multiply (short)	MER	RR F	S,U,E
Multiply (short)	ME	RX F	P,A,S,U,E
Divide (long)	DDR	RR F	S,U,E,FK
Divide (long)	DD	RX F	P,A,S,U,E,FK
Divide (short)	DER	RR F	S,U,E,FK
Divide (short)	DE	RX F	P,A,S,U,E,FK
Store (long)	STD	RX F	P,A,S
Store (short)	STE	RX F	P,A,S

Notes

A	Addressing exception
C	Condition code is set
E	Exponent-overflow exception
F	Floating-point feature
FK	Floating-point divide exception
LS	Significance exception
P	Protection exception
S	Specification exception
U	Exponent-underflow exception

TABLE 3.9 EXTENDED PRECISION FLOATING-POINT ARITHMETIC INSTRUCTIONS

Name	*Mnemonic*	*Type*	*Exceptions*
Load rounded (extended to long)	LRDR	RR X	S, E
Load rounded (long to short)	LRER	RR X	S, E
Add normalized (extended)	AXR	RR X,C	S,U,E,LS
Subtract normalized (extended)	SXR	RR X,C	S,U,E,LS
Multiply (extended)	MXR	RR X	S,U,E
Multiply (long/extended)	MXDR	RR X	S,U,E
Multiply (long/extended)	MXD	RX X	P,A,S,U,E

Notes

A	Addressing exception
C	Condition code is set
E	Exponent-overflow exception
LS	Significance exception
P	Protection exception
S	Specification exception
U	Exponent-underflow exception
X	Extended precision feature

TABLE 3.10 LOGICAL INSTRUCTIONS

Name	Mnemonic	Type		Exceptions	
Move	MVI	SI		P,A	
Move	MVC	SS		P,A	
Move numerics	MVN	SS		P,A	
Move zones	MVZ	SS		P,A	
Move long	MVCL	RR	C	P,A,S	
Compare logical	CLR	RR	C		
Compare logical	CL	RX	C	P,A,S	
Compare logical	CLI	SI	C	P,A	
Compare logical	CLC	SS	C	P,A	
Compare logical long	CLCL	RR	C	P,A,S	
Compare logical characters under mask	CLM	RS	C	P,A	
AND	NR	RR	C		
AND	N	RX	C	P,A,S	
AND	NI	SI	C	P,A	
AND	NC	SS	C	P,A	
OR	OR	RR	C		
OR	O	RX	C	P,A,S	
OR	OI	SI	C	P,A	
OR	OC	SS	C	P,A	
Exclusive OR	XR	RR	C		
Exclusive OR	X	RX	C	P,A,S	
Exclusive OR	XI	SI	C	P,A	
Exclusive OR	XC	SS	C	P,A	
Test under mask	TM	SI	C	P,A	
Insert character	IC	RX		P,A	
Store character	STC	RX		P,A	
Insert characters under mask	ICM	RS	C	P,A	
Store characters under mask	STCM	RS	C	P,A	
Load address	LA	RX			
Translate	TR	SS		P,A	
Translate and test	TRT	SS	C	P,A	
Edit	ED	SS	T,C	P,A,	D
Edit and mark	EDMK	SS	T,C	P,A,	D
Shift left single logical	SLL	RS			
Shift right single logical	SRL	RS			
Shift left double logical	SLDL	RS			S
Shift right double logical	SRDL	RS			S

Notes

A	Addressing exception
C	Condition code is set
D	Data exception
P	Protection exception
S	Specification exception
T	Decimal feature

Logical Operations

Logical instructions perform logical, data movement, editing, shifting, testing, and translating operations. In general, operands are regarded as 8-bit bytes, although the logical shift and some of the logical arithmetic instructions use general registers. Variable-length operands are processed from left to right and may extend for a maximum of 256 bytes; two exceptions exist: compare logical long (CLCL) and move long (MVCL). Both instructions use general registers to hold the specifications for the instruction and permit bytes to be compared or moved for a length limited only by the amount of main storage. The operands for storage-to-storage operations may overlap and the result is dependent upon the respective operation being executed. Except for the editing instructions, operands are not treated as numbers but as a sequence of bits or bytes. The edit instruction (ED) requires a packed decimal field as one operand and yields a field of zoned decimal digits in EBCDIC format. Logical instructions are listed in Table 3.10.

Summary of Processing Unit Functions

As described here, processing unit functions involve the instruction sets and instruction formats and include the fixed-point, decimal, floating-point, and logical instructions. Branching and control instructions are also executed by the CPU as are instructions to initiate input and output. Both topics are treated separately because of the key roles they play in programming and in systems design.

3.5 BRANCHING AND CONTROL FUNCTIONS

The normal sequential order of execution of computer instructions is altered in three ways: by a branch instruction, with an instruction that specifies indirect execution, and by an interruption. The execution of programs is affected indirectly by control operations, used primarily by an operating system control program to monitor the operation of the computer system.

Conditional Branching

The design of System/370 includes four instructions that permit conditional branching. The branch-on-condition instructions (BCR and BC) include a mask field that is used in conjunction with the condition code (CC) setting to branch to a given storage address when a specified condition is met. Depending upon the setting of the mask bits, the branch-on-condition instruction can also be used as an unconditional branch instruction or a no-operation instruction.

Iterative and looping procedures require instructions that update a counter value concurrently with a branch instruction or immediately preceding it. This need is satisfied by three versatile instructions: branch on count (BCTR and BCT), branch on index high (BXH), and branch on index low or equal (BXLE). All three instructions update a counter that is maintained in a general register and branch conditionally to a specified address.

Table 3.11 lists the branching instructions. Type RR format instructions use an effective address for branching that is maintained in a general register.

TABLE 3.11 BRANCHING INSTRUCTIONS

Name	*Mnemonic*	*Type*	*Exceptions*
Branch on condition	BCR	RR	
Branch on condition	BC	RX	
Branch and link	BALR	RR	
Branch and link	BAL	RX	
Branch on count	BCTR	RR	
Branch on count	BCT	RX	
Branch on index high	BXH	RS	
Branch on index low or equal	BXLE	RS	
Execute	EX	RX	P,A,S, EX

Notes

A	Addressing exception
EX	Execute exception
S	Specification exception
P	Protection exception

Subroutine Linkage and Indirect Execution

Table 3.11 additionally lists the branch-and-link instructions (BALR and BAL) that store a return address prior to a branch to a specified address in main storage. Subroutine arguments (or an address pointer to them) are normally carried in the general registers. During the execution of a branch-and-link instruction, the condition code is stored along with the instruction address (i.e., the rightmost half of the PSW) in the specified link register. Thus, the called subroutine is provided with the current status of the CPU and a means of returning to the calling program when the execution of the subroutine has been completed.

The execute instruction (EX) permits the execution of a single instruction outside of the current instruction sequence. The subject instruction is executed as though it had been in the normal instruction sequence. The execute instruction is also listed in Table 3.11.

The branch instructions are provided as a part of the standard instruction set.

Control Instructions

Most, but not all, of the control instructions are privileged so that they can be used only when the CPU is in the supervisor state. Collectively, the control instructions control CPU execution by modifying the PSW and storage keys, by loading and storing the control registers, by allowing CPU and channel IDs to be inspected, by maintaining the time-of-day clock, by allowing programs to be shared, by permitting two CPUs to communicate directly with each other, by providing a diagnostic checkout instruction for the CPU, and by enabling a program running in the problem state to effectively communicate with an operating system control program. Control instructions are listed in Table 3.12.

TABLE 3.12 CONTROL INSTRUCTIONS

Name	*Mnemonic*	*Type*		*Exceptions*
Load PSW	LPSW	SI	L	M,P,A,S
Set program mask	SPM	RR	L	
Set system mask	SSM	SI		M,P,A
Supervisor call	SVC	RR		
Set storage key	SSK	RR	Z	M, A,S
Insert storage key	ISK	RR	Z	M, A,S
Write direct	WRD	SI	Y	M,P,A
Read direct	RDD	SI	Y	M,P,A
Diagnose	—	SI		M,P,A,S
Test and set	TS	SI	C	P,A
Load control	LCTL	RS		M,P,A,S
Store control	STCTL	RS		M,P,A,S
Set clock	SCK	SI	C	M,P,A,S
Store clock	STCK	SI	C	P,A
Store CPUID	STIDP	SI		M,P,A,S
Store channel ID	STIDC	SI	C	M
Monitor call	MC	SI		S

Notes

A	Addressing exception
C	Condition code is set
L	New condition code loaded
M	Privileged operation exception
P	Protection exception
S	Specification exception
Y	Direct control feature
Z	Protection feature

3.6 SUMMARY

The architecture of System/370 satisfies the need for a family of compatible computers that can support large main storage sizes, provide for simple relocation of programs and data, and support storage protection and monitor control requirements over a broad spectrum of applications. The requirements are met through a combination of multiple accumulators, a flexible instruction set, an automatic interrupt system, a variety of data formats, a simple main storage addressing scheme, and a control structure that is independent of the cost/performance index of a specific model.

The flexibility of System/370 is also inherent in the channel organization and input/output system and in the operating systems required to control and monitor system operation. These topics are covered in subsequent chapters and the appendices.

REFERENCES

1. Amdahl, G.M., "The structure of System/360: Part III—Processing unit design considerations," *IBM Systems Journal*, **3,** (2) (1964).
2. Blaauw, G.A., and F.P. Brooks, Jr., "The structure of System/360: Part I—Outline of the logical structure," *IBM Systems Journal*, **3** (2) (1964).
3. Flores, I., "Computer Organization," Prentice-Hall, Inc., Englewood Cliffs, N.J., 1969.
4. IBM System/370 publications: "System Summary," Form GA22-7001; "Principles of Operation," Form GA22-7000. IBM Corporation, Data Processing Division, White Plains, N.Y., 1970.
5. IBM System/360 publications: "Principles of Operations," Form GA22-6821; "Introduction to System/360 Architecture," Form C20-1667-1. IBM Corporation, Data Processing Division, White Plains, N.Y., 1968.

4 CHANNEL ORGANIZATION AND INPUT/OUTPUT

4.1 INTRODUCTION

Modern computing systems support a variety of input/output devices in a complex operating environment. As a result, most IO systems are exceedingly complicated; in fact, most programming systems tend to obscure the true "nitty-gritty" from the applications programmer and problem solver through easy-to-learn and easy-to-use programming language statements, such as the following example of an input statement from PL/I:

GET LIST(A,B,C);

The task of IO organization is usually relegated (but not always) to systems programmers or operations management. The efficiency of input and output operations is a prime determinant of overall system performance and an important factor in computer systems architecture.

IO Requirements

Multiprogramming and time-shared operating systems require IO device independence, asychronous execution of IO operations, storage protection for nonoperating programs, and the capability of attaching a variety of devices with totally different operating characteristics. Concurrent IO operations must be supported along with device-dependent operations when required by a particular application. On the other hand, low speed and control operations should not be permitted to monopolize IO channel facilities. System/370 satisfies these requirements with an efficient IO system that functions with a minimum amount of supervision by an operating system control program.

IO Organization

Input and output operations are executed by IO channels, control units, and IO devices operating under control of an IO control program that executes in the CPU. Most functional units are treated as independent entities by other functional units in the system.

Storage devices, external to the computer, are referred to as IO devices —regardless if they are used for input or output or as a mass storage medium. In other words, the terms input and output refer to an operational procedure rather than a functional assignment. IO devices most frequently take the form of card equipment, tape units, printers, and direct-access devices, but may also include optical/visual/audio devices and a variety of card, tape, and keyboard units.

An IO device is attached to an IO channel through an IO control unit that contains data buffers and the logical circuitry necessary to operate the device and perform control functions. Information is transferred between the IO control unit and the IO channel over a standard connection termed the *IO interface.* The interface allows one byte (eight data bits plus one parity bit) to pass between the two units at one time. The standard IO interface is common to all channels and to all device types.

The connection between an IO channel and main storage is not standard and varies from one System/370 model to another. In general, the amount of data passing over the channel/storage interface at one time is dependent upon storage design and the access width.

Not all IO operations involve the transfer of information; some perform a control function such as tape rewind or a disk seek. A control function is performed by an IO control unit independently of CPU and other channel operations. A control unit may be shared or nonshared. A nonshared control unit, often referred to as *unipath*, controls only one device. A shared control unit may be shared-path or multipath but controls several devices—each with the same or similar characteristics. A *shared-path* control unit permits only one device to operate at any one time and usually restricts the devices to be of the same type; magnetic tape units frequently share a shared-path control unit. A *multipath* control unit allows several devices to operate concurrently and usually permits different but functionally similar devices to be attached to it; a common example of a multipath control unit is the IBM 2821 that controls card reader/punches and line printers.

IO Operation

The CPU initiates an IO operation by specifying the channel* and device to be used and by indicating to the channel the main storage location of

*In discussions of input and output, an IO channel is frequently referred to as simply a channel.

the beginning of a channel program. The channel program specifies the IO operation(s) that are to take place and exists as a series of channel command words (CCWs). A CCW specifies an operation, flags, a count, and a storage location. Six IO operations are defined: read, write, read backward, control, sense, and transfer in channel. *Read* and *read backward* operations transfer information from an IO device to main storage. A *write* operation transfers information from main storage to an IO device. A *control* operation passes an *order* to a control unit that decodes it and performs a non-data operation. A write operation and a control order are processed in the same way by the IO channel. An IO operation signals a termination by interrupting the CPU; status information on the IO operation that caused the interruption is stored as a channel status word (CSW), discussed later. Additional information of a device-dependent nature is provided by the control unit and is available to the CPU with a *sense* operation. Read and sense operations are also processed similarly by the channel. A channel program is a series of CCWs, stored normally in sequential locations. When the execution of one CCW has been completed, the channel goes to the next CCW or terminates operation, depending upon the setting of flag bits and upon channel connections. When the next CCW is not stored in the next sequential location, then a *transfer in channel* (TIC) CCW is used to direct channel control to a specified location in main storage.

IO operations are initiated in CPU with a start IO instruction. Other CPU instructions that govern IO operations are start IO fast release, test channel, test I/O, halt I/O, and halt device. IO programming is presented in Section 4.4.

4.2 IO CHANNEL ORGANIZATION

An IO channel directs and controls the flow of information between main storage and IO devices and permits CPU processing to proceed concurrently with IO operations. An IO channel is designed to perform a variety of functions—most of which require logical circuitry* and storage facilities.† The manner in which these facilities are implemented varies between the different models of System/370 and between the different types of channels. The channel may be a functionally independent unit or may time-share certain facilities with the CPU. Similarly, some types of channels operate differently from others and the method of operation determines the kinds of devices that can be attached to it.

*The logical circuitry must provide the following kinds of capabilities: address modification, counting, assembly and disassembly of data, and facilities for transferring data between main storage and IO devices.

†Storage facilities include: a counter, a main storage address for data transfer, the address of the current CCW, and other storage facilities for status information and flags.

This section concerns the organization of System/370 IO channels; each channel is designed to perform the following functions:*

Accept an IO instruction from the CPU.
Address an IO device specified by an IO instruction.
Fetch CCWs from the channel program in main storage.
Decode CCWs.
Test a CCW for validity.
Execute CCW functions.
Place control signals on the IO interface.
Accept control signals over the IO interface.
Transfer information between main storage and an IO device.
Check the parity of bytes transferred.
Count the number of bytes transferred.
Accept and maintain IO device status information.
Send interruption requests to the CPU.
Sequence and control IO interruptions from devices.
Update main storage location 64 with status information for accepted interruptions.
Store status information in main storage location 64 when requested by the CPU.

Channel Design

System/370 has three types of IO channels:† byte multiplexer, selector, and block multiplexer. Each type of channel is characterized by its mode of operation (byte, burst, or both) and the manner in which it responds to CPU requests and IO device activity. The *byte mode* is used with low-speed devices, such as a card reader, and effectively allows information from different devices to be interleaved as it passes through the channel—thus sharing channel facilities. The byte mode is available with the byte multiplexor channel. The *burst mode* is used with higher-speed devices, such as magnetic tape or disk storage, and utilizes all channel facilities during the transfer of a block of data. All three types of channels can operate in the burst mode.

Channel Operation

The mode of operation (i.e., byte or burst) is completely transparent to the programmer and is determined by the operational characteristics of devices and the architecture of the computing system. Another feature that cannot be controlled by the programmer is that of a subchannel—generally defined to be the channel facilities associated with single IO oper-

*See reference 3 form GA22-6962, p. 5.

†Chapter 1 includes an introduction to the different types of IO channels.

ation. An *unshared subchannel* can be used with a single IO device. A *shared subchannel* can be used with a set of devices and is commonly used with a shared-path IO control unit. A selector channel can have only one subchannel. Byte and block multiplexer channels have one or more subchannels.

Each channel has logical circuitry and internal registers for holding and maintaining the following information for an active IO operation:

protection key,
data address,
command code operation,
CCW flags,
byte count,
channel status, and the
address of the next CCW.

In the case of a selector channel, the preceding information is maintained in channel registers for as long as the channel is in operation since only one subchannel need be sustained. In byte and block multiplexer channels, the control information must be maintained for each subchannel in operation.

In systems with integrated channels, storage for the control information is provided in control storage or as an extension to main storage. In either case, however, the storage, frequently referred to as "bump" storage, is not addressable by the programmer. When control information for an operating subchannel is stored by a channel in bump storage, it is referred to as a *unit control word* (UCW). In general,* each operating subchannel requires a UCW, and the total number of UCWs in a computer system is dependent upon the amount of control storage allocated for that purpose or on the amount of main storage. (Each 1024-byte section of main storage provides for one additional UCW; the upper limit on the number of UCWs is 1024.) The UCWs for a given computer are assigned when the equipment is installed.

The subchannel capacity of a functionally independent IO channel is fixed for that device and is discussed, as required, in Part Three.

Byte Multiplexer Channel

A byte multiplexer channel in System/370 can be integrated into the CPU or utilize the IBM 2870 Multiplexer Channel. Up to 256 subchannels may be supported depending upon the model selected. In either case, a single data path is shared among several IO devices when the channel is operating in the multiplex (or byte) mode; when the channel is operating

*Some minor exceptions are considered later.

in the burst mode, the data path is monopolized by a single device. An IO control unit determines whether a byte multiplexer operates in the burst or byte modes for devices under its control. Figure 4.1 depicts a simplified view of byte multiplexer channel operation.

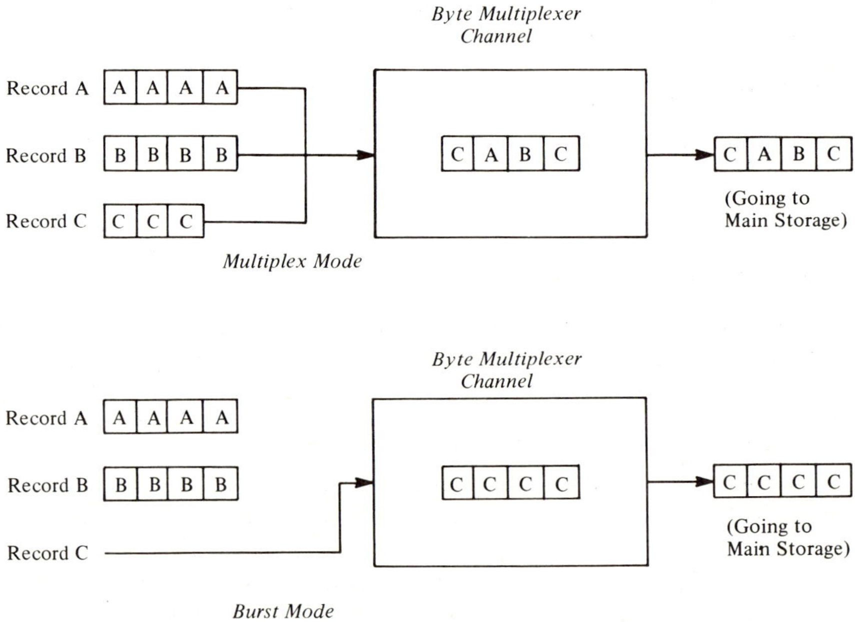

Figure 4.1 Simplified view of byte multiplexer channel operation.

Selector Channel

A selector channel can also be integrated into the CPU or be implemented as a stand alone unit. In the latter case, the IBM 2860 Selector Channel, designed for System/360, is used. Each selector channel can be used to attach up to 8 IO control units and up to 256 IO devices to a System/370 computer. Only one IO device assigned to a selector channel can be transmitting information at a given time, although several selector channels can be operating concurrently.

Block Multiplexer Channel

A block multiplexer channel is designed to operate, concurrently, several high-speed IO devices over a single data path and is implemented as an integrated channel or as a functionally independent unit,* depending

*The IBM 2880 Block Multiplexer Channel is used with System/370 Model 165 and is also available with several models of System/360.

upon the model of System/370. A block multiplexer channel operates in one of two modes: selector or block multiplex. The mode is set by bit 0 of control register 0. If the mode bit is zero when a start IO instruction is issued for a device attached to a block multiplexer channel, then that channel operates in the selector mode and is functionally equivalent to a selector channel. If the mode bit is one, then the operations of the addressed device are block multiplexed with other IO operations in the same channel. The *block multiplex* mode is characterized in several ways:

1. Channel programs are initiated sooner than they would be in the selector mode.
2. Data blocks are interleaved.
3. Channel facilities are freed sooner after a data transfer operation.
4. Channel facilities are released for certain non-data operations.

Block multiplexing operates in conjunction with rotational position sensing and multiple requesting to improve the effective data rate of a given system. These topics are discussed further in Part Three under *Direct-Access Devices*.

Channel Features

System/370 channel design also includes a *command retry* facility that works in conjunction with certain IO control units to retry an improperly executed channel command automatically without requiring an IO interruption and a programmed error recovery procedure. The model 165 includes an optional *extended channel feature* that permits up to 12 IO channels to be attached to that computer. A *channel-to-channel* adapter feature is also available to provide two System/370s with interchannel communications. Another optional feature on the Model 165 is a 2-byte interface between a channel and control units that increase the effective data rate of the IBM 2880 Block Multiplexer Channel from 1.5 megabytes* per second to 3 megabytes per second.

IO channel facilities are presented in more detail in Part Three with respect to specific models of System/370.

4.3 IO ADDRESSING, INSTRUCTIONS, AND COMMANDS

The properties of the System/370 input/output system are considered from two points of view; static and operational. Static properties are included in this section and present the IO device addressing conventions, CPU instructions, and channel command formats. Operational properties are discussed in the next section, *IO Programming and Operations*.

*The term megabyte is an accepted abbreviation for one million bytes.

IO Addressing

An IO device and an access path to it via an IO channel are specified by a 16-bit IO address. The high-order 8 bits denote a channel address and the low-order 8 bits denote a control unit and an IO device attached to that particular channel. In multiplexer channels,* the device address also identifies the subchannel as well as the device address. A device address with a zero in the high-order position of the device address field denotes a nonshared subchannel. A device address with a one in the high-order position of the device address field may be shared or nonshared, depending upon settings made at installation time. Shared subchannels are assigned contiguous device addresses.

Channel 0 is normally reserved for the first byte multiplexer channel. Channels numbered 1–6 may be either byte multiplexer, selector, or block multiplexer as determined by a particular System/370 model. An extended channel feature allows channels 7–11 to be assigned on the Model 165. Channels numbered 13–255 may not be assigned even though control register 2 contains mask bits for channels 0–31. The following list contains some typical IO addresses:

IO Address				
Channel	*Device*	*Hex Value*	*Channel*	*Note*
00000000	00001111	000F	0	Nonshared
00000001	10000000	0180	1	Shared or nonshared
00000001	10000001	0181	1	Shared or nonshared
00000110	00000100	0604	6	Nonshared

The IO System additionally permits a given IO control unit to be attached to two or more channels and a specific IO device to be attached to two or more control units. Device and unit control word (UCW) assignment is considered with respect to specific models of System/370 in Part Three.

IO Instructions

Input and output operations are controlled by five privileged CPU instructions that are used to initiate and halt IO processing and to selectively test IO conditions. All IO instructions fall into the storage-immediate (SI) category and have the format depicted in Figure 4.2.

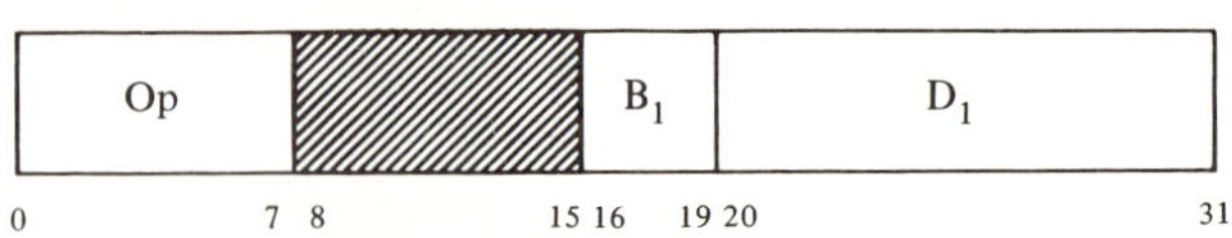

Figure 4.2 IO instruction format.

*That is, both byte and block multiplexer channels.

The effective address formed as the sum of the contents of register B_1 and the contents of the D_1 field specify the IO address. The 24-bit address is used as follows:

Bits 8–15 of the effective address are ignored by the CPU. The IO instructions are listed in Table 4.1.

TABLE 4.1 IO INSTRUCTIONS

Name	*Mnemonic*	*Type*	*Exception*
Start IO	SIO	SI,C	M
Start IO fast release	SIOF	SI,C	M
Test IO	TIO	SI,C	M
Halt IO/Halt device	HIO/HDV	SI,C	M
Test channel	TCH	SI,C	M

Notes

C Condition code is set

M Privileged-operation exception

The *start IO* (SIO) instruction initiates an IO operation on the IO device and subchannel specified by the effective address. The start IO instruction sets a condition code* that can be used to determine the state of the addressed device and to verify that the instruction was accepted.† If the start IO is accepted by the addressed channel and device, a protection key and the main storage address of the first channel command word (CCW) is obtained from a 4-byte channel address word (CAW) located at address 72 in main storage. The CAW format is depicted in Figure 4.3.

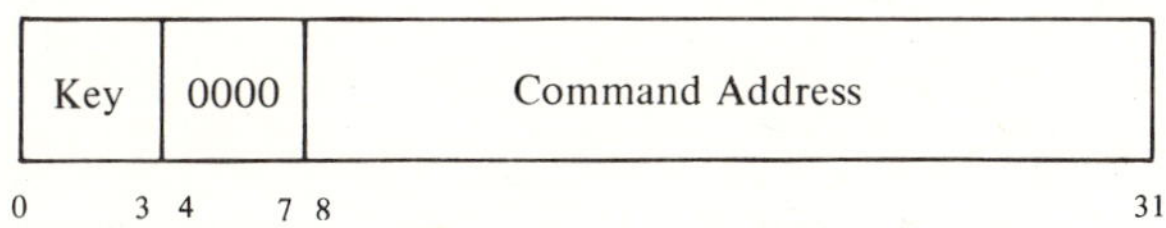

Figure 4.3 Channel address word (CAW) format.

*The fact that the IO instructions set the condition code in the PSW enables a branch-on-condition (BC or BCR) instruction to be used for decision making.

†In a sense, the implementation of the start IO instruction is designed to protect both the user and the system against inadvertently creating undesirable IO conditions and to facilitate IO control by an operating system.

The protection key is used by an IO channel to access protected main storage blocks in the same way that the protection key in the PSW is used.

The *start IO fast release* (SIOF) instruction is a variation to the start IO instruction that allows the next sequential instruction to be executed sooner. If the addressed channel is not busy when the SIOF instruction is executed, the assumption is that the IO can be initiated and the CPU is not held up waiting for a reply from an IO control unit. An IO interruption is generated if it is later determined that the IO operation could not be initiated. SIOF is designed for use with block multiplexer channels and is executed as a start IO instruction when the addressed channel is not in the block multiplex mode.*

The *test IO* (TIO) instruction tests the state of the IO system and sets the condition code accordingly. The resultant condition code setting can indicate that the channel is available, the channel is busy, the channel is not operational, or that a channel status word (CSW) is stored. The CSW gives the status of an IO device or the conditions under which an IO operation was terminated. It is considered later as a separate topic.

The *halt IO* (HIO) and halt device (HDV) instructions terminate either a channel or device operation, depending upon the type of channel and channel conditions. A halt device instruction issued to a device connected to either a byte multiplexer channel or a block multiplexer channel operating in the block multiplex mode causes the IO operation on the device addressed to be stopped without interfering with other IO operations in progress on the channel.

The *test channel* (TCH) instruction sets the condition code to indicate the state of the addressed channel. The state of the channel is not affected by the operation. The TCH instruction is designed to indicate one of the following conditions: channel available, interruption pending in channel, channel operating in burst mode, or channel not operational.

As a whole, the IO instructions serve to control IO operations in a System/370 computer. IO channels perform actual IO processing as directed by a series of channel commands—collectively termed a channel program.

Channel Commands

A channel command word (CCW) provides information to an IO channel for an IO operation that should be executed or for an action that should be taken by that channel. A CCW may be located anywhere in main storage as long as it is placed on a double word boundary. The address of the first CCW in a CCW chain is specified in the channel address word

*As mentioned earlier, the block multiplex mode is entered by setting bit 0 of control register zero to one prior to executing an SIO or SIOF instruction.

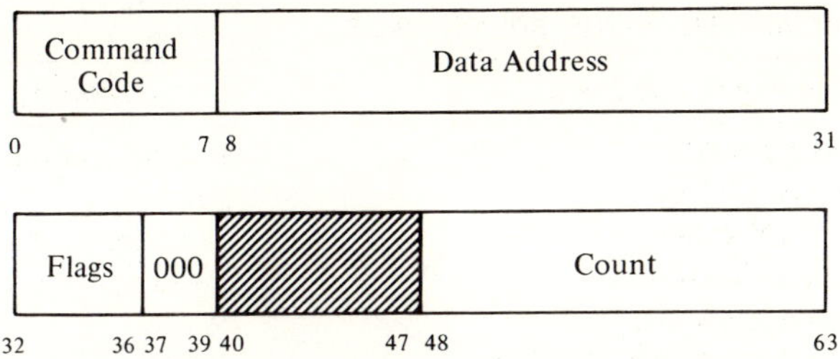

Figure 4.4 Channel command word (CCW) format.

(CAW) when a start IO instruction or a start IO fast release instruction is executed. The format of a CCW is given in Figure 4.4. The fields of a CCW are defined as follows:

Field	*Bit Positions*	*Function*
Command code	0–7	Specifies operation to be performed.
Data address	8–31	Specifies beginning or end of data area in main storage.
Chain data flag (CD)	32	Specifies data chaining.
Chain command flag (CC)	33	Specifies command chaining.
Suppress-length-indicator (SLI)	34	Specifies whether an incorrect length condition should be reported.
Skip flag (SKIP)	35	Suppresses transfer of data to main storage.
Program controlled interruption flag (PCI)	36	Causes the channel to generate an interruption condition when the CCW takes control of channel.
Count	48–63	Specifies the number of main storage bytes used in the IO operation.
	37–39	Must be zero.
	40–47	Ignored by the channel.

As stated earlier, several commands appear the same to an IO channel and its degree of participation in CCW processing is minimal. In fact, the channel recognizes only four distinct operations: output forward (for write and control commands), input forward (for read and sense commands), input backward (for a read backward command), and branching (for a transfer in channel command). The channel uses the two low-order bits of the command code field, and when these bits are 00, the four low-order bits, to identify the operation and initiate the required channel processing. However, all 8 bits of the command code are sent to the IO device—that is, except for the transfer in channel command which is handled entirely by the channel. The high-order bits of the command

TABLE 4.2 COMMAND CODE BIT SETTINGS

Command Code Field	*Command*
XXXX0000	Invalid command
AAAA0100	Sense
XXXX1000	Transfer in channel
AAAA1100	Read backward
AAAAAA01	Write
AAAAAA10	Read
AAAAAA11	Control

Notes

X denotes the bit position is ignored.
A denotes a modifier bit.

code are used as modifier bits and vary between devices. The command code bit settings are listed in Table 4.2.

The CCW flags are discussed under *IO Programming and Operations*. Two minor points should be mentioned before the different commands are discussed. For write, read, control, and sense operations, the locations specified in the data address field are accessed in ascending order. The count field is decremented during information transfer operations. The only exception is the read backward operation that uses main storage locations in descending order. The final point is that the count field of a CCW must never be zero and a channel program cannot use that field to specify an operation in which no data are transferred.

The System/370 channel commands are listed in Table 4.3. The commands form a basic set with any complications being related to the characteristics of a particular device. In general, a simple IO device requires a relatively unsophisticated channel program; a more complicated device, such as a disk storage drive, frequently requires a sophisticated channel program.

The *write command* transfers data from main storage to the addressed IO device. Data bytes from main storage are selected by ascending order of addresses. The first byte transferred is the one addressed by the data address field of the CCW.

The *read command* transfers data from the addressed IO device to main storage; storage locations are filled in ascending sequence beginning with the data address field in the CCW.

The *read backwards* command transfers data from an IO device to main storage; storage locations are filled in descending sequence beginning with the data address field in the CCW. The read backwards command is designed for use with magnetic tape devices that permit the operation to be performed with the tape moving backwards.

The *control command* is used to initiate an IO operation at an IO device that does not involve the transfer of data. For most control operations, the nature of the operation is specified by modifier bits in the command code—although in some cases, the operation does require the transfer of control information from locations in main storage specified by the data address field of the CCW.

TABLE 4.3 CHANNEL COMMANDS

Name	*Flags*
Write	CD CC SLI PCI
Read	CD CC SLI SKIP PCI
Read backward	CD CC SLI SKIP PCI
Control	CD CC SLI PCI
Sense	CD CC SLI SKIP PCI
Transfer in channel	

Notes

CD	Chain data
CC	Chain command
SLI	Suppress length indication
SKIP	Skip
PCI	Program-controlled interruption

The *sense command* provides information on IO device conditions and unusual conditions in the addressed device. The information is more detailed than that stored in the channel status word. Two bytes of status information are usually transmitted to main storage with additional information being of a diagnostic nature. The first six bits of sense data are common to all devices and are listed as follows:

Bit	*Condition*
0	Command reject
1	Intervention required
2	Bus-out check
3	Equipment check
4	Data check
5	Overrun

The sense command is commonly used when an unusual condition exists at the device level and more information is required. For example, it is the means that the computer operating system control programs use to determine that more paper is needed at the printer; a message is usually sent to the operator informing him of the situation. The precise meaning of each of the sense conditions as well as other sense data is described in appropriate reference manuals on the System/370 and on the particular device involved.

The *transfer in channel* command instructs the channel to fetch the next CCW from the locations specified in the data address field. Neither the

CCW addressed by the channel address word (CAW) nor the CCW addressed by a transfer in channel command may specify a transfer in channel operation.

The operational properties of the System/370 IO system are described in the next section.

4.4 IO PROGRAMMING AND OPERATION

This section describes basic IO programming and the operational properties of the IO system. IO instructions are privileged and can be executed only when the CPU is in the supervisor state. However, the IO system is an important aspect of the architecture of System/370 and an understanding of its operational properties is essential for effective systems design, development, and evaluation.

The procedures given do not pertain to any specific device but rather to any device that can be attached to a System/370 computer. In general, specific procedures are not given except for direct-access devices which are considered in a later chapter.

States of IO System

The state of the IO system specified by a given IO address is determined jointly by the states of the channel, subchannel, and IO device. Each of

TABLE 4.4 STATES OF THE IO SYSTEM

State	*Component*	*Description*
Available (A)	Channel, subchannel, or IO device	None of the other states
Interruption pending (I)	Channel	IO interruption immediately available from channel
	Subchannel	Information for CSW available in subchannel
	IO device	Interruption condition pending in device
Working (W)	Channel	Channel operating in burst mode
	Subchannel	Subchannel executing any operation
	IO device	Device executing an operation
Not operational (N)	Channel	Channel not operational
	Subchannel	Subchannel not operational
	IO device	IO device not operational

these components can assume one of four states that affect the response that is generated to an IO instruction; the various states are listed in Table 4.4. If the response to an IO instruction can be determined from the state of a channel or a subchannel, then other components in the IO chain are not interrogated. Of the 64 possible states, 10 composite states are identified. They are described in more detail in reference 4 and are listed with condition code settings in Table 4.5.

TABLE 4.5 COMPOSITE STATES OF THE IO SYSTEM AND CONDITION CODE SETTINGS FOR IO INSTRUCTIONS[a]

Conditions	*State Abbreviation*	*SIO SIOF*[b]	*TIO*	*HIO*	*HDV*	*TCH*
Available	AAA	0,1[c]	0	1[c]	1[c]	0
Interruption pending in device	AAI	1[c]	1[c]	1[c]	1[c]	0
Device working	AAW	1[c]	1[c]	1[c]	1[c]	0
Device not operational	AAN	3	3	3	3	0
Interruption pending in subchannel	AIX[d]					
For the addressed device		2	1[c]	0	0	0
For another device		2	2	0	0	0
Subchannel working	AWX[d]					
With the addressed device		2	2	1[c,e]	1[c,e]	0
With another device		2	2	1[c,e]	0	0
Subchannel not operational	ANX[d]	3	3	3	3	0
Interruption pending in channel	IXX[d]	--------See Note--------				1
Channel working	WXX[d]					
With the addressed device		2	2	2	[f]	2
With another device		2	2	2	[g]	2
Channel not operational	NXX[d]	3	3	3	3	3

[a] Reprinted by permission from "IBM System/370 Principles of Operation," Form GA22-7000-0.

[b] START IO FAST RELEASE may cause the same condition code to be set as for START IO or may cause condition code 0 to be set.

[c] The CSW or its status portion is stored at location 64 during execution of the instruction.

[d] The symbol X stands for A, I, W, and N, and indicates that the state of the corresponding component is not significant. As an example, AIX denotes the states AIA, AII, AIW, and AIN, while IXX represents a total of 16 states, some of which do not occur.

[e] When a "device not operational" response is received in selecting the addressed device, condition code 3 is set.

[f] The condition cannot be identified during execution of the instruction.

[g] The condition code depends on the state of the subchannel, the channel type, and system model. If the subchannel is not operational, a condition code 2 or 3 is set. If the subchannel is available or working with the addressed device, a condition code 2 is set. Otherwise, a condition code 0 or 2 is set.

The condition code depends on the IO interface sequence, the channel type, and the system model. If the channel ascertains that the device received the signal to terminate, a condition code 1 is set and the CSW stored. Otherwise, a condition code 2 is set.

NOTE. For the purpose of executing START IO, START IO FAST RELEASE, TEST IO, HALT DEVICE, and HALT IO, a channel containing a pending interruption condition appears the same as an available channel, and the condition-code setting depends on the states of the subchannel and device. The condition codes for the IXX states are the same as for the AXX states, where the X's represent the states of the subchannel and the device. As an example, the condition code for the IAA state is the same as for the AAA state, and the condition code for the IAW state is the same as for AAW.

Basic Programming Procedures

A simple example of a data transfer operation is given along with the actions taken by the IO system. The operation transfers a block of data from an input device to main storage. For the actual IO operation the programmer does the following:

1. Creates an appropriate CCW on a double word boundary in main storage. A series of CCWs, called a channel program, may be required. The CCWs may be assembled by the assembler program or synthesized during program execution.
2. Sets the CAW in location 72 by loading the protection key (if used) and the address of the first CCW in the channel program.
3. Loads channel and device address information into a base register for the start IO instruction.
4. Disables IO interruptions.
5. Issues the start IO instruction.
6. Tests the condition code to determine the result of start IO:
   - cc 0 denotes the IO was accepted.
   - cc 1 denotes the CSW has been stored and its status bytes should be examined—the start IO was not accepted.
   - cc 2 denotes the channel or subchannel was busy.
   - cc 3 denotes the IO address is not operational.
7. Enables IO interruptions if cc 0 is received, and the CPU program can continue. If another condition code value is received, appropriate procedures are initiated.

After the start IO instruction is issued by the executing program, the CPU seeks a response from the addressed device to determine its status.* The following steps take place in the computer system:

1. The CAW is fetched by the channel and checked for validity.
2. The CCW is fetched by the channel and checked for validity.
3. The condition code is set in the PSW. (Ordinarily the execution of the start IO instruction is completed here and the CPU can proceed.)
4. The operation is executed by the device.
5. The data transfer of the operation is completed by the channel and the channel-end status bit is set to one.
6. The completion of the operation at the device is indicated by setting the device-end status bit to one.
7. An IO interruption is initiated by the channel.
8. When the IO interruption is accepted, the PSWs are switched and the CSW is stored.

*It is here that the start IO fast release (SIOF) instruction allows the CPU program to continue.

The channel status word (CSW), IO termination, and IO interruptions are presented in succeeding paragraphs.

Channel Status Word

A channel status word (CSW) is stored in response to an IO interruption or as a result of an IO instruction. The CSW occupies a double word beginning at fixed location 64. Figure 4.5 depicts the CSW format; the fields are defined as follows:

Field	*Bit Positions*	*Function*
Protection key	0–3	Protection key (from CAW) used by the subchannel
	4–7	Must be zero
Command address	8–31	Address of the last CCW used plus 8
Status bits	32–47	Specify device and channel conditions. Bits 32–39 are obtained over the IO interface; bits 40–47 are provided by the channel. (See Table 4.6)
Count	48–63	Residual count for the last CCW used

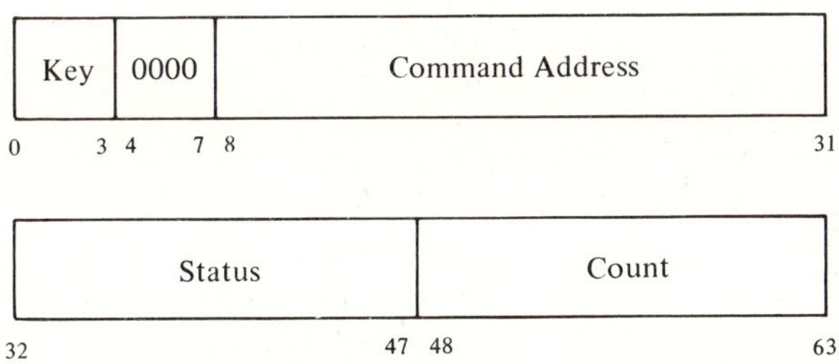

Figure 4.5 Channel status word (CSW) format.

When a CSW is stored in response to an IO instruction (such as a start IO), the IO device is the one specified by the instruction itself. If the CSW results from an IO interruption, then the IO address of the operation causing the interruption is specified in the interruption code field of the old IO PSW. Thus by keeping a table of outstanding IO operations, the IO control program can associate an interruption with a particular program. In a small way, this explains how IO for several programs can proceed concurrently in a complex operating environment.

System/370 architecture also includes a *limited channel logout* (LCL) function that stores information relevant to machine check error conditions that affect IO operations. The LCL field occupies permanent storage byte locations 176–179 and is stored only when the CSW, or part of it, is stored. The reader is referred to reference manuals for detailed information on limited and full channel logouts under machine check conditions.

The conditions represented by the CSW status bits are listed in Table 4.6. The indicators demonstrate the kind of information that is available from the IO system. The precise meaning of each status indicator is dependent upon the equipment involved and the event that caused the CSW to be stored.

Channel Programming

Clearly, a channel program must be executed whenever it is desired to perform any kind of IO operation—regardless if data are being transferred or not. A channel program can consist of one CCW or several CCWs, depending upon the needs of the user and the type of IO process that must be performed. A channel is programmed in much the same way that the CPU is programmed.

TABLE 4.6 CSW STATUS BIT DESIGNATIONS[a]

Bit	*Designation*
32	Attention
33	Status modifier
34	Control unit end
35	Busy
36	Channel end
37	Device end
38	Unit check
39	Unit exception
40	Program controlled interruption
41	Incorrect length
42	Program check
43	Protection check
44	Channel data check
45	Channel control check
46	Interface control check
47	Chaining check

[a] Reprinted by permission from "IBM System/360 Principles of Operation," Form GA22-6821-8. © 1970 by International Business Machines Corporation.

The use of one or more of the flag bits in a CCW increases the scope of IO functions that can be performed. When the channel completes the operation specified by a CCW, it can terminate IO operations on the addressed device or continue depending upon the settings of the CD (bit 32) and CC (bit 33) flags. The process is called chaining and involves fetching the next CCW in sequence (called the new CCW) from main storage.

When *data chaining* is specified by setting the CD bit to one, the new

CCW defines a new storage area for the original IO operation.* The new storage area is used when the data transfer specified by the count field of the current CCW has been completed; the operation of the IO device is not affected by the new CCW. Data chaining is commonly used with *scatter read* and *scatter write* operations (Figure 4.6). Scatter read is frequently used in an operating system to bring in distinct routines with a single IO instruction.

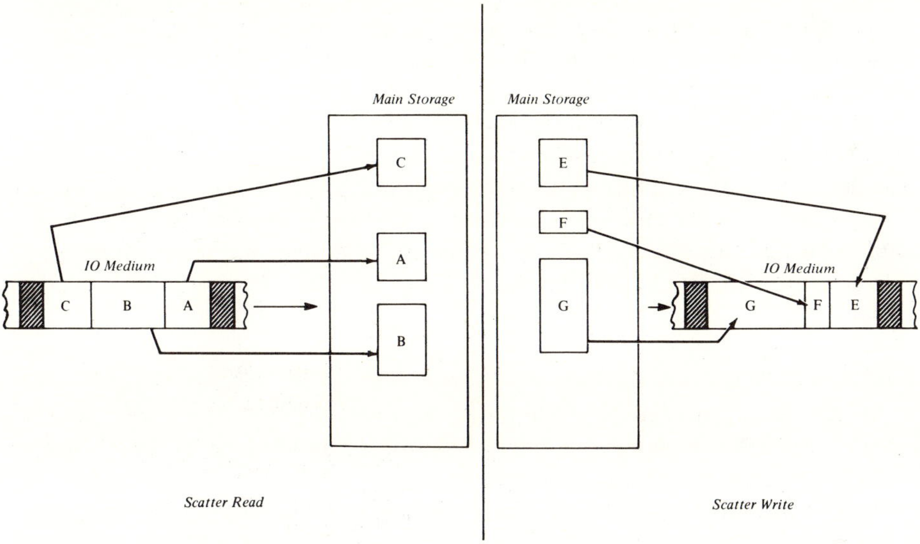

Figure 4.6 Scatter read and scatter write are specified by data chaining in a channel program.

When *command chaining* is specified by setting the CC bit to one in the current CCW, the new CCW specifies a new IO operation on the device addressed by the original start IO instruction. No IO interruption is normally generated when the first IO operation has been completed. Command chaining is frequently used to print multiple lines on the line printer without interfering with CPU operation—that is, only one start IO instruction is required for, perhaps, an entire page of printing. Command chaining is also used with heavily used storage devices such as the paging device in a virtual memory operating system. All the IO control program need do to initiate another data transfer operation is add a new CCW to a channel program currently being executed.

If a transfer in channel command is recognized by the channel during either command or data chaining, the CCW addressed by the transfer in channel is used as the new CCW.

*The command code in the new CCW is not used.

The SKIP flag (bit 35) in the CCW causes suppression of main storage accesses by the IO channel during an IO operation and effectively allows data to be passed over on a storage medium. Skipping is strictly a channel function; device operation proceeds normally and control information is maintained in the usual fashion. Skipping takes place when the skip flag is one. The SKIP flag may assume different values in chained CCWs.

The PCI* flag (bit 36) instructs the channel to initiate an IO interruption when a CCW with that bit set to one is encountered. The setting of the PCI bit in a CCW does not affect the execution of the IO operation. Multiple program controlled interruptions can be initiated in a single channel program.

The status information in the channel status word contains an incorrect length indicator that is set when the number of bytes specified in the CCW is not equal to the number of bytes expected by the IO device (during a write) or is inconsistent with the block size (during a read). Setting of the SLI (bit 34) flag in the CCW to one causes the incorrect length indicator to be suppressed. The SLI flag is commonly used with command and data chaining.

IO Termination

An IO operation can be terminated at one of three times: during IO initiation, after the operation has been initiated and before it is completed, and after it has been completed.

IO termination during IO initiation is caused by an improperly specified start IO instruction or an error in command chaining. IO termination after a start IO instruction is indicated by the condition code setting in the PSW. IO termination during command chaining causes an IO interruption to be generated and the subchannel to become unavailable.

An operation that does not require the use of the IO channel (such as control operation to rewind a magnetic tape) causes the channel to signal a channel-end condition (see Table 4.6) indicating that the channel is no longer in use. Later when the non-data operation is complete, the device or control unit then signals with a control unit-end or device-end signal.

Termination of a data transfer operation is normally indicated by two conditions: channel end and device end. The *channel-end* condition denotes that the data transfer portion of the operation is complete and channel facilities are no longer needed. The *device-end* condition indicates that the operation has been completed at the IO device. In general, the termination of a data transfer operation is recognized by the hardware in one of two ways (in the absence of data or command chaining): the byte count in the CCW has been exhausted or, in cases where a storage

*PCI stands for program controlled interruption.

medium recognizes a physical data block, the transfer of a complete data block has been completed. Some IO devices require the use of control unit facilities after a channel-end condition. Two familiar examples are the backspace operation on tape which requires control unit functions and use of the IBM 2702 Transmission Control Unit, which may monitor a large number of teleprocessing lines. Thus, another signal, *control unit end*, is provided, in some cases, to signal that the control unit is free and may be used by another device that shares it. Channel, control unit, and device end indicators are stored as part of the channel status word (CSW).

IO operations can also be terminated by issuing a halt IO or halt device instruction to a specific subchannel and device, by a channel equipment malfunction, or by a system reset.

IO Interruption

An IO interruption can be initiated by an IO device or an IO channel. When an interruption originates from a channel, other channel conditions may be indicated in the channel status word (CSW), but none of the device status indicators are set. When an interruption originates from an IO device, both channel and device indicators are set in the CSW. An IO interruption request is generated under the following conditions: channel end, control unit end, device end, and attention. During command chaining the following conditions also generate interruption requests: unit check, unit exception, device busy, program check, and protection check. A channel also initiates an IO interruption when it detects a PCI flag in a CCW or when a halt IO instruction is issued on a channel operating in the selector mode.

The manner in which the CPU functions after receiving an IO interruption has been discussed previously. The current PSW is stored at location 56 and the CSW is stored at location 64. A new PSW is loaded from location 120. The channel address of the IO device that caused the interruption is stored in bit positions 16–23 of the old PSW and the device address is stored in bit positions 24–31 of the old PSW. If the interruption was caused by a control unit end, then the control unit address is stored instead of the channel address.

The priority of interruption requests by IO channels is based upon the type of channel and its channel address. Within devices on a single channel, priority is determined by interruption condition, position on the IO interface cable, and the order in which an IO device responds to the channel with an interruption request.

4.5 SUMMARY

The use of the channel concept for controlling input and output operations in a computing system provides the capability for increased system performance but also increases the complexity of the programming and operational procedures required.

An input and output (IO) system is composed of three types of functional units: IO channels, IO control units, and IO devices. An IO channel is classed as either a byte multiplexer channel, a selector channel, or a block multiplexer channel. The three types of channels differ in their operational properties and the number of concurrent IO operations that they can support. An IO control unit connects an IO device to an IO channel and controls the operation of that device. A control unit may support a single device or a family of similar devices.

The IO system is programmed by instructions, commands, and orders. Instructions are executed by the CPU; commands are executed by a channel; and orders are executed by a control unit. An IO operation is initiated by an IO instruction and proceeds under control of a channel program composed of channel commands. The channel is programmed in much the same manner that the CPU is programmed.

IO operations are interrupt-driven in the sense that IO operations and CPU processing proceed concurrently. When an IO operation requires the services of the CPU, an IO interruption is generated so that the CPU can perform the required service. The CPU can ascertain the status of the IO system through status information provided with the interruption and sense data that may be obtained from the IO device causing the interruption condition.

Detailed information on channel organization and IO programming should be obtained from appropriate reference manuals.

REFERENCES

1. Flores, I., "Data Structure and Management," Prentice-Hall, Inc., Englewood Cliffs, N.J., 1970.
2. Padegs, A., "The structure of System/360: Part IV—Channel design considerations," *IBM Systems Journal*, **3,** (2) (1964).
3. IBM System/370 publications: "IBM System/370 System Summary," Form GA22-7001; "IBM System/370 Principles of Operation," Form GA22-7000; "IBM System/370 Model 155 Channel Characteristics," Form GA22-6962. IBM Corporation, Poughkeepsie, N.Y., 1970.
4. IBM System/360 publications: "IBM System/360 Principles of Operation," Form GA22-6821. IBM Corporation, Poughkeepsie, N.Y., 1970.

PART THREE:
SYSTEM/370
SYSTEMS AND DEVICES

5 SYSTEM/370 MODEL 135

5.1 INTRODUCTION TO THE MODEL 135

The Model 135 is the fourth model to be announced in IBM's System/370 family of compatible computers; it is upwards compatible with the architecture of System/360 computers and most 360/370 input/output devices are supported. System/360 user programs and programming systems, except for those dependent upon system configurations and the timing properties of specific models, will operate on the Model 135 without modification. In addition, the advanced features of the Model 135 are supported by two IBM provided operating systems: DOS and OS/MFT.* Integrated emulators for earlier IBM computers that operate under control of either DOS or OS/MFT and a DOS emulator that operates under control of OS/MFT are available for facilitating the transition to the Model 135.

The System/370 Model 135 is a small-to-medium scale general-purpose data processing system designed for commercial, scientific, and data communications applications. The high internal speeds of the system permit fast IO devices to be attached and sufficient main storage is available to support several levels of multiprogramming. Integrated file and communication adapters are provided as options for attaching direct-access devices and communications lines, respectively, to the system without

*DOS (Disk Operating System) and OS/MFT (Operating System/Multiprogramming with a Fixed Number of Tasks) are introduced in Appendix B. DOS is a low-entry operating system and OS is a comprehensive large-scale operating system.

requiring additional equipment. The Model 135 supports the standard System/370 architecture and incorporates many of the design features of the Models 145, 155, and 165.

System Specifications

The Model 135 has a variable length CPU cycle time ranging from 275 nanoseconds to 1430 nanoseconds, depending upon the operation performed. Data paths within the CPU are two bytes wide and are parity checked. The fetch cycle time of main storage is 770 nanoseconds for two bytes. If the two bytes fetched are located on a double word boundary, then the adjacent two bytes can be fetched in an additional 165 nanoseconds. The store cycle time is 935 nanoseconds for two bytes. Main storage is available in four capacities:

*Model Designation**	*Capacity*
FE135	98,304 bytes (96K)
GD135	147,456 bytes (144K)
GF135	196,608 bytes (192K)
DH135	245,760 bytes (240K)

One byte multiplexer channel with 16 subchannels is standard on the Model 135. The system can support up to 64 subchannels on the byte multiplexer channel, an integrated file adapter, one or two selector channels, and an integrated communications adapter. The integrated file adapter allows 2314-type disk storage to be attached to the Model 135 without requiring a selector channel or a disk control unit—thereby lowering costs. The integrated communications adapter is functionally a part of the CPU but operates as a transmission control unit attached to the byte multiplexer channel; it permits up to eight low or medium speed communications lines to be directly attached to the Model 135. The selector channels can be installed with a block multiplexer option for use with rotational position sensing devices. Channel facilities are discussed later in this chapter.

System Design Features

The design of the Model 135 contains many of the architectural features of System/370 as standard items:

commercial instruction set,
storage and fetch protection,

*The convention used for specifying the model designation is easily recognized. D denotes 16K, E denotes 32K, F denotes 64K, G denotes 128K, H denotes 256K, etc. The letters are combined as roman numerals where the decimal value of a roman numeral is the sum of the equivalent decimal values of its characters with the following exception. If a letter is followed by one with a higher value, then its value is subtracted rather than added to the sum.

byte-oriented operand feature,
error checking and correction (ECC) facilities,
instruction retry,
channel/control unit retry capability,
interval timer,
time-of-day clock,
byte multiplexer channel (Channel 0),
console file, and
OS/DOS compatibility.

Most of these features are not unique to the Model 135 and were presented in Part Two. A description of other model-dependent features is included as required.

All system storage in the Model 135 is synthesized using monolithic technology, referred to as monolithic system technology (MST). System storage includes main storage, local storage, and control storage. The major advantages in implementing main storage from monolithic technology rather than from discrete ferrite cores* are that distances between storage elements are shorter and that read-out is nondestructive and does not require a write-back half cycle. Thus, storage speeds are inherently faster. Unlike core storage, monolithic storage is volatile and information is lost when power is turned off.

Control storage is separate from main storage (unlike the Model 145) and holds the microprograms and temporary storage areas that control the operation of the CPU and IO channels. Control storage and main storage share ECC logic and address and data paths. The unit control words necessary for channel multiplexing are also held in control storage, which is reloadable from the system console and is referred to as *reloadable control storage* (RCS). The organization of control storage is considered in more detail later.

The IO channels in the Model 135 are integrated with the CPU and share the use of control storage, data paths, and the arithmetic logical unit. Both channels (i.e., byte multiplexer and selector) and the integrated file adapter interfere with the CPU during channel activity, which includes data servicing and status requests. Channel operations are presented in the section "IO Channels." Installation of a selector channel (optionally, either one or two is allowed) permits the 3330 direct-access storage facility to be attached to a Model 135 system. When the block multiplex feature is installed on a selector channel and when operating under control of OS/MFT, the system can take advantage of block multiplexing and rota-

*MST is also used for main storage in the Model 145; however, the Models 155 and 165, which provide larger main storage sizes, utilize ferrite cores and a MST buffer storage hierarchy system. An obvious conclusion that one could reach, here, is that for *large* main storage sizes, ferrite cores continue to be a cost-effective technology.

tional position sensing to increase the rate at which information can enter or leave the system.

CPU hardware errors detected during the execution of most instructions are retried automatically using hardware facilities in conjunction with system microcode (i.e., micrograms) held in reloadable control storage (RCS). Retry procedures operate in conjunction with an extended machine check interruption system that facilitates error recording or error recovery procedures, as required. RCS also holds the microprograms for the OS/DOS compatibility feature and the 1401/1440/1460 compatibility feature.

In addition to suitable microprograms, the *OS/DOS compatability feature* includes an OS processing program that effectively allows a DOS operating system to operate under OS control. The feature, referred to as the *DOS emulator*, allows a DOS system with associated problem programs to be multiprogrammed in an OS environment without requiring changes to the DOS system, programs, job control statements, or data files. The DOS emulator provided with the Model 135 is the same DOS emulator that is available for the Models 145 and 155. The DOS emulator feature is intended to allow a smooth transition from DOS to OS operating environments.

The contents of reloadable control storage are loaded from a small read-only disk device, called the *console file*, located at the system console. An *initial microprogram loading* (IMPL) sequence is initiated when power is applied to the system or the console file start key is pressed.

Optional features for the Model 135 include:

scientific instruction set,
extended-precision floating-point,
one or two selector channels,
block multiplexer feature on selector channels,
integrated file adapter,
additional (48) byte multiplexer subchannels,
integrated communications adapter,
control storage to support optional Model 135 features,
direct control,
3210 Model 1 adapter for the 3210 console printer-keyboard model 1 or the 3215 adapter for the 3215 console printer-keyboard (one console is required), and
1401/1440/1460 compatibility.

The *extended-precision floating-point option* provides up to 34 decimal digits of precision for a comprehensive set of arithmetic operations. This feature requires the floating-point option.

The *integrated file adapter* (IFA) allows three, four, or five 2314-type disk drives* to be attached to a Model 135 computer without requiring a selector channel or disk control unit. The basic unit is an IBM 2319 Direct-Access Storage Facility (DASF) consisting of three drives that are compatible with the 2314A series disk drives and also use the removable 2316 disk pack. Up to two additional drives can be added to the 2319 DASF configuration with the 2312 unit (one drive) or the 2318 unit (two drives). 2314 disk storage facilities can also be added to a Model 135 system using selector channel facilities.

One *integrated communications adapter* (ICA) can be attached to a Model 135 via a byte multiplexer channel. The ICA permits up to eight half-duplex communications lines that operate at low or medium speeds to be operated without additional communications equipment. Start/stop, binary synchronous, and alphanumeric type communications devices are supported.

Another 360/370 CPU can communicate with the Model 135 in either of two ways. With the *direct control feature*, a single byte of data is transferred between an external device and the main storage of another system. This feature includes external interruption lines and read direct and write direct instructions. A Model 135 IO channel can also be connected to an IO channel of another 360/370 computer that has the channel-to-channel adapter feature installed. The channel-to-channel adapter cannot be installed on a Model 135.

A relocatable emulator for the 1401/1440/1460 computers that operates under DOS or OS control is available to Model 135 users. The emulators are integrated in the sense that they do not require a standalone machine and execute in a multiprogramming environment. The 1401/1440/1460 compatibility feature uses emulator processing programs (simulation routines), microprograms, the Model 135 instruction set, and operating system facilities to emulate a given computer.

System Structure

The major components of a System/370 Model 135 are the processing unit,† main storage, control storage, IO channels, the system control panel and operator's console, a console file (for loading microcode), and a power supply unit. The functional components of the processing unit, storage, IO channels, and IO adapters are all housed within the central processing unit cabinets. The power supply unit and operator's console

*2314-type disk drives use the 2316 removable disk pack, each of which has the following characteristics: 20 recording surfaces, 200 recording tracks on each surface, 7294 bytes per track—for a total capacity of over 20 megabytes per pack.

†The term processing unit refers to the central processing unit discussed earlier.

are housed externally to the CPU. The power supply unit is used to supply and regulate electrical power to the CPU during normal circumstances and when variations occur in line voltage. The operator's console is located adjacent to the central processing unit. The system control panel is attached to the end of the CPU and contains the dials, lights, and switches necessary to operate the system. The console file is located in the system control panel.

A complete description of IO devices supported by the Model 135 is beyond the scope of this book. However, two devices (the 3330 disk storage and the 3211 line printer) of several that are new with the System/370 series are described in Chapters 9 and 10. The 2305 fixed-head storage is not supported in a Model 135 system.

5.2 PROCESSING UNIT

The Model 135 central processing unit (CPU) controls the operation of the Model 135 by decoding and executing instructions held in main storage, and by monitoring the operation of IO channels and IO devices. All CPU functions and channel operations are controlled by a microprogram held and executed in two-byte (18 bits) control words in reloadable control storage (RCS).

Local and Working Storage

Local storage is shared by the CPU, the integrated channels, and the integrated IO adapters. Local storage contains the general and floating-point registers and work areas for the CPU, channels, and IO adapters.

The Model 135 uses two (0 and 14) of the 32-bit control registers defined with System/370. The status of a Model 135 when the operating state (see Chapter 3) is reflected in the 64-bit program status word.

Integrated IO Adapters

The Model 135 design includes four adapters that allow IO devices to be attached directly to the CPU. The *console file adapter* is used to load reloadable control storage (RCS) from the system console. The *console printer/keyboard adapter* supports an on-line communications device for the system operator. The *integrated file adapter* allows the 2319 DASF to be attached to the system without an IO channel or control unit. The *integrated communications adapter* permits direct attachment of up to eight low and medium speed data communications lines without an IO channel or transmission control unit.

Data Checking

Data paths in the CPU and between the CPU and main storage are parity checked by byte. Microcode words and adder sums are also parity checked and most CPU instructions are retried if a hardware error occurs during their execution.

Interruptions

The move long and compare logical long instructions that are a part of the System/370 extensions to System/360 architecture are interruptable on the Model 135.* If an IO or external interruption condition arises during execution of either instruction and the CPU is enabled for that type of interruption, then the interruption is taken and the general registers, used by the instruction, are incremented accordingly. As a result, the instruction can be re-executed and processing will resume at the point of interruption.

CPU Features

Many of the other Model 135 features are implemented in the CPU: the interval timer, the time-of-day clock, the scientific instruction set, the extended-precision floating-point feature, direct control, IO channel features, and the relocatable emulators. System/370 also includes several new instructions over its predecessor, the System/360. The reader is directed to reference manuals for more detailed information.

5.3 STORAGE AND THE CONSOLE FILE

The Model 135 storage system consists of reloadable control storage and main storage†—both implemented in monolithic technology. Reloadable control storage contains microprograms and storage areas for system control functions. Main storage is used for holding programs and data for use by the CPU. Control storage is separate from main storage and is contained in one basic storage module. This section is primarily concerned with control storage and the console file. However, some key facts on main storage should be mentioned.

The byte-oriented operand feature is supported and allows operands for nonprivileged instructions to reside on byte boundaries without causing a specification program interruption. Byte boundary alignment does not apply to CPU instruction (which must be aligned on a half word boundary), and the operands of privileged instructions.

Error checking and correction circuitry, which is shared by main storage and control storage, is used for validity checking as data enter and leave storage. Main and control storage also share address and data paths to and from the CPU.

*The move long and compare logical long instructions are interruptable on the Models 145, 155, and 165, as well.

†Main storage is also called processor storage.

Control Storage Organization and Requirements

The amount of control storage required in a Model 135 system is directly related to the features installed in that system. A standard 24K of control storage, which supports standard features of the Model 135 and some optional features, is provided with the system. The amount of control storage can be extended to 36K or 48K (i.e., in 12K increments) to support additional optional features. The first 24K of control storage is divided into a fixed area and a variable area. The fixed area supplies basic Model 135 functions and is packaged optimally. It is not modified under normal circumstances. The variable area provides certain optional features selected by the user. As listed in Table 5.1, other optional features require that control storage be extended to 36K or 48K.

TABLE 5.1 MODEL 135 CONTROL STORAGE REQUIREMENTS

Standard *24K*	*First 12K Increment* *36K*	*Second 12K Increment* *48K*
Fixed area:	Any of the following:	Either of the following combinations:
Standard Model 135 instruction set (including decimal arithmetic and protection instructions)	3215 console *and* scientific instruction set	1401/1440/1460 compatibility and the ICA with the Synchronous Data Adapter
16 byte multiplexer UCWs	Extended-precision floating-point	Any three of the following: 1. Block multiplexing
OS/DOS Compatibility	Additional 48 byte multiplexer UCWs	2. 1401/1440/1460 Compatibility 3. ICA with the Synchronous Data Adapter Type II
Variable area:	Block multiplexing[a]	4. ICA with Terminal Adapter Type I
3210 Model 1 or 3215 console	Integrated Communications Adapter (ICA)[a]	5. ICA with Terminal Adapter Type III
Integrated File Adapter (IFA)		
Direct Control		
Selector Channels	1401/1440/1460 Compatibility[a]	
Scientific instruction set (if 3210 is selected)		

[a] May require the second 12K increment.

Disk Cartridges

Disk cartridges containing system microcode are supplied by IBM to meet the requirements of a given installation. A given Model 135 system can use more than one disk cartridge, but not at the same time, provided that the necessary system components are available to support the microcode on each cartridge.

The use of reloadable control storage and changeable disk cartridges have several happy consequences over conventional circuitry and read-only storage:

1. The system is made potentially more versatile by allowing different combinations of optional features.
2. Engineering changes can be distributed by supplying a new disk cartridge to an installation.
3. More comprehensive and efficient microprograms that serve diagnostic and check-out functions are available for scheduled and unscheduled maintenance.

A disk cartridge, often called a *floppy disk*, has the capacity for approximately 65K bytes of microcode.* It is housed in an 8-inch square casing, as depicted in Figure 6.2. The disk is read by the console file as it rotates inside the casing.

Disk cartridges are prewritten and cannot be read or written by a computer program. A disk cartridge normally contains an initial microprogram load procedure, system microdiagnostics to insure that the system is operating correctly, and the microcode for a given system configuration.

Console File

The disk cartridge is read by the console file located in the system control panel. Since monolithic storage is volatile, reloadable control storage must be reloaded each time power is applied to the system. As a result, the console file is activated automatically during the power-up sequence. The process of loading RCS from the console file is referred to as the *initial microprogram load* (IMPL) sequence. IMPL takes about one minute and includes time for the disk cartridge to come up to speed and for system microdiagnostics to be performed. Data are read from the disk cartridge at 33,300 bits per second. When the system is in the operating state (the power is turned on), the IMPL sequence is initiated by pressing the start console file key.

During normal operation of the system, the disk cartridge will stay mounted in the console file. The disk cartridge will be changed only when system maintenance is performed.

5.4 IO CHANNELS AND ADAPTERS

Model 135 channels and IO adapters are integrated into the CPU and share control storage, data paths, and arithmetic logical facilities. The

*See Chapter 6 for a more precise description of the capacity of a disk cartridge.

number of concurrent IO operations that can be sustained is dependent upon the number and types of channels, the data rates of the attached IO devices, and the amount of reloadable control storage allocated to unit control words. All channel activity, which includes data transfer operations and status requests, interferes with normal CPU operation.

Cycle Stealing

When an IO request must be serviced, CPU operation is suspended by a hardware-controlled function known as *cycle stealing.* During a cycle steal, normal microprogram activity is suspended and either one or two bytes of data are transferred between main storage and the IFA or a channel. The cycle steal takes 660 nanoseconds during which time the data count and storage address for that operation are modified accordingly. Two or more cycle steals may take place successively before microprogram activity is resumed.

A servicing priority is established among the channels and IO adapters for use in cases when IO requests occur simultaneously. The byte multiplexer channel and the integrated communications adapter are assigned the lowest priority. Cycle steal requests from the IFA and the channels are handled in the following manner:

1. Cycle steal requests from the IFA and the channels are sampled.
2. Outstanding requests are ordered in priority sequence from high to low: IFA, first channel, second channel.
3. Requests are serviced in priority sequence, until all outstanding requests have been satisfied, before requests are again sampled.

Thus, a channel or the IFA is allowed in the worst case, every third cycle steal.

Byte Multiplexer Channel

The byte multiplexer channel is designed to control multiple low-speed IO devices and operates in either the byte-interleaved mode or the burst mode, depending upon the needs of a particular IO device. In the byte-interleaved mode, several low-speed devices operate concurrently and share channel facilities. In the burst mode, only one medium-to-high speed device operates at one time. Even though the byte multiplexer channel can operate in the burst mode, most unbuffered devices requiring the burst mode of operation will overrun* and should be attached to a selector channel. In either mode, data are transferred between main storage and the byte multiplexer channel at a rate of one byte per storage cycle.

*Informally, overrun refers to the case where main storage/channel speed can not satisfy IO speeds.

The byte multiplexer channel is addressed as channel 0 and can have 16 or 64 subchannels. The number of subchannels present determines the maximum number of IO devices that can be attached to the byte multiplexer channel. Each subchannel requires a 16-byte unit control word (UCW) that is used to record addresses, count, and status and control information for each active IO operation. When a subchannel is not active, its UCW is held in control storage. When the byte multiplexer channel requires the use of control information* for an IO operation, the UCW for the associated device is read from control storage and held in appropriate registers in local storage. When the device no longer requires services of the channel, the updated control information is returned to its UCW area in control storage.

The amount of control storage allocated to UCWs is not a function of the size of main storage but must be specified when the microcode disk cartridge is ordered.

The console printer/keyboard requires one multiplexer subchannel as does each communications line attached to the integrated communications adapter.

Integrated Communications Adapter

The integrated communications adapter (ICA) was introduced earlier as a low-cost means of attaching up to eight communications lines to the Model 135. The system can support one ICA. Lines connected to the ICA are addressed as channel 0 (byte multiplexer channel) and are assigned device positions 01 through 08. Each communications line uses one byte multiplexer UCW. The ICA supports half-duplex communications lines and provides three types of terminal adapters:

1. Terminal Adapter Type I for start/stop terminals;
2. Terminal Adapter Type III for alphanumeric display units; and
3. Synchronous Data Adapter Type II for binary synchronous communications.

Any combination of the three types is permitted in a single Model 135 computer.

Integrated File Adapter

The integrated file adapter (IFA) is a means of attaching disk storage units to a Model 135 computer without requiring an IO channel or control unit. Disk storage units attached to the IFA (i.e., the 2319 DASF plus other optional units) operate as a single channel and single control unit so that only one disk module can be active at a given time. The IFA, if present in

*Control information includes: protection key, data address, command code indicator, CCW flags, byte count, channel status, and the address of the next CCW.

a system, is addressed as channel 1 and is programmed as though the channel and control unit were available.

The integrated file adapter uses the hardware-controlled cycle stealing function and one byte of information is transferred between the IFA and main storage in one storage cycle. A data rate of 312 kilobytes per second can be sustained with the IFA.

Selector Channels

A Model 135 selector channel can control a single high-speed IO operation on a single data path. A selector channel operates in the burst mode and can support a maximum data rate of 1.3 megabytes per second as the first selector channel and 1.2 megabytes per second as the second selector channel. The maximum combined data rate is 2.4 megabytes per second which can be maintained concurrently with a data rate of 312 kilobytes per second on the IFA.

One or two selector channels can be installed. When the integrated file adapter (IFA) is not present, the selector channels are addressed as channels 1 and 2. If the IFA is present, the selector channels are addressed as channels 2 and 3. Each selector channel contains a four byte buffer and data is transferred between it and main storage, using cycle stealing, at a rate of one or two bytes per storage cycle. Double byte transfers are made whenever possible.

Block Multiplexer Channels

A selector channel with the block multiplex feature operates in the block multiplex mode or the selector mode, depending upon the setting of bit 0 in control register 0 when the start IO for that channel is issued. In the block multiplex mode, the channel can support interleaved, concurrent execution of multiple channel programs and the concurrent operation of multiple high-speed IO devices. Each channel program requires a subchannel and a unit control word (UCW). The block multiplex feature is required when the 3330 disk storage is installed and OS/MFT is used.

A selector channel with the block multiplex feature operating in the selector mode is busy during the entire execution of a channel program. When operating in the block multiplex mode, the channel can disconnect for non-data operations during operation of one channel program so that a data transfer operation can be executed for another channel program. During the execution of a channel program with multiple command channel CCWs, the channel disconnects from that program when a channel end is received without a concurrent device end. The channel is then available for another IO operation; the status of the disconnected operation is saved in its UCW. When the disconnected operation is again ready to use the channel, the control unit attempts to regain use of the channel facilities. If the channel is free, the channel registers are reloaded from the UCW and execution of that channel program is resumed. If the channel is busy at the time, the device must wait. Block multiplex operations are controlled by channel and control unit hardware.

Each selector channel with the block multiplex feature provides 17 unit control words (UCWs) for use during block multiplexing. Sixteen of the UCWs are nonshared and are assigned permanently to control units capable of block multiplexing. The seventeenth UCW is shared and is assigned dynamically to one of a set of devices.* A device assigned to a shared UCW does not operate in the block multiplex mode.

5.5 SYSTEM RELIABILITY AND AVAILABILITY

The Model 135 computer includes error recovery and recording features designed to improve reliability, availability, and serviceability of the system hardware. The above features operate in conjunction with an expanded machine check interruption facility to provide a level of software support previously unavailable in data processing systems.

CPU Retry

A CPU error detected during the execution of an instruction causes that instruction to be retried up to eight times if an established threshold point for that instruction was not passed or if storage or a register was not altered by the operation. If storage or a register is altered, a microcoded routine is used to determine if one of the source operands has been changed. If the operands are not changed, then the instruction is retried. If eight instruction retries are unsuccessful, the threshold point is passed, or source operands are altered, then a hard machine check interruption is initiated. If retry is successful, a soft machine check interruption is initiated so that the occurrence of the error can be recorded by the software.

Storage Error Checking and Correction

Eight bits of error checking and correction (ECC) code is maintained with each double word of main and control storage. Checking on an 8-byte basis, rather than a single byte basis, allows single bit errors to be corrected and all double bit and most multiple bit errors to be detected. Internally to the CPU, a parity bit is maintained with each byte. A conversion between byte parity and ECC code is made as each double word enters and leaves control or main storage. A single bit error detected by

*A shared UCW is usually assigned to a control unit with multiple devices attached to it —only one of which can be in operation at a time.

ECC logic is corrected automatically and the valid doubleword is sent to the CPU. Main or control storage is not corrected.

The design of the Model 135 includes an *error frequency limit* (EFL) of 256 single bit errors in 416 microseconds. If the limit is exceeded, a machine check interruption is initiated (if enabled) and the counter is reset

TABLE 5.2 MODEL 135 FIXED STORAGE LOCATIONS

Decimal Address	*Length*	*Purpose*
0	2 wds	IPL PSW
8	2 wds	IPL CCW1
16	2 wds	IPL CCW2
24	2 wds	External old PSW
32	2 wds	SVC old PSW
40	2 wds	Program old PSW
48	2 wds	Machine check old PSW
56	2 wds	IO old PSW
64	2 wds	CSW
72	1 wd	CAW
76	1 wd	Unused
80	1 wd	Interval timer
84	1 wd	Unused
88	2 wds	External new PSW
96	2 wds	SVC new PSW
104	2 wds	Program new PSW
112	2 wds	Machine check new PSW
120	2 wds	IO new PSW
128–159	—	Unused
160	2 wds	Reserved
168	1 wd	Channel ID
172	1 wd	Unused
176	1 wd	Limited channel logout (ECSW)
180	1 wd	Reserved
184	1 wd	IO address
188	1 wd	Reserved
192–231	—	Reserved
232	2 wds	Machine check code
240	2 wds	Unused
248	1 wd	Failing storage address
252	1 wd	Unused
256–267	—	CPU logout
268–277	—	Extended channel logout
352–383	8 wds	Floating-point register save area
384–447	16 wds	General register save area
448–511	16 wds	Control register save area

to zero. Error correction continues after the EFL is reached and another EFL interruption may be subsequently initiated.

IO Errors

IO channel errors and CPU errors associated with a channel operation are accompanied by an IO interruption during which the channel status word (CSW) and the extended channel status word (ECSW) are stored (see Table 5.2). The CSW and ECSW are used by error recovery routines to retry failing IO operations.

IO command retry is provided with certain control units and IO devices, automatically, without an IO interruption or programmed error recovery procedures.

Machine Check Interruptions

Five types of machine check interruptions are defined in the Model 135. They are listed in Table 5.3 and classified by whether they are hard or soft.

TABLE 5.3 MODEL 135 MACHINE CHECK INTERRUPTIONS

Mask Bits	*Interruption Type*	*Machine Check*
PSW bit 13 CR[a]14 bit 4	System recovery	Soft
PSW bit 13 CR 14 bit 6	Internal timer damage	Soft
PSW bit 13 CR 14 bit 6	Time-of-day clock damage	Soft
PSW bit 13	System damage (irreparable hardware malfunction)	Hard
PSW bit 13	Instruction processing damage (CPU, storage, or protect key)	Hard

[a] CR—Control register.

A *hard machine check* interruption follows an unsuccessful retry attempt. A *soft machine check* interruption follows a successful retry effort and is initiated so that the error condition can be recorded.

A machine check interruption, accepted by the CPU, is accompanied by a machine check logout to the fixed logout area (main storage bytes 232–511). Model 135 fixed storage locations are depicted in Table 5.2. IO interruptions cause a logout to the IO communications area that occupies byte locations 160–191.

The *machine check code* stored in byte locations 232–239 of the fixed logout area is of special concern since it indicates the state of the hardware when the interruption occurred. The bit settings provide the condition that caused the interruption and the validity of certain fields in the fixed logout area. Model 135 machine check codes are identical to Model 145 machine check codes that are presented in Figure 6.4.

5.6 SUPPORT FACILITIES

The System/370 Model 135 is supported by programming systems as well as by additional advanced hardware facilities. In addition to the IBM 3330 Disk Storage Facility,* the IBM 3211 Printer, and the IBM 3210 and 3215 consoles, several IO devices were announced after the Model 145 announcement. The 3803/3420 Magnetic Tape Subsystem provides data rates of 120, 200, and 320 kilobytes per second at a density of 1600 bytes per inch along with several advanced features in magnetic tape system engineering. The 3505 Card Reader reads 80-column cards at either 800 or 1200 cards per minute. The 3525 Card Punch punches 80-column cards at either 100, 200, or 300 cards per minute. Both of the latter IO devices also include advanced features in engineering design.† The reader is directed to the appropriate reference manuals for more detailed information.

The Model 135 supports two multiprogramming operating systems: DOS/360 and OS/360 (MFT). An integrated emulator for the 1401/1440/1460 systems is available that operates under either DOS or OS control in a multiprogramming environment. In addition, a DOS emulator that operates under OS control is a standard feature.

The IO devices are presented in Chapters 9 and 10; programming systems and emulators are introduced in the appendices.

REFERENCES

IBM System/370 publications: "Principles of Operation," Form GA22-7000; "A Guide to the System/370 Model 135," Form GC20-1738. IBM Corporation, Data Processing Division, White Plains, N.Y., 1971.

*For a brief discussion of these devices, the reader is directed to Chapters 9 and 10.

†All devices mentioned here are available for other models of System/370.

6 SYSTEM/370 MODEL 145

6.1 INTRODUCTION TO THE MODEL 145

The IBM System/370 Model 145 computer is characterized in a variety of ways:

1. It is a medium-scale, general-purpose data processing system designed for commercial, real-time, and certain classes of scientific applications.
2. The system supports a wide variety of input/output and mass storage devices including a new line printer, a new console keyboard, and new direct-access storage devices.
3. The system is upward program compatible with System/360 models, fully compatible with other System/370 models, and most System/360 input/output devices can be attached.
4. Emulators for several earlier IBM computers are provided that operate under operating system control.
5. A compatibility feature is available that supports emulation of a DOS operating system under OS control.*

System Specifications

The Model 145 has a variable-length CPU cycle time ranging from 202.5 nanoseconds to 315 nanoseconds. Four distinct cycle times (202.5, 247.5,

*DOS stands for disk operating system, a low-entry operating system for System/360 users. OS stands for operating system, a comprehensive and powerful System/360 operating system.

Two models of System/370. Upper: Model 145. Lower: Model 155. (Courtesy of International Business Machines Corporation.)

292.5, and 315) are defined and the time necessary to perform a CPU operation is a combination of these cycle times.* Main storage is available in six capacities:

Model Designation	*Capacity*
FED145	114,688 bytes
GE145	163,840 bytes
GFD145	212,992 bytes
H145	262,144 bytes
HG145	393,216 bytes
I145	524,288 bytes

The fetch cycle time of main storage is 540 nanoseconds for 4 data bytes and 8 instruction bytes. The store cycle time is 607.5 nanoseconds for 4 data bytes.

One byte multiplexer channel with 16 subchannels and one selector channel are standard on the Model 145. The system can support one byte multiplexer channel and as many as four selector channels or one byte multiplexer channel, an integrated file adapter, and two selector channels. The integrated file adapter allows disk storage to be attached to the Model 145 without a selector channel or disk control unit. Channel capacities are discussed later in this chapter.

System Design Features

The design of the Model 145 contains many of the architectural features of System/370 as standard items:

- commercial instruction set,
- storage protection (including fetch protect),
- byte-oriented operand feature,
- error checking and correction (ECC),
- instruction retry,
- channel retry information,
- command retry,
- interval timer,
- time-of-day clock,
- byte multiplexer channel (Channel 0),
- first selector channel (Channel 1 or Channel 2 if the integrated file adapter is installed),
- console file, and
- OS/DOS compatibility.

*In general, machine cycle time is an indirect measure of system performance. For example, an RR-type load instruction takes .923 microseconds (923 nanoseconds), an RR-type fixed-point add takes 1.373 microseconds, and an RR-type floating-point multiply takes 19.929 microseconds. The actual machine cycles required by an instruction are dependent upon the nature of the operation and the data involved.

Most of these features are not unique to the Model 145 and were presented in Part Two. A description of other model-dependent features is included as required.

All system storage in the Model 145 is synthesized using monolithic technology. Included in this category are main storage, control storage, and local storage. The major advantages in implementing main storage from monolithic technology rather than from discrete ferrite cores are that distances between storage elements are shorter and that read-out is nondestructive and does not require a write-back half cycle. Thus, storage speeds are inherently faster.

Control storage is implemented as an extension to main storage and holds the microprograms that control the operation of the CPU and IO channels. The unit control words necessary for channel multiplexing are also held in control storage, which is reloadable from the system console and is referred to as *reloadable control storage* (RCS). Storage is considered in more detail later.

The IO channels in the Model 145 are integrated with the CPU and share the use of control storage, data paths, and the arithmetic logical unit. A byte multiplexer channel interferes with the CPU when it requires one of the shared facilities; a selector channel and the integrated file adapter interfere with both the CPU and the byte multiplexer channel. CPU interference takes place when an IO operation is initiated, when it is completed, and when one of the IO channels references main storage. Selector channel design permits the installation of a block multiplexer feature that enables the channel to operate in the block multiplexer mode. When the block multiplexer feature is installed on a selector channel, the 3330 and 2305 Model 2 direct-access facilities can be installed and the system can take advantage of rotational position sensing and multiple requesting to increase the effective data rate of the system.

CPU errors detected during the execution of certain instructions* are automatically retried using microprogram logic held in reloadable control storage (RCS). RCS also holds the microprograms for the OS/DOS standard compatibility feature and those required for the emulation of other computers.

The *OS/DOS compatibility feature* includes an OS/DOS processing program and microprograms that effectively allow the DOS operating system to operate under OS control. The feature is intended for installations that desire to upgrade their operating system from DOS to OS without requiring extensive reprogramming.

The contents of reloadable control storage are loaded from a small read-only disk device, called the *console file*, located at the system console.

*All but four CPU instructions can be retried.

An *initial microprogram loading* (IMPL) sequence is initiated when power is applied to the system or the console file start key is pressed.

Optional features for the Model 145 include:

- scientific instruction set,
- universal instruction set,
- extended precision floating point,
- block multiplexer feature on selector channels,
- selector channels (maximum of three additional for channels 2, 3, and 4; or when the integrated file adapter is installed, one additional plus the standard on channel 2),
- direct control,
- channel-to-channel adapter,
- 3210 Model 1 adapter for the 3210 console printer/keyboard model 1 or the 3215 adapter for the 3215 console printer/keyboard (one of these units is required),
- 3210 Model 2 adapter for the standalone 3210 console printer/keyboard,
- integrated file adapter,
- word buffer,
- 1401/1440/1460 compatibility, and
- 1401/1440/1460, 1410/7010 compatibility.

The *direct control feature* allows two CPUs to communicate by transferring a single byte of data between an external device and the main storage of another system. Included with this feature are read direct and write direct instructions and six external interruption lines.

The *channel-to-channel adapter* allows two 360/370 computers to be coupled into a multisystem configuration (see Chapter 2) or permits moving blocks of information from one area of main storage to another in the same system. Thus, the two channels connected need not be attached to different systems. The adapter occupies one control unit position on each channel.

The *integrated file adapter* (IFA) allows from three to eight 2314A-type disk drives* to be attached to a Model 145 computer without requiring a selector channel or disk control unit. The basic unit is an IBM 2319 Direct Access Storage Facility (DASF) consisting of three drives. Up to five additional 2314A-type drives can be added to the 2319 DASF con-

*2314A-type disk drives use a removable disk pack each with the following characteristics: 20 recording surfaces, 200 recording tracks on each surface, 7294 bytes per track—for a total capacity of over 29 megabytes per pack. Average access time is 60 milliseconds and average rotational delay is 12.5 milliseconds.

figuration with the following units: 2312 (one drive), 2313 (four drives), and 2318 (two drives).

Ordinarily, data are transferred between a Model 145 IO channel and main storage on a byte basis—that is, the CPU is interrupted and one byte is transferred. The *channel word-buffer feature*, effective on *all* selector and block multiplexor channels, permits the assembly of 4 data bytes before requesting a storage cycle to transfer the data. The word-buffer feature allows the IBM 2305 Model 2 Fixed Head Storage Facility to be attached to a Model 145 computer.

Relocatable emulators for the 1401/1440/1460 and 1410/7010 systems that operate under DOS or OS control are available to Model 145 users. The emulators are integrated in the sense that they do not require a stand-alone machine and execute in a multiprogramming environment. Two emulator features are available: 1401/1440/1460 emulator for use in the emulation of 1401/1440/1460 systems, and the 1401/1440/1460/1410/7010 emulator for use in emulation of 1401, 1440, 1460, 1410, or 7010 systems. The emulation features use emulator processing programs (simulation routines), emulator feature microprograms, the Model 145 instruction set, and operating system facilities to emulate a given computer.

System Structure

The major component of a System/370 Model 145 is the 3145* processing unit that contains up to 256K bytes of main storage, depending upon the model. Addition of the 3345 processor storage unit increases main storage to 384K bytes and the 3346 processor storage unit (instead of the 3345) provides a total of 512K bytes of main storage. The 3145 processing unit contains the arithmetic and logical circuits, local storage, control storage (up to 32K bytes), IO channels, and the integrated file adapter. Additional control storage (up to 64K bytes) decreases the amount of main storage available for programs and data.

A complete description of IO devices that can be attached to the Model 145 is beyond the scope of this book. However, several devices, new to the System/370 series, are described in Chapters 9 and 10.

6.2 PROCESSING UNIT

The 3145 central processing unit (CPU) controls the operation of the Model 145 by decoding and executing instructions, held in main storage, and by monitoring the operation of IO channels and IO devices. All CPU

*The term processing unit refers to the central processing unit discussed earlier.

functions and channel operations are controlled by a microprogram held and executed in 36-bit reloadable control storage (RCS).

Local Storage

Local storage is shared by the CPU and the integrated channels. Local storage contains the general and floating-point registers, subchannel storage facilities for selector channels, and working storage for the CPU and the byte multiplexer channel. A set of monolithic-register stacks, called *external registers*, is implemented to reduce the use of temporary storage during the sharing of CPU facilities.

Working Registers

Working registers include control registers 0, 2, 14, and 15 and an instruction counter.

Integrated IO Adapters

The Model 145 design includes three adapters that allow IO devices to be attached directly to the CPU. The *console file adapter* is used to load reloadable control storage (RCS) from the system console. The *console printer/keyboard adapter* supports an on-line communications device for the system operator. The *integrated file adapter* allows the 2319DASF to be attached to the system without an IO channel or control unit.

Data Checking

Data paths in the CPU and between the CPU and main storage are priority checked by byte. Microcode words and adder sums are also priority checked and most CPU instructions are retried if a hardware error occurs during their execution.

CPU Features

Many of the other Model 145 features are implemented in the CPU: the interval timer, the time-of-day clock, the extended precision feature, direct control—to name only a few. System/370 also includes several new instructions over its predecessor, the System/360. The reader is directed to reference manuals for more detailed information.

6.3 STORAGE AND THE CONSOLE FILE

The Model 145 storage system consists of control storage and main storage—both implemented in monolithic technology. Control storage contains microprograms and storage areas for system control functions. Main storage is used for holding programs and data for use by the CPU. Control storage is constructed as an extension to main storage; the boundary between the two is established at initial microprogram load (IMPL) time and is dependent upon the system configuration of a particular installation. This section describes storage organization and the control storage required by the various computing system functions. The console file used to load control storage is also discussed. First, some general comments on main storage are required.

The byte-oriented operand feature is supported and allows operands for nonprivileged instructions to reside on byte boundaries without causing a specification program interruption. The feature does not apply to CPU instructions (which must be aligned on a half word boundary), CCWs (which must be aligned on a double word boundary), and the operands of privileged instructions. Error checking and correction circuitry applies to all stores and fetches to main storage; it is considered, along with permanent storage assignments, in the section on reliability.

Storage Organization

The amount of control storage required in a Model 145 system is directly related to the features installed in that system. As noted in Table 6.1, 32K bytes of control storage are automatically provided with every Model 145 computer. Additional control storage (up to a total of 64K bytes) can be defined by a particular installation but the amount over 32K is subtracted from the main storage available for programs and data. Main storage is allocated as control storage in 2K increments.

TABLE 6.1 MODEL 145 STORAGE CAPACITIES

Model Designation	*Main Storage*	*Control Storage*	*Total Storage*
FED145	112K	32K	144K
GE145	160K	32K	192K
GFD145	208K	32K	240K
H145	256K	32K	288K
HG145	384K	32K	416K
I145	512K	32K	544K

Control storage is assigned from upper storage locations, as depicted in Figure 6.1. The CPU maintains an address check boundary (in an address check boundary register) that is established when the microcode is loaded. If a CPU instruction or an IO operation attempts to reference storage above the address check boundary, an address check program interruption is initiated. If a microprogram attempts to reference control storage below the address check boundary, a machine check condition is generated. When either the 3345 or the 3346 processor storage unit is installed, the low-order storage addresses are in that unit.

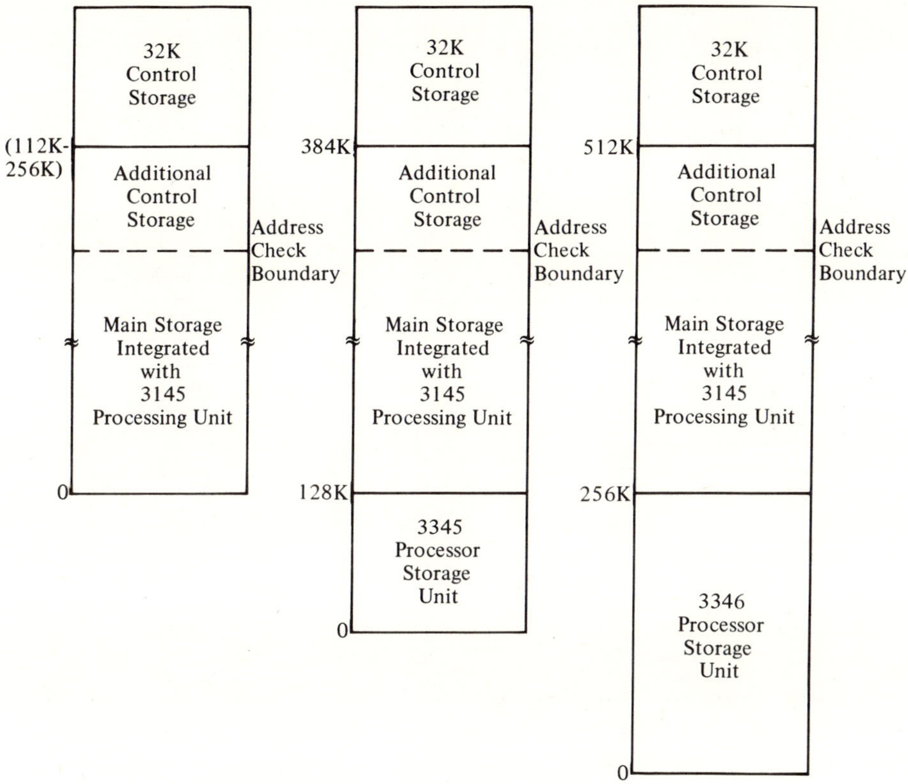

Figure 6.1 Model 145 storage organization.

Control Storage Requirements

The operation of a Model 145 computer is controlled by microcode stored in reloadable control storage (RCS). That microcode is required and enables the computer to operate as a System/370 (or any other computer, as a matter of fact). Microprogram loading is introduced in the next section. Microcode is provided by IBM and varies in form and size, depending upon a particular configuration. RCS requirements are the sum of the bytes of control storage required by the following functions:

basic system microcode,
byte multiplexer channel UCWs,
console printer/keyboard features,
base block multiplexer channel microcode,
block multiplexer channel UCWs,
integrated file adapter,

compatability features,
floating-point arithmetic, and
direct control.

Table 6.2 lists the bytes of control storage required by each of the above functions.

TABLE 6.2 MODEL 145 CONTROL STORAGE REQUIREMENTS

Function	*Bytes of Control Storage Required*
Basic system microcode	24,600
Byte multiplexer channel UCWs:	
16 subchannels	256
32 subchannels	512
64 subchannels	1024
128 subchannels	2048
256 subchannels	4096
Console printer/keyboards:	
3210 Model 1	3040
3210 Model 1 with 3210 Model 2	3160
3215 Model 1	3620
3215 Model 1 with 3210 Model 2	4180
Block multiplexer channel microcode	2100
Block multiplexer channel UCWs:	
Group of 8 UCWs	64
Integrated file adapter	8800
Compatibility features:	
1401/1440/1460	4800
1401/1440/1460 and 1410/7010	6000
Floating-point arithmetic (with extended precision)	2240
Direct control	120

Console File

Microcode is loaded into reloadable control storage (RCS) from a console file when electrical power is applied to the Model 145 computer or when the start console file key is depressed. The process is termed initial microprogram load (IMPL).

Microcode is stored on a removable disk cartridge* (Figure 6.2) and read into the Model 145 RCS by a read-only disk device called a *console file*, located beneath the operator's console table. The cartridge has a capacity of 65,280 10-bit bytes (8 data bits, one parity bit, and a start bit)

*The disk cartridge is often called a "floppy disk."

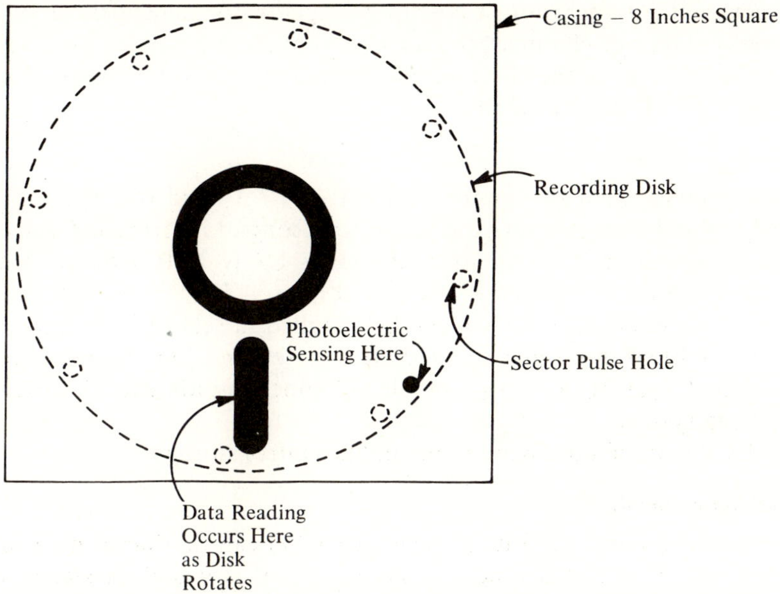

Figure 6.2 Disk cartridge for the console file. Shaded areas represent recording disk showing through cutout areas in casing. Dotted lines show recording disk inside the casing. Eight holes in the periphery of the disk generate, via photoelectric sensing, sector pulses to indicate beginning of sector. (Courtesy of IBM Corporation.)

and is read at 33,300 bits per second. Approximately 32K bytes of RCS can be loaded in 45 seconds.

The address check boundary is determined by microcoded information stored on the disk cartridge.

The use of RCS and the disk cartridge has several distinct advantages:

1. An installation can order several disk cartridges to satisfy the needs of various applications.
2. Disk cartridges can be used to hold system diagnostic microprograms for use during system maintenance.
3. Engineering changes can be distributed easily by providing a new disk cartridge.

6.4 IO CHANNELS

Model 145 channels are integrated into the CPU and share reloadable control storage, data paths, and arithmetic logical facilities. The number of concurrent IO operations that can be sustained is dependent upon the number and type of channels, the data rates of the IO devices attached to these channels, and the amount of reloadable control storage that is allocated to unit control words.

Unit Control Words

Associated with each subchannel is a unit control word (UCW), used to record the addresses, count, and status and control information for each active IO operation. Each byte multiplexer UCW is 16 bytes in length and the maximum number of byte multiplexer UCWs permitted in a Model 145 system is 256. They can be installed in sets of 16, 32, 64, 128, or 256. A block multiplexer UCW is 8 bytes and can be installed in multiples of 8 up to a maximum of 512 block multiplexer UCWs per Model 145 system.

All UCWs are maintained in reloadable control storage.

Shared Subchannels

A shared subchannel (and its associated UCW) can be shared by a set of devices, one device at a time. A shared UCW is usually assigned to a control unit with similar characteristics, such as those for tape units and direct-access devices without rotational positional sensing (see Chapter 10). Shared subchannels have been discussed previously under System/370 channel architecture.

A nonshared subchannel (and its associated UCW) is attached to a single IO device—such as each disk module in an IBM 3330 facility (a block of 8 UCWs is always required) or IBM 3211 printer.

Selector Channels

A Model 145 selector channel can control a single high-speed IO operation on a single data path. A selector channel operates in the burst mode and can sustain a data rate of 820,000 bytes per second with an aggregate channel data rate, per Model 145 system, of 1,850,000 bytes per second. When a selector channel is operating, data are transferred between main storage and the channel on a byte basis. In most cases, CPU processing and other IO activity proceeds concurrently with selector channel operation. If the channel word-buffer feature is installed, the data rates increase to 1,850,000 and 5,000,000 bytes per second, respectively.

A selector channel does not require unit control words.

Block Multiplexer Channels

A selector channel with the block multiplex feature operates in the block multiplex mode or the selector mode, depending upon the setting of bit 0 in control register 0 when the start IO for that channel is issued. In the block multiplex mode, the channel can support interleaved, concurrent execution of multiple-channel programs and the concurrent operation of multiple high-speed IO devices. Each channel program requires a subchannel and a unit control word.

Shared subchannel UCWs are assigned in groups of eight and must be specified when a microcode disk cartridge is ordered. A shared UCW requires an 8-byte UCW area plus an additional byte so that a group of eight UCW areas provides seven shared UCWs. Shared subchannels are designed for use with shared control units.

Nonshared subchannel UCWs are not assigned to a specific channel and are pooled for assignment on a dynamic basis. When a start IO instruction is issued for a nonshared device, a group of eight UCWs is assigned to the range of addresses in which that device address is contained. Subsequent start IOs to that group of device addresses do not require the assignment of additional UCWs. When the pool of UCWs is exhausted, the next start IO issued causes the channel-not-operational condition code to be set (condition code 3).

A selector channel with the block multiplex feature operating in the selector mode is busy during the entire execution of a channel program. When operating in the block multiplex mode, the channel can disconnect for non-data operations during the operation of one channel program so that a data transfer operation can be executed for another channel program. During the execution of a channel program with multiple command channel CCWs, the channel disconnects from that program when a channel end is received without a concurrent device end. The channel is then available for another IO operation; the status of the disconnected operation is saved in its UCW. When the disconnected operation is again ready to use the channel, the control unit attempts to regain use of the channel facilities. If the channel is free, the channel registers are reloaded from the UCW and execution of that channel program is resumed. If the channel is busy at the time, the device must wait. Block multiplex operations are controlled by channel and control unit hardware.

Byte Multiplexer Channels

The byte multiplexer channel is designed to control multiple low-speed IO devices and operates in either the byte-interleaved mode or the burst mode, depending upon the needs of a particular IO device. In the byte-interleaved mode, several low-speed devices operate concurrently and share channel facilities. In the burst mode, only one medium- to high-speed device operates at one time. In either mode, data are transferred between main storage and byte multiplexer channel at a rate of one byte per storage cycle.

A maximum of 256 subchannels is permitted. As with block multiplexer channels, subchannels may be shared or nonshared. However, the number and type of subchannels must be specified when the "floppy disk" is ordered.

When the byte multiplexer channel requires the use of control information* the UCW for the associated device is read from control storage and held in appropriate registers in local storage. When the device no longer requires services of the channel, the updated control information is returned to its UCW area in control storage.

The maximum data rate of a byte multiplexer channel is 50,000 bytes per second in the multiplex mode and 180,000 bytes per second in the burst mode.

Integrated File Adapter

The integrated file adapter (IFA) was introduced earlier as a means of attaching disk storage units to a Model 145 computer without requiring an IO channel or control unit.

Disk storage units attached to the IFA (i.e., the 2319DASF plus other optional units) operate as a single channel and single control unit device so that only one disk module can be active at a given time. The IFA feature has a data rate of 312,000 bytes per second.

The IFA is specified as Channel 1 and is program and data compatible with 2314-A series disk units.

6.5 SYSTEM RELIABILITY AND AVAILABILITY

The Model 145 is designed for use in an on-line data processing environment in which high availability is required. The system includes advanced features for error recognition, retry, and recovery.

CPU Retry

CPU errors detected during the execution of an instruction cause that instruction to be retried automatically up to eight times before a "hard" machine check interruption is initiated. Retry procedures operate under microprogram control and provide the ability to recover from intermittent CPU failures that would ordinarily cause a system halt. Successful retries generate a "soft" machine check interruption so that error conditions can be recorded.

*Control information includes: protection key, data address, command code indicator, CCW flags, byte count, channel status, and the address of the next CCW.

Storage Error Checking and Correction

Eight bits of error checking and correction (ECC) code are maintained with each double word of main and control storage. Checking on an 8-byte basis, rather than a single-byte basis, allows single-bit errors to be corrected and all double-bit and most multiple-bit errors to be detected. Internally to the CPU, a parity bit is maintained with each byte. A conversion between byte parity and ECC code is made by a *storage adapter unit* as each double word enters and leaves control or main storage.

After a single-bit error is corrected by the *correcter unit* in the storage

Decimal locations					
0	IPL PSW				Fixed Area 0-127 • Model independent among System/360 and System/370 models except for PSW bit 12 • Processed by the control program
8	IPL CCW 1				
16	IPL CCW 2				
24	External old PSW				
32	SVC old PSW				
40	Program old PSW				
48	Machine check old PSW				
56	IO old PSW				
64	Channel status word – CSW				
72	Channel address word – CAW	76 Unused			
80	Interval timer	84 Unused			
88	External new PSW				
96	SVC new PSW				
104	Program new PSW				
112	Machine check new PSW				
120	IO new PSW				
128	128–159 Unused				
160	Reserved				IO Communications Area 160-191
168	Channel ID	172 IO extended logout pointer			
176	Limited channel logout	180 Reserved			
184	IO address	188 Reserved			
192	192–231 Reserved				
232	Machine check code				Fixed Logout Area 232-511 • Layout is model independent among System/370 models Fields and bits used vary slightly by model • Always logged on a machine check interrupt
240	Unused				
248	Failing processor storage address	252 Failing control storage address	Bit corrected	Type of storage error	
256	Unused				
352	Floating point register save area				
384	General purpose register save area				
448	Control register save area				
512	CPU extended logout area – 192 bytes (Pointer in control register 15 set to 512 at IPL and on system reset)				CPU Extended Logout Area • Model dependent • Logged on all machine checks and first and eighth CPU retry if not disabled

Figure 6.3 Model 145 fixed storage locations. (Reprinted by permission from "A Guide to the IBM System/370 Model 145," Form GC20-1734-0. ©1970 by International Business Machines Corporation.)

adapter unit, it is sent back to storage and then to the CPU to continue the operation. The storage operation is also retried to determine if the storage error is intermittent or solid.

IO Errors

IO channel errors and CPU errors associated with a channel operation are accompanied by an IO interruption during which the channel status word (CSW) and the extended channel status word (ECSW) are stored (see Figure 6.3). The CSW and ECSW are used by error recovery routines to retry failing IO operations.

IO command retry is provided with certain control units and IO devices, automatically, without an IO interruption or programmed error recovery procedures.

Machine Check Interruptions

Five types of machine check interruptions are defined in the Model 145. They are listed in Table 6.3 and classified by whether they are hard or soft. A *hard machine check* interruption follows an unsuccessful retry attempt. A *soft machine check* interruption follows a successful retry effort and is initiated so that the error condition can be recorded.

TABLE 6.3 MODEL 145 MACHINE CHECK INTERRUPTIONS

Mask Bits	*Interruption Type*	*Machine Check*
PSW bit 13 CR[a] bit 14	System recovery	Soft
PSW bit 13 CR bit 6	Internal timer damage	Soft
PSW bit 13 CR bit 6	Time-of-day clock damage	Soft
PSW bit 16	System damage (irreparable hardware malfunction)	Hard
PSW bit 13	Instruction processing damage (CPU, storage, or protect key)	Hard

[a]CR stands for control register.

A machine check interruption, accepted by the CPU, is accompanied by a machine check logout to the fixed logout area (main storage bytes 232–511). Model 145 fixed storage assignments are depicted in Figure 6.3. IO interruptions cause a logout to the IO communications area that occupies byte locations 160–191.

Machine check codes are depicted in Figure 6.4. A model-dependent CPU extended logout occurs in fixed storage locations 512–703 (unless changed by programming) with certain types of machine check interruptions if bit 1 of control register 14 (synchronous machine check

Fixed Logout Area Locations 232-239

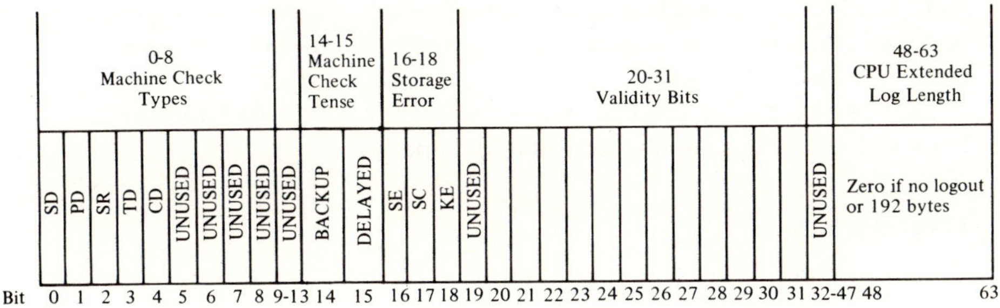

Bit	Iterrrupt Type
0	SD – System Damage
1	PD – Instruction Processing Damage
2	SR – System Recovery
3	TD – Timer Damage
4	CD – Time of Day Clock Damage

Bit	Storage Error
16	Storage Error Uncorrected
17	Storage Error Corrected
18	Key in Storage Error Uncorrected

Bit	Valid Fixed Area Data
20-23	Machine Check Old PSW (48-55) 20 AMWP 21 Masks and Protect Key 22 Program Mask and Condition Code 23 Instruction Address
24	Failing Storage Address (248, 249)
25	Region Code (252-255)
26	Unused
27	Floating Point Registers (352-383)
28	General Purpose Registers (384-447)
29	Control Registers (448-511)
30	CPU Extended Logout
31	Storage (Validity of processor storage being processed by instructions when interrupt occured)

Figure 6.4 Model 145 machine check codes. (Reprinted by permission from "A Guide to the IBM System/370 Model 145," Form GC20-1734-0. ©1970 by International Business Machines Corporation.)

extended logout mask) or if bit 8 of control register 14 (asychronous machine check extended logout mask) is set. The CPU extended logout is intended for use by operating system recovery management routines.

6.6 SUPPORT FACILITIES

The System/370 Model 145 is supported by programming systems as well as by additional advanced hardware facilities.

The Model 145 supports the IBM 2305 Fixed Head Storage Facility Model 2, which has a data rate of 1.5 megabytes per second, the IBM 3330 Disk Storage Facility, with a storage capacity of 800,000,000 bytes, the IBM 3211 Printer, which prints at speeds of 2000 lines per minute, and either the IBM 3210 pedestal-mounted console printer/keyboard, with a printing speed of 85 characters per second (CPS), or the IBM 3215 microprogrammed tabletop console printer/keyboard, which prints at a speed of 15 CPS.

The Model 145 supports two multiprogramming operating systems: DOS/360 and OS/360. Integrated emulators for the 1401/1440/1460 and 1410/7010 system are available that operate under either DOS or OS control in a multiprogramming environment. In addition, a DOS emulator that operates under OS control is a standard feature.

The IO devices are presented in Chapters 9 and 10; programming systems and emulators are introduced in the appendices.

REFERENCES

1. IBM System/370 publications: "Principles of Operation," Form GA22-7000; "Model 145 Functional Characteristics," Form GA24-3557; "Guide to the IBM System/370 Model 145," Form GC20-1734; "System Summary," Form GA22-7001. IBM Corporation, Data Processing Division, White Plains, N.Y., 1970.

7 SYSTEM/370 MODEL 155

7.1 INTRODUCTION TO THE MODEL 155

The IBM System/370 Model 155 computer is characterized in a variety of ways:

1. It is a high-performance data processing system designed for commercial, scientific, and real-time applications.
2. The system supports a wide variety of input/output and mass storage devices including a new line printer, a new console keyboard, and new direct-access storage devices.
3. The system is upward program compatible with System/360 models, fully program compatible with other System/370 models, and most System/360 input/output devices can be attached.
4. Emulators for several earlier IBM computers are provided that operate under operating systems control.
5. A compatibility feature is available that supports emulation of a DOS operating system under OS control.*

System Specifications

The major machine cycle time of a Model 155 is 115 nanoseconds, making the system appropriate for a wide range of scientific applications that

*DOS stands for Disk Operating System, a low-entry operating system for System/360 users. OS stands for Operating System, a comprehensive and powerful System/360 operating system.

require a high-performance CPU.* Main storage is available in seven capacities:

Model Designation	*Capacity*
H155	262,144 bytes
HG155	393,216 bytes
I155	524,288 bytes
IH155	786,432 bytes
J155	1,048,576 bytes
JI155	1,572,864 bytes
K155	2,097,152 bytes

The main storage cycle time is 2.07 microseconds for an access width of 16 bytes (one *quad word*). Thus 16 bytes can be fetched every 2.1 microseconds without interference. However, data can actually be obtained by the CPU from main storage in a shorter time for nonconsecutive storage references: 4 bytes can be obtained in 1.49 microseconds, 8 bytes in 1.61 microseconds, and 16 bytes in 1.96 microseconds. A buffer storage system is implemented to reduce effective access time to approximately $\frac{1}{4}$–$\frac{1}{3}$ of the storage cycle time. The storage buffer has a capacity of 8192 bytes. Four bytes can be fetched from the buffer by the CPU in 230 nanoseconds and 8 consecutive bytes can be fetched in 345 nanoseconds. Model 155 IO channels can transfer 16 bytes of data to or from main storage in each storage reference. Data flow in the Model 155 is discussed in a later section. One byte multiplexer channel and two block multiplexer channels are standard on the Model 155. The system can support one byte multiplexer channel and as many as five block multiplexer channels or two byte multiplexer channels and up to four block multiplexer channels.

System Design Features

The design of the Model 155 includes most of the System/370 architecture as standard features. This category includes:

universal instruction set,
storage protection (including fetch protect),
byte-oriented operand feature,
error checking and correction (ECC),
instruction retry,
channel retry,
command retry,
interval timer,

*In general, machine cycle time is only an indirect measure of system performance. Most nonarithmetic RR-type instructions (such as *load*) take one machine cycle; some fixed-point arithmetic instructions take two machine cycles. Other CPU instructions take several machine cycles depending upon the nature of the operation and the data involved.

time-of-day clock,
first byte multiplexer channel (Channel 0), and
two block multiplexer channels (Channels 1 and 2).

Most of these features are not unique to the Model 155 and were presented in Part Two. A description of other model-dependent features is included as required.

A two-level storage hierarchy system (see Figure 7.1), directly address-

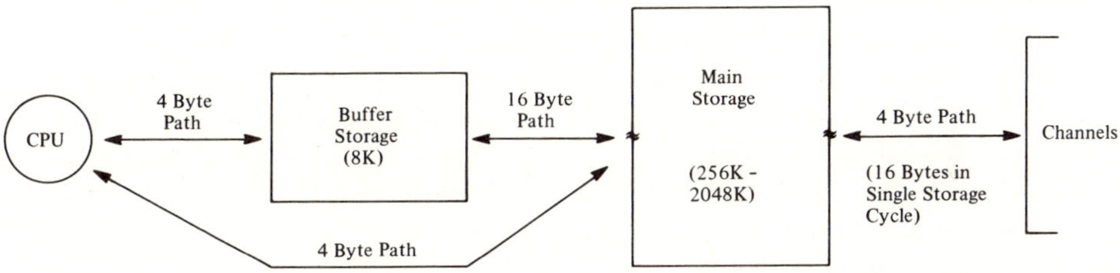

Figure 7.1 Model 155 storage hierarchy system. (Courtesy of International Business Machines Corporation.)

able by the CPU, is implemented as a standard feature. Main storage is synthesized from discrete ferrite cores and can range in size from 256K bytes to 2048K bytes. The 8K buffer storage is implemented using monolithic storage technology.

The IO channels in the Model 155 are integrated with the CPU and share control storage, data paths, and the arithmetic logic unit. A byte multiplexer channel interferes with the CPU when it requires one of the shared facilities; a block multiplexer channel interferes with both the CPU and the byte multiplexer channel. CPU interference takes place when an IO operation is initiated and when it is completed. The CPU and channels compete for access to main storage within the following priority structure: block multiplexer channels, byte multiplexer channels, the CPU.

CPU and channel operations are controlled by microprograms held in capacitor read-only storage (ROS). A loaded ROS—also called *control storage*—is provided with the computer and is not modified by the user under normal circumstances. Instruction retry procedures are also coded as microprograms and increase the overall reliability of a Model 155 computer. When an internal CPU error is encountered during the execution of an instruction, a microprogram routine returns CPU control to a point where the operation (or parts of it) can be attempted again. Emulator microprograms, when ordered as an optional feature, are held in control storage and used by the CPU during emulation.

Optional features for the Model 155 include:

extended precision floating point,
direct control,
channel-to-channel adapter,
1401/1440/1460 and 1410/7010 compatibility,
OS/DOS compatibility,
block multiplexer channel (Channel 3),
block multiplexer channel or second byte multiplexer channel (Channel 4),
block multiplexer channel (Channel 5),
3210 Model 1 adapter for the 3210 console printer/keyboard Model 1 or the 3215 adapter for the 3215 console printer/keyboard (one of these units is required),
3210 Model 2 adapter for the stand alone 3210 console printer/keyboard, and
emergency power-off control.

The *direct control* feature allows two CPUs to communicate by transferring a single byte of data between an external device and the main storage of another system. Included with this feature are read direct and write direct instructions and six external interruption lines.

The *channel-to-channel adapter* allows two 360/370 computers to be coupled into a multisystem configuration (see Chapter 2). A single adapter may be installed on a Model 155 and it occupies one control unit position on either a byte or block multiplexer channel.

The *1401/1440/1460*, *1410/7010*, and *OS/DOS compatibility* features allow programs and operating systems, written for earlier systems, to be executed on the Model 155. These emulators are integrated in the sense that they operate in a multiprogramming environment and do not require a standalone machine.

The *emergency power-off control* feature allows the emergency power-off switches of several cable-connected systems to be combined as a single power-off switch.

Channel and IO features are considered as separate sections.

Notes:

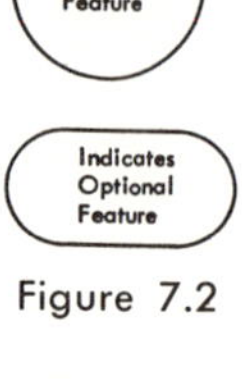

1. The System/370 universal instruction set includes the System/360 universal instruction set and the 15 enhancement instructions, which include halt device and redefined halt I/O.
2. The channel-to-channel adapter (one per system, attachable to byte or block multiplexer channel) permits interconnection of two channels. One control unit position on the Model 155 channel can connect to one control unit position on any other System/370 or System/360 channel. Only one adapter is needed per connection; it counts as one control unit on both channels.
3. Attaches as many as eight control units; available subchannels are shown on chart.
4. Operates either in burst mode or in byte mode; multiplexing capability on bytes, groups of bytes, or blocks.
5. Operates in burst mode only; multiplexing capability on blocks or multiple blocks. Available subchannels are shown on chart.

Figure 7.2 IBM System/370 Model 155 configurator. (Courtesy of International Business Machines Corporation.)

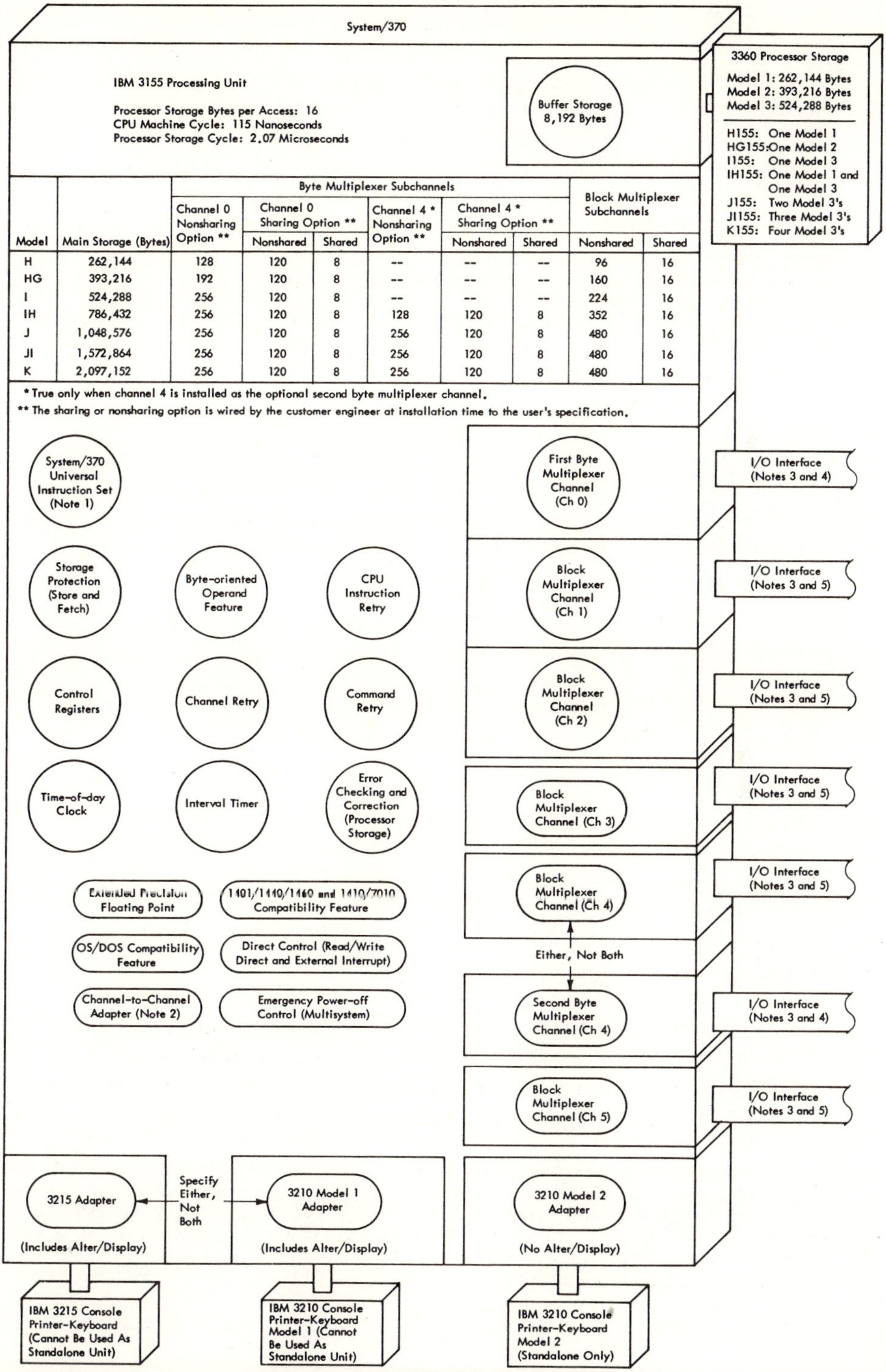

Model	Main Storage (Bytes)	Byte Multiplexer Subchannels: Channel 0 Nonsharing Option **	Channel 0 Sharing Option **: Nonshared	Channel 0 Sharing Option **: Shared	Channel 4 * Nonsharing Option **	Channel 4 * Sharing Option **: Nonshared	Channel 4 * Sharing Option **: Shared	Block Multiplexer Subchannels: Nonshared	Block Multiplexer Subchannels: Shared
H	262,144	128	120	8	--	--	--	96	16
HG	393,216	192	120	8	--	--	--	160	16
I	524,288	256	120	8	--	--	--	224	16
IH	786,432	256	120	8	128	120	8	352	16
J	1,048,576	256	120	8	256	120	8	480	16
JI	1,572,864	256	120	8	256	120	8	480	16
K	2,097,152	256	120	8	256	120	8	480	16

* True only when channel 4 is installed as the optional second byte multiplexer channel.

** The sharing or nonsharing option is wired by the customer engineer at installation time to the user's specification.

System Structure

The major components of a System/370 Model 155 are the 3155 processing unit,* the 3360 processor (main) storage Models 1–3†, and IO control units and devices. The 3155 processing unit contains the arithmetic and logical circuits, control storage, local storage, and at least three IO channels. Figure 7.2 depicts the Model 155 configurator; the buffer storage system is considered to be a part of the processing unit in that diagram.

A complete description of System/370 IO devices is beyond the scope of this book. However, several devices, new to the System/370 series, are described in Chapters 9 and 10.

7.2 PROCESSING UNIT

The 3155 central processing unit (CPU) controls the operation of the Model 155 by decoding and executing instructions, held in main storage, and by monitoring the operation of IO channels and IO devices. The functional components and storage facilities necessary to perform these tasks include:

data gates and buses,
working registers,
adder,
1-bit shifter,
4-bit shifter,
mover,
byte counters,
CPU local storage,
IO local storage, and
I-fetch logic.‡

All CPU functions, channel operations, and data gates are controlled by a microprogram held in 72-bit control words in control storage. Essentially, the microprogram uses the above components to make the Model 155 operate as a System/370 computer.

*The term processing unit refers to the central processing unit discussed earlier.

†The 3360 Models 1, 2, and 3 provide 262,144 bytes, 393,216 bytes, and 524,288 bytes of storage, respectively. They are combined in a given computer system to supply the main storage sizes mentioned previously.

‡I-fetch stands for instruction fetch.

Local Storage

The microprogram has access to two local storage areas: CPU local storage and IO local storage. The *CPU local storage* consists of 64 words and contains the 16 general registers, the 4 floating-point registers, and certain channel control data. The *IO local storage* also consists of 64 words and is controlled by channel hardware so that it can be used concurrently with CPU operation. It contains storage areas for block multiplexer channel buffering and working storage for byte multiplexer channel operation.

Working Registers

Working registers include control registers 0, 2, 8,* 14, and 15 and a 2-byte PSW register. The PSW register is used to control current CPU functions and holds bytes 0 and 1 of the current PSW. The remainder of the PSW is held in active CPU registers or in CPU local storage. When an interruption is accepted by the CPU, the old PSW is assembled by the CPU and stored in main storage. The new PSW is fetched from main storage, disassembled, and routed to the required registers and local storage areas in the CPU.

Instruction Fetch

The I-fetch section uses three one-word instruction buffers to overlap instruction fetches and decoding with the execution of previous instructions. However, operands are not prefetched and imprecise interruptions† do not occur.

I-fetch logic also includes two instruction counter registers that retain the storage address of prefetched instructions and are used to re-store the instruction counter during instruction retry.

CPU Data Flow

The architectural design of the Model 155 CPU is inherent in the data paths used to move data between the functional components. Three data paths are implemented: a 4-byte path, a 1-byte path, and an instruction path for instruction fetches. The Model 155 data flow is depicted in Figure 7.3.

The 4-byte data path is used for references to main storage, for control functions, and for the processing of fixed-point and floating-point in-

*Control register 8 is used with the monitor call instruction. The Model 155 is the only system for which this feature has been announced.

†An interruption is classified as imprecise when insufficient information is available to determine which instruction caused the interruption.

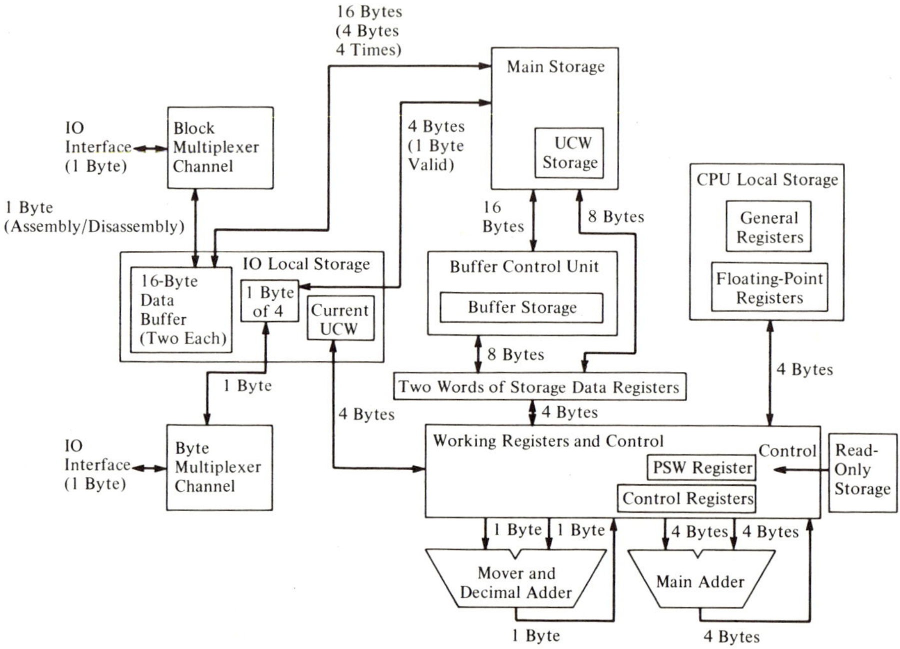

Figure 7.3 Model 155 data flow.

structions. Two 4-byte *storage data registers* are used to buffer-down the 8-byte paths from the buffer storage control unit and from main storage.* The 4-byte data path connects the external switch, working registers, adder, shifters, local storage, and the adder output bus.

The 1-byte data paths permit operations to be executed on variable-length fields and are used during emulation under microprogram control. One-byte paths are used primarily with the *mover*, a 1-byte binary adder with two 1-byte inputs and one 1-byte output. The mover is used to perform logical and arithmetic functions and serves to move information in the CPU.

Every data path in the CPU and between the CPU and main storage is parity checked by byte. The adder is parity checked, as is data and control information as it leaves the buffer control unit.†

*This explains how 4 bytes can be obtained from the buffer in 230 nanoseconds and 8 consecutive bytes take only 345 nanoseconds.

†The buffer control unit houses the buffer storage system. It is discussed in the next section.

CPU Features

Many of the other Model 155 features are implemented in the CPU: the interval timer, the time-of-day clock, the extended precision feature, direct control—to name only a few. System/370 also includes several new instructions over its predecessor, the System/360. The reader is directed to reference manuals for more detailed information.

7.3 STORAGE

The main storage hierarchy system in the Model 155 was introduced earlier. This section describes its organization and the manner in which it operates. First, some comments on the general subject of main storage are necessary.

The byte-oriented operand feature is supported and allows operands for nonprivileged instructions to reside on byte boundaries without causing a specification program interruption. The feature does not apply to CPU instructions (which must be aligned on a half word boundary), CCWs (which must be aligned on a double word boundary), and the operands of privileged instructions. Error checking and correction circuitry applies to all stores and fetches to main storage; it is considered, along with permanent storage assignments, in the section on reliability.

Operation of the Buffer Storage System

The objective of the buffer storage system is to increase the frequency with which main storage requests can be satisfied from the higher-speed unit. When a request for data is made by the CPU, the buffer control unit determines if the requested data are in the buffer. If the data are in the buffer, they are transmitted to the CPU without a main storage access. If the requested data are not in the buffer, a main storage fetch is initiated and the data are sent directly to the CPU. A buffer location is also determined and the data are stored there for subsequent references. The buffer storage is maintained dynamically by the CPU and is transparent to the programmer. When data are stored by the CPU, the buffer is also updated if the locations being changed are currently held in the buffer.

If an IO channel stores data in locations being maintained in the buffer, then appropriate bits are set to invalidate those buffer entries. IO channels, in the Model 155, access only main storage.

Buffer Control Unit

The 8K monolithic buffer storage is functionally a component of a *buffer control unit* (BCU) that serves as a high-speed interface between main storage and the CPU. The BCU additionally includes logical circuitry, an index array, and control information for maintaining the buffer storage. The BCU was shown conceptually in Figure 7.3. Its components are considered separately.

Storage Organization

Main storage and the buffer are both divided into 4K *rows*—each row containing 128 32-byte *blocks*. Each block is further divided into 16-byte *half blocks*—the unit of transfer between main storage and the BCU. It follows that the buffer contains two rows and that the number of rows in main storage depends on its size, ranging from 64 rows in a 256K system to 512 rows in a 2048K system. The blocks, numbered 0–127, that comprise a row can be referred to as columns.

Figure 7.4 depicts a main storage address. Bits 11–19 denote the row

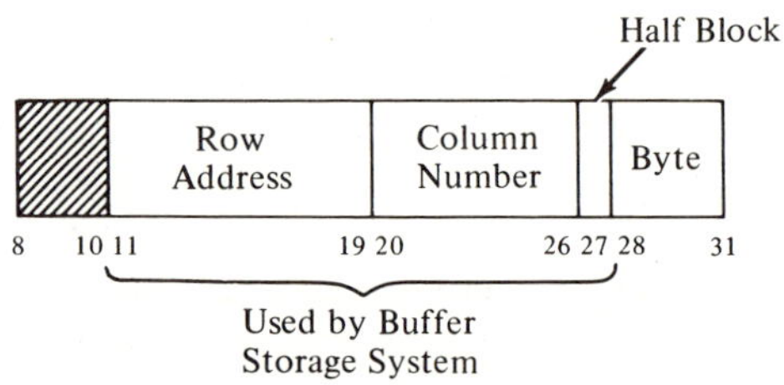

Figure 7.4 Main storage address.

address. Within a row, bits 20–26 denote its column index (or block number), which falls in the range 0–127. Bit 27 specifies a half block within a block and bits 28–31 allow addressing within a 16-byte half block. Only bits 11–27 of a main storage address are used by the buffer storage system.

Buffer storage is managed with the help of an *index array* that contains an entry for each block in the buffer. The index array also contains 2 rows and 128 columns and it corresponds with buffer storage blocks one-for-one. Figure 7.5 shows an index array entry. The *row address* field contains the main storage address of the data block that occupies the respective position in the buffer. The leftmost valid bit is associated with the high-order half block and the rightmost valid bit is associated with the low-order half block. The OK bit denotes that the corresponding positions in the buffer and in the index array are functioning correctly.

Figure 7.6 depicts the relationship of main storage, buffer storage, and the index array. The buffer storage system is maintained on a columnwise basis—that is, each column of main storage competes for a position in that column of the buffer.

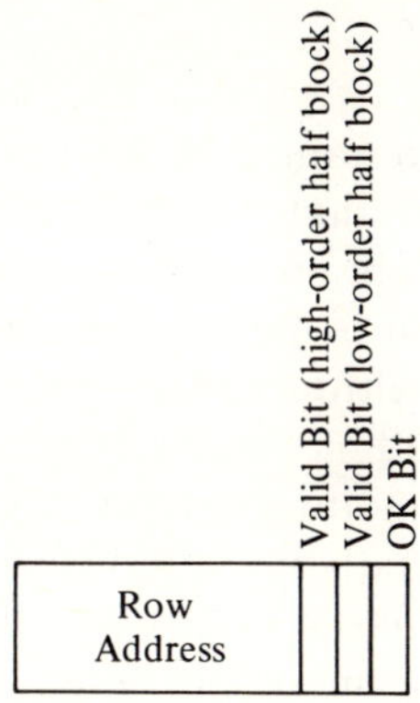

Figure 7.5 Index array entry.

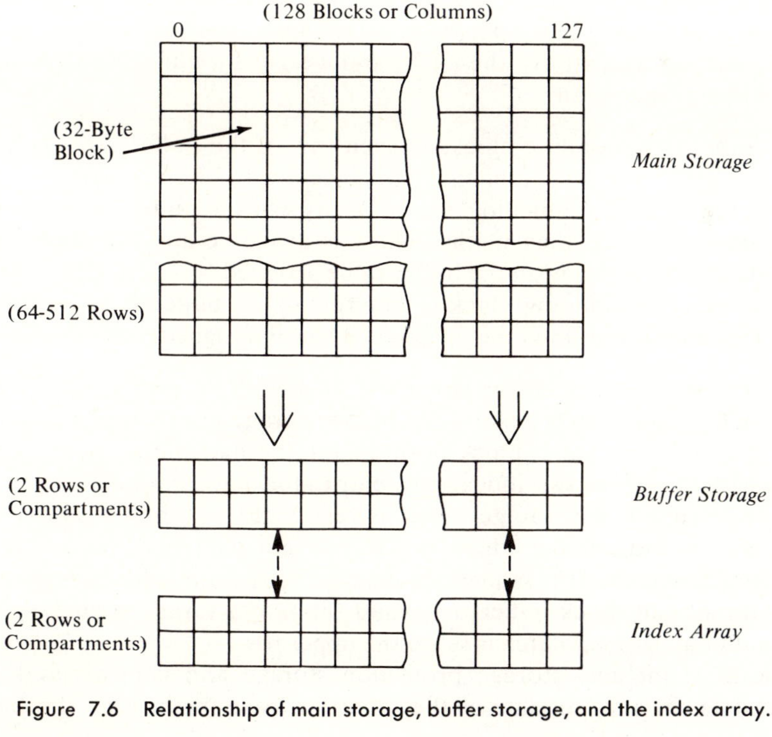

Figure 7.6 Relationship of main storage, buffer storage, and the index array.

Maintenance of Buffer Storage

A block of main storage is assigned to the buffer when bits 11–19 of its main storage address are contained in the row address field of one of the two index array entries for that column (denoted by bits 20–26 of the address) and one of the half block valid bits is set. The assignment of that block to that buffer position is made when either one of its half blocks is referenced by the CPU. Although the entire block is considered to be assigned, only the referenced half block is actually loaded into the buffer. In general, the buffer is maintained on a half block basis using row address, column, and the half block indicators. The BCU also uses an assignment latch to determine which row (compartment) of the buffer is to be assigned. Initially, upon system reset, the latch is set to the upper row (compartment).

When main storage is referenced by the CPU, the two index array entries for the buffer column denoted by bits 20–26 of the effective address are compared with bits 11–19 of the effective address. If the row addresses and the half block agree, the half block is sent to the CPU from the storage buffer and main storage need not be referenced. If the row addresses or the half block positions do not agree, then the data is fetched from main storage, sent to the CPU, and assigned a buffer location using the following algorithm:

1. If the corresponding blocks in each row of the buffer are available, the buffer assignment latch denotes the row to be assigned.
2. If the corresponding blocks in both rows of the buffer have one half block assigned, then neither block is available and the latch again determines the row in the buffer to be assigned.
3. If the corresponding block in one row of the buffer is assigned and the other is not, then the unassigned row is assigned.

Similarly, index array entries are used by the BCU during CPU store operations to main storage, and the buffer storage unit is updated only if the row address and half block position for the half block being altered agree with one of the two index array entries for that column.

When a row of the storage buffer is referenced, the buffer assignment latch is set to indicate the other row (the row not referenced last). System reset (including the IPL sequence) sets the index array addresses to zero, turns off all half block indicators (valid bits), and turns on all OK bits. The buffer assignment latch is set to the upper row.

The BCU includes storage protection storage and controls and performs data checking on data as they enter or leave the buffer. If a buffer component fails, the OK bit for that block is set to off and a machine check interruption occurs. The OK bit for a block of the buffer storage unit must be set to on before it is used by the BCU. The entire buffer storage facility can be disabled by console switch or under microprogram control. In that case, the CPU functions normally but performance is degraded.

7.4 IO CHANNELS

Model 155 channels are integrated into the CPU and share its control storage, data paths, and arithmetic logical facilities. The number of concurrent IO operations that can be sustained is dependent upon the number and type of channels, the data rates of the IO devices attached to these channels, and the size of main storage.

Unit Control Words

Associated with each subchannel is a unit control word (UCW), used to record the addresses, count, and status and control information for each active IO operation. The UCW is stored in an extension to main storage, referred to as "bump storage." The capacity of bump storage is related to the size of main storage. In general, each 1024-byte section of main storage provides one UCW, up to a limit of 1024 UCWs. Half of the UCWs are assigned to byte multiplexer channels and the other half are assigned to block multiplexer channels.

Shared Subchannels

A shared subchannel (and its associated UCW) can be shared by a set of devices, one device at a time. A shared UCW is usually assigned to a control unit with similar characteristics, such as those for tape units and direct-access devices without rotational positional sensing (see Chapter 9). Shared subchannels have been discussed previously under System/370 channel architecture.

A nonshared subchannel (and its associated UCW) is attached to a single IO device—such as each disk drive in an IBM 3330 facility (a block of 8 UCWs is always required) or IBM 3211 printer.

Block Multiplexer Channels

The block multiplexer channel operates in the block multiplex mode or the selector mode, depending upon the setting of bit 0 in control register 0 when the start IO for that channel is issued. In the block multiplex mode, the channel can support interleaved, concurrent execution of multiple high-speed channel programs and the concurrent operation of multiple high-speed IO devices. Each channel program and IO operation requires a subchannel; Table 7.1 lists the number of block multiplexer subchannels and UCWs available to a Model 155 system.

The 16 shared subchannels are fixed at installation time by plugcard wiring. Each shared subchannel refers to a set of 16 contiguous device addresses.

TABLE 7.1 SUBCHANNELS AND UCWS AVAILABLE FOR MODEL 155 BLOCK MULTIPLEXER CHANNELS

Model	*Storage Size (bytes)*	*Total Nonshared*	*Total Shared*
H155	262,144	96	16
HG155	393,216	160	16
I155	524,288	224	16
IH155	786,432	352	16
J155	1,048,576	480	16
JI155	1,572,864	480	16
K155	2,097,152	480	16

Nonshared subchannel UCWs are pooled and are assigned dynamically as start IO instructions are issued for different devices. UCWs for certain multipath devices (such as the 3330 disk facility) are assigned in blocks to cover the range of device addresses assigned to that device. When the pool of UCWs is exhausted, the next IO operation initiated is executed in the selector mode since no UCW is available for storage during block multiplexing.

A block multiplexer channel operating in the selector mode is busy during the entire execution of a channel program. When operating in the block multiplex mode, the channel can disconnect for non-data operations during the operation of one channel program so that a data transfer operation can be executed for another channel program. During the execution of a channel program with multiple command chained CCWs, the channel disconnects from that program when a channel end is received without a concurrent device end. The channel is then available for another IO operation; the status of the disconnected operation is saved in its UCW. When the disconnected operation is again ready to use the channel, the control unit attempts to regain the channel facilities. If the channel is free, the channel registers are reloaded from the UCW and execution of that channel program is resumed. If the channel is busy at that time, the device must wait. Block multiplex operations are controlled by channel and control unit hardware.

Byte Multiplexer Channels

The byte multiplexer channel operates in the byte interleaved mode or the burst mode depending upon the needs of a particular IO operation.

Up to 8 control units and 256 IO devices can be attached to a byte multiplexer channel, depending upon the size of main storage. A second byte multiplexer channel (Channel 4) can be installed on IH155 models and up, permitting from 384 to 512 subchannels. The number of subchannels available with a Model 155 is listed in Table 7.2. As with block multiplexer channels, byte multiplexer subchannels may be shared or nonshared; however, all subchannels are wired at installation time.

TABLE 7.2 SUBCHANNELS AND UCWS AVAILABLE FOR MODEL 155 BYTE MULTIPLEXER CHANNELS

Model	*Storage Size (bytes)*	*Channel 0*	*Channel 4*
H155	262,144	128	
HG155	393,216	192	
I155	524,288	256	
IH155	786,432	256	128
J155	1,048,576	256	256
JI155	1,572,864	256	256
K155	2,097,152	256	256

7.5 SYSTEM RELIABILITY AND AVAILABILITY

The Model 155 is designed to operate reliably in an operating environment where high availability is required. The system contains a variety of recovery features and provides information for repair when automatic recovery is not possible.

CPU Retry

CPU hardware errors are retried automatically under microprogram control up to eight times before a machine check interrupt is initiated. All hardware errors are retried except those encountered during the execution of the following instructions: diagnose, test and set, read direct, and write direct. The system provides facilities whereby successful retries can be recorded and unsuccessful retries can invoke programmed recovery procedures.

Storage Error Checking and Correction

Eight bits of ECC code are associated with each double word of main storage. Checking on an 8-byte basis, instead of a single-byte basis, allows single-bit errors to be corrected and all double-bit and most multiple-bit errors to be detected. Double and multiple-bit errors are not corrected. Internally to the CPU, a parity bit is maintained with each byte. A conversion between byte parity and ECC code is made by a *storage adapter unit* as each double word enters and leaves main storage.

Automatic Buffer Block Deletion

The buffer control unit maintains an OK bit for each 32-byte block of buffer storage. A failing buffer storage block causes the OK bit to be set to off and a soft machine check to be generated.

Decimal loactions					Area
0	IPL PSW				Fixed Area 0–127 ● Model independent among System/360 and System/370 models except for PSW bit 12 ● Processed by the control program
8	IPL CCW 1				
16	IPL CCW 2				
24	External old PSW				
32	SVC old PSW				
40	Program old PSW				
48	Machine check old PSW				
56	IO old PSW				
64	Channel status word – CSW				
72	Channel address word – CSW		76 Unused		
80	Interval timer		84 Unused		
88	External new PSW				
96	SVC new PSW				
104	Program new PSW				
112	Machine check new PSW				
120	IO new PSW				
128	128 – 167 Unused				
168	Channel ID		172 Unused		
176	Extended CSW		180 Unused		Fixed Logout Area 176–511 ● Layout is model independent among System/370 models ● Fields and bits used vary slightly by model ● Always logged on a machine check interrupt
184	184 – 231 Unused				
232	Machine check code				
240	Unused				
248	Failing storage address	252 Buffer degrade	Bit corrected	TOD log	
256	Unused				
352	Floating point register save area				
384	General purpose register save area				
448	Control register save area				
512	CPU extended logout area – 640 Bytes (Pointer in control register 15 set to 512 at IPL and on system reset)				CPU Extended Logout Area ● Model dependent ● Logged on all hard machine checks and first and eighth CPU retry if not disabled

Figure 7.7 Model 155 fixed storage locations. (Reprinted by permission from "A Guide to the IBM System/370 Model 155," Form GC20-1729-0. Copyright 1970 by International Business Machines Corporation.)

IO Errors

IO channel errors and CPU errors associated with a channel operation are accompanied by an IO interrupt during which the channel status word (CSW) and the extended channel status word (ECSW) are stored (see Figure 7.7). The CSW and ECSW are used by an error recovery routine to retry failing IO operations.

IO command retry is provided with certain control units and IO devices, automatically without an IO interrupt or programmed error recovery procedures.

Machine Check Interruptions

Seven types of machine check interruptions are defined in the Model 155. They are listed in Table 7.3 and classified by whether they are hard or

TABLE 7.3 MODEL 155 MACHINE CHECK INTERRUPTIONS

Subclass	*Mask Bits*	*Interruption Type*	*Machine Check*
Internal	PSW bit 13	System damage (irreparable hardware malfunction)	Hard
Internal	PSW bit 13	Instruction processing damage (CPU, storage, or protect key)	Hard
Internal	PSW bit 13 CR[a] 14 bit 4	System recovery	Soft
External	PSW bit 13 CR 14 bit 6	Internal timer damage	Soft
External	PSW bit 13 CR 14 bit 6	Time-of-day clock damage	Soft
External	PSW bit 13 CR 14 bit 6	External damage (error not affecting CPU)	Soft
Alert	PSW bit 13 CR 14 bit 5	Automatic configuration (buffer block deletion)	Soft

[a] CR stands for control register.

soft. A *hard machine check interruption* follows an unsuccessful retry attempt. A *soft machine check interruption* follows a successful retry procedure and is initiated so that the occurrence of the error condition can be recorded.

A logout to the fixed logout area (main storage bytes 176–511) is made

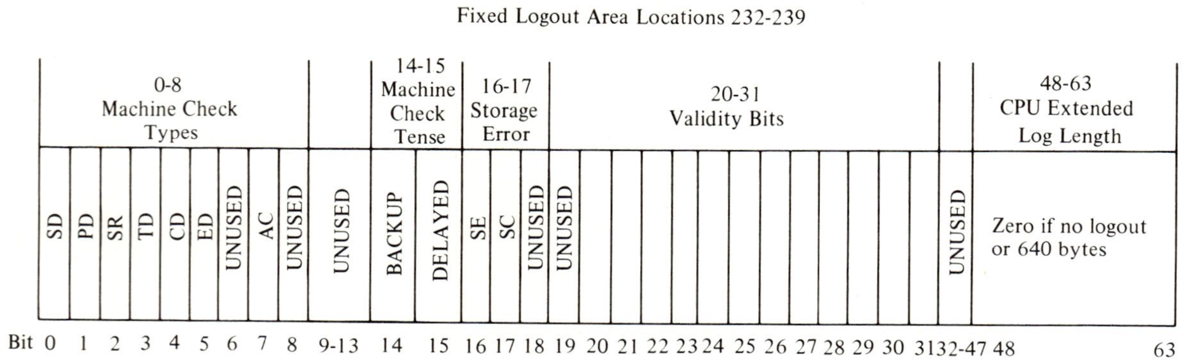

Subclass	Bit	Interrupt Type
Internal	0	SD – System Damage
	1	PD – Instruction Processing Damage
	2	SR – System Recovery
External	3	TD – Timer Damage
	4	CD – Time of Day Clock Damage
	5	ED – External Damage
	6	Unused
Alert	7	AC – Automatic Configuration

Bit	Storage Error
16	Storage Error Uncorrected
17	Storage Error Corrected

Bit	Valid Fixed Area Data
20-23	Machine Check Old PSW (48-55) 20 AMWP 21 Masks and Protect Key 22 Program Mask and Condition Code 23 Instruction Address
24	Failing Storage Address (248, 249)
25	Region Code (252-255)
26	Unused
27	Floating Point Registers (352-383)
28	General Purpose Registers (384-447)
29	Control Registers (448-511)
30	CPU Extended Logout
31	Storage (Validity of main storage being processed by instructions when interrupt occured)

Figure 7.8 Model 155 machine check codes. (Reprinted by permission from "A Guide to the IBM System/370 Model 155," Form GC20-1729-0. Copyright 1970 by International Business Machines Corporation.)

when any type of machine check interruption is accepted by the CPU. Model 155 fixed storage assignments and machine check codes are depicted in Figures 7.7 and 7.8, respectively.

A model-dependent CPU extended logout occurs with certain types of machine check interruptions if bit 1 of control register 14 (synchronous machine check extended logout mask) or bit 8 of control register 14 (asychronous machine check extended logout mask) is set to one. The extended logout area is intended for use by operating system recovery management routines.

7.6 SUPPORT FACILITIES

The System/370 Model 155 is supported by programming systems as well as by additional advanced hardware facilities.

The Model 155 supports the IBM 2305 Fixed Head Storage Facility Model 2, which has a data rate of 1.5 megabytes per second, and the IBM 3330 Disk Storage Facility, with a storage capacity of 800,000,000 bytes, the IBM 3211 Printer, which prints at a speed of 2000 lines per minute, and either the IBM 3210 pedestal-mounted remote console printer/keyboard with a printing speed of 85 characters per second (CPS), or the IBM 3215 microprogrammed tabletop console printer/keyboard, which prints at a speed of 15 CPS.

The Model 155 supports two multiprogramming operating systems: DOS/360 and OS/360. Integrated emulators for the 1401/1440/1460 and 1410/7010 system are available that operate under either DOS or OS control in a multiprogramming environment. In addition, a DOS emulator is available that operates under OS control.

The IO devices are presented in Chapters 9 and 10; programming systems and emulators are introduced in the appendices.

REFERENCES

1. IBM System/370 publications: "Principles of Operation," Form GA22-7000. "Model 155 Function Characteristics," Form GA22-6942; "Model 155 Channel Characteristics," Form GA22-6962; "Guide to the IBM System/370 Model 155," Form GC20-1729; "System Summary," Form GA22-7001. IBM Corporation, Data Processing Division, White Plains, N.Y., 1970.

8 SYSTEM/370 MODEL 165

8.1 INTRODUCTION TO THE MODEL 165

The IBM System/370 Model 165 is a high-performance computing system designed for large-scale scientific and business applications. The system is organized to achieve the maximum in computing power from high-speed components and efficient computational algorithms. The Model 165 features a storage hierarchy system, concurrent CPU operations, and interleaved storage facilities. Standard System/370 mass storage and input/output devices are supported and a compatibility feature for emulating earlier computers is available. The Model 165 is upward program compatible with System/360 computers and fully program compatible with other System/370 models.

System Specifications

The CPU machine cycle time of the Model 165 is 80 nanoseconds, supported by internal logic that allows many CPU functions to be performed in one machine cycle.* Main storage is available in five capacities:

Model Designation	*Capacity*	*Interleaving*
I165	524,288 bytes	Four way
J165	1,048,576 bytes	Four way

*In general, machine cycle time is only an indirect measure of system performance. In the Model 165, most RR-type instructions require a single CPU cycle (80 nanoseconds). For example, a fixed-point RR-type add operation is executed in 80 nanoseconds. The execution times for other instructions is dependent upon the nature of the operation and the characteristics of the data involved.

Model Designation	*Capacity*	*Interleaving*
JI165	1,572,864 bytes	Four way
K165	2,097,152 bytes	Four way
KJ165	3,145,728 bytes	Four way

The main storage cycle time is 2 microseconds for an access width of 8 data bytes. However, storage is four-way interleaved and the CPU can reference storage every machine cycle. Thus, 32 consecutive bytes can be accessed concurrently. The four-way interleaved storage is organized so that 32 consecutive bytes are spread over four storage units—8 bytes in each unit. Assume the storage units are identified as *a*, *b*, *c*, and *d*. Then, location 0 is in *a*; location 8 is in *b*; location 16 is in *c*; location 24 in in *d*; location 32 is in *a*; etc. Data paths within the CPU and between the CPU and storage are also 8 bytes wide and operate in parallel.

The effective main storage access time is significantly reduced with a high-speed buffer storage system. The buffer storage unit is available in sizes of 8K and 16K and has a cycle time of 80 nanoseconds. Eight bytes can be fetched from the buffer by the CPU in two cycles, or 160 nanoseconds, and a fetch can be initiated every machine cycle. Thus, 8 bytes can be obtained from the buffer in 160 nanoseconds and 16 bytes can be obtained in 240 nanoseconds. Main storage can also be accessed concurrently by one or more IO channels and the CPU; 32 bytes of information can be transferred between the channels and main storage in 2 microseconds.

Seven IO channels can be attached to a Model 165 computer, and if an extended channel feature is installed, the number is increased to 12. The IO channels are not integrated into the CPU and compete with the CPU for access to storage. An IO channel does not reference the buffer storage directly—only main storage—but causes the buffer to be updated when it performs a store operation into locations currently being held in the buffer. The set of channels that can be attached to a specific model is a combination of the following:

Two byte multiplexer channels (the first must have address 0; the second can be assigned an address from 1 to 6).
Six selector channels (addresses 1–6).
Eleven block multiplexer channels (addresses 1–11).

System Design Features

The design of the Model 165 incorporates practically all of the architectural features of System/370. Included are:

universal instruction set,
storage protection (including fetch protect),

byte-oriented operand feature,
error checking and correction,
instruction retry,
channel retry,
command retry,
interval timer,
time-of-day clock,
IO channel adapters (three—one for each type of channel),
system console,
direct control, and
extended precision floating-point arithmetic.

Most of these features are not unique to the Model 165 and were presented in Part Two. A description of other model-dependent features is included as required.

A two-level storage hierarchy system (see Figure 8.1), directly addressable by the CPU, is implemented to reduce the access time to frequently used data. An 8K storage buffer is standard. Main storage is four-way interleaved and managed by a storage control unit (SCU) that controls all storage references by the CPU and the channels. The SCU also contains the buffer storage system and channel IO buffers.

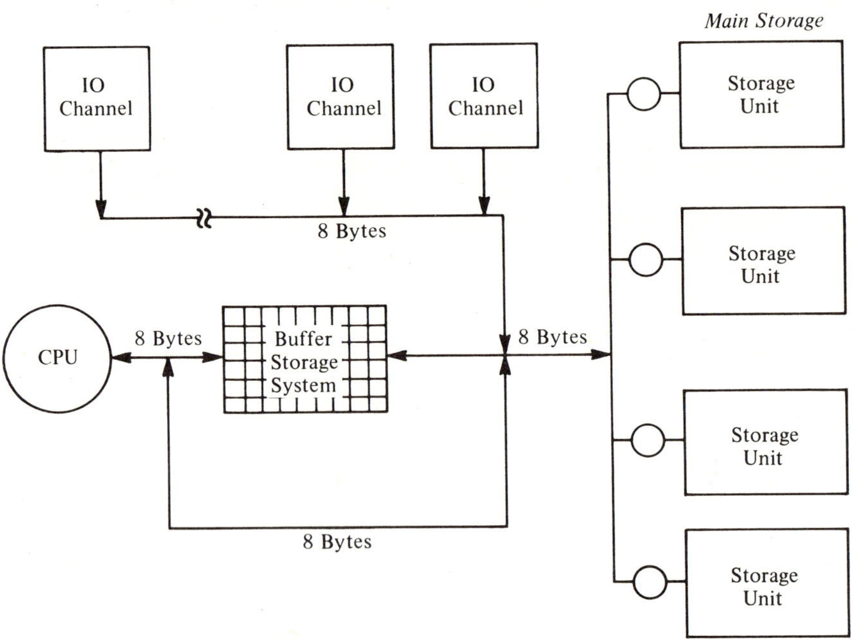

Figure 8.1 Data flow in the Model 165 utilizing a buffer storage system.

IO channels are implemented as standalone functional units—each with a model number. The byte multiplexer channel is the 2870; the selector channel is the 2860; and the block multiplexer is the 2880. All channels contain their own registers, temporary storage facilities, and logical circuitry. Thus, interference with the CPU is reduced to the case where a channel and the CPU attempt to reference the same logical memory unit at the same time.

The CPU is controlled by microprograms held in capacitor read-only storage (ROS) and in monolithic writable control storage (WCS). A loaded ROS is provided with the computer and is not modified by the user under normal circumstances. Writable control storage is loaded from the system console and supports basic system control, diagnostic capability, and a compatibility feature. Instruction retry procedures are also coded as microprograms and increase the overall reliability of a Model 165 computer. When an internal CPU error is encountered during the execution of an instruction, a microprogram routine returns CPU control to a point where the operation (or parts of it) can be attempted again.

Functionally, the CPU is divided into six independent units: an instruction unit, an execution unit, a storage control unit, main storage, buffer storage, and control storage. The instruction and execution units can operate concurrently and operands can be prefetched and held in operand buffers in the execution unit.

The remote standalone *system console* can be located up to 25 feet from the CPU and contains the following facilities: standard console lights, buttons, and switches; a CRT display and keyboard; a microfiche viewer; a device for loading microcode; a system activity monitor; and a configuration plugboard. The configuration plugboard allows the main storage configuration to be varied according to the immediate needs of the installation.

The *direct control feature* allows two CPUs to communicate by transferring a single byte of data between an external device and the main storage of another system. Included with this feature are read direct and write direct instructions and six external interruption lines.

The *extended precision floating-point feature* permits floating-point arithmetic operations to be executed on 128-bit floating-point operands, equal in precision to approximately 34 decimal digits.

Optional features for the Model 165 include:

buffer storage extension to 16,384 bytes,
high-speed multiply feature,
extended channel feature,
7070/7074 compatibility,
7080 compatibility,

709/7090/7094/7094II compatibility, and
channel-to-channel adapter.

The *buffer storage extension* and the *high-speed multiply* are performance features. The larger buffer increases the frequency that needed data are found in the high-speed buffer storage. The high-speed multiply feature reduces the time for a long-precision (64 bits) floating-point multiply from 1.87 microseconds to .61 microseconds. The same feature reduces the time for a fixed-point multiply from .78 microseconds to .42 microseconds.

The *extended channel feature* permits 12 IO channels to be installed on a Model 165 instead of 7.

The *compatibility* features are mutually exclusive and provide the capability of emulating earlier large-scale IBM computers. In each case, the emulation process involves an emulator program that runs under OS* control in addition to the hardware feature, implemented in microcode and executed out of control storage.

The *channel-to-channel adapter* allows two 360/370 computers to be coupled into a multisystem configuration (see Chapter 2) or permits moving blocks of information from one area of main storage to another in the same system. Thus, the two channels connected need not be attached to different systems. The adapter occupies one control unit position on each channel.

System Structure

The major components of a System/370 Model 165 are the 3165 processing unit,† the 3360 processor (main) storage,‡ a system console, and the following IO channels: 2860 selector channel, 2870 byte multiplexer channel, and 2880 block multiplexer channel. The 3165 processing unit contains arithmetic and logical components, main storage, control storage, and local storage. Figure 8.2 depicts the Model 165 configurator; most features including the buffer storage system are considered to be part of the CPU in that diagram.

A complete description of IO devices that can be attached to the Model 165 is beyond the scope of this book. However, several devices, new to the System/370 series, are described in Chapters 9 and 10.

*OS stands for Operating System and refers to OS/360—a comprehensive operating system for System/360 computers.

†The term processing unit refers to central processing unit, as discussed earlier.

‡The 3360 Models 4 and 5 provide 262,144 bytes and 524,288 bytes of storage, respectively. They are combined in a given computer system to supply the main storage sizes mentioned previously. Each storage unit is organized as two logical memories so that an even number of units is required to achieve four-way interleaving. Thus, an I165 system (524,288 bytes of storage) uses two 3360-4 storage units.

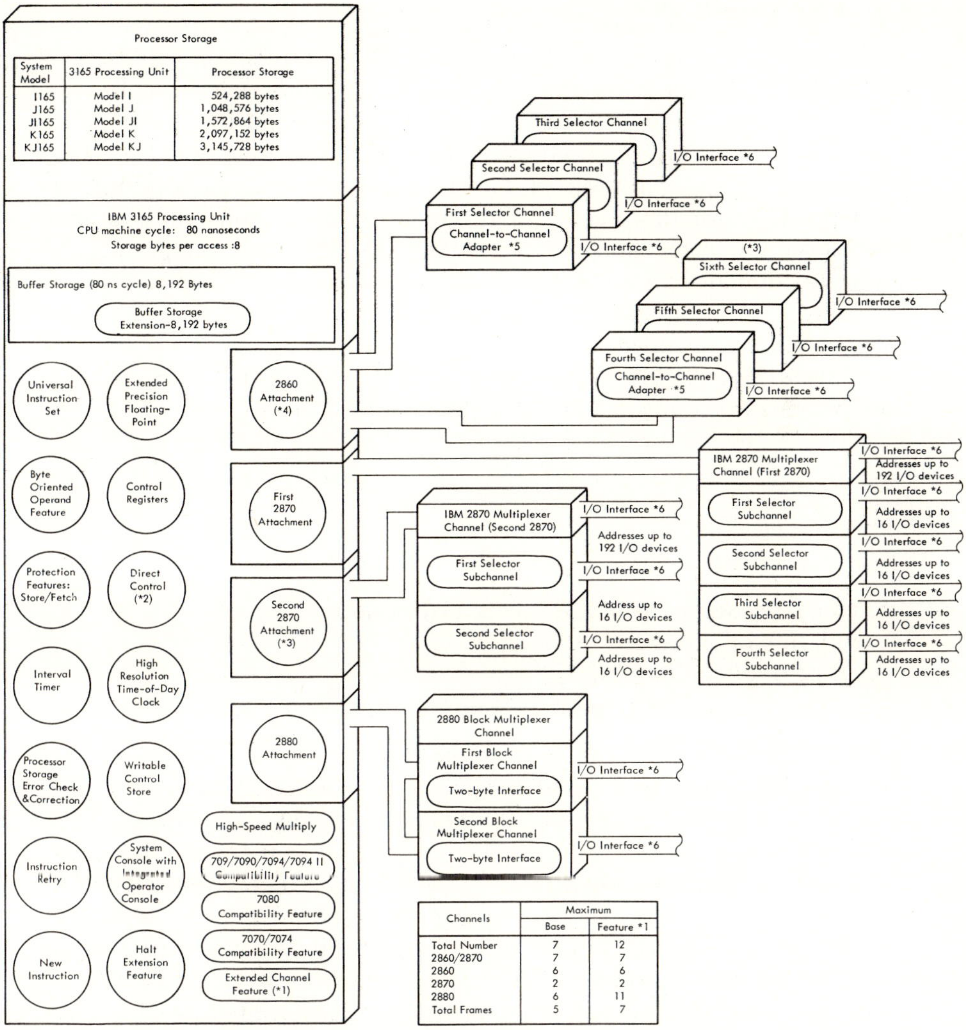

Channels	Maximum Base	Maximum Feature *1
Total Number	7	12
2860/2870	7	7
2860	6	6
2870	2	2
2880	6	11
Total Frames	5	7

Notes:

(Circle) Indicates Standard Feature

(Rounded box) Indicates Optional Feature

*1. The Extended Channel Feature permits connection of five additional/2880 channels; see chart above.

*2. Read/Write Direct and External Interrupt.

*3. A system with the first 2870 may attach up to six selector channels; a system with the first and second 2870 may attach up to five selector channels.

*4. Each selector channel addresses up to 256 I/O devices, one at a time. Operation is in burst mode with overlapped processing. The IBM 2860 Selector Channel is available in three models: Model 1 provides one channel, Model 2 provides two channels, and Model 3 provides three channels in one unit. The system attaches a maximum of two units and a minimum of one unit, or one 2870 with the optional selector subchannel feature installed, or one 2880 Block Multiplexer Channel.

*5. A Channel-to-Channel Adapter option (one per 2860 channel) permits interconnection of two channels. One channel position can connect to one channel position on any other IBM System/370 channel. Only one Channel-to-Channel Adapter is needed per connection; it counts as one control unit on each channel.

*6. Up to eight control units may be attached. Input/Output control units and devices are shown on the IBM System 360/370 Input/Output Configurator, GA22-6972

Figure 8.2 Model 165 configurator. (Courtesy of International Business Machines Corporation.)

8.2 PROCESSING UNIT

The Model 3165 central processing unit (CPU) controls the operation of the Model 165 by decoding and executing instructions, held in main storage, and by monitoring the operation of IO channels and IO devices. The organization and implementation of the CPU is oriented towards high performance: The operation of the instruction and execution units is overlapped; instructions are prefetched down both paths of a branch instruction; the instruction unit contains a special adder for performing address arithmetic; general registers can be referenced simultaneously by five sources within the CPU; and operands are prefetched. The execution unit, which is controlled by a microprogram held in control storage, is synthesized from highly parallel components; as a result, many instructions require only one machine cycle (80 nanoseconds) for execution. The execution of the instruction unit is controlled by logical circuitry.

Instruction Unit

The instruction unit performs the following functions:

fetching, decoding, and buffering of instructions,
calculation of effective addresses,
fetching of operands, and
initiating the execution of instructions by the execution unit.

The working storage necessary for these tasks is depicted in Figure 8.3. The *main instruction buffer* and the *auxiliary instruction buffer* are each 16 bytes in length and are used to hold prefetched instructions. The *instruction register* (4 bytes) holds each instruction as it is being decoded; it is filled from the main instruction buffer. The *queue registers* buffer an instruction before it is moved to the execution unit. The instruction unit also contains a 24-bit three-input adder for performing address arithmetic, four 24-bit address registers, an incrementer, and an instruction decoder.

During instruction decoding, an instruction is moved from the main instruction buffer to the instruction register for decoding by the decoder. The decoding process normally takes one machine cycle but may be delayed for one of the following reasons:

1. Address calculation is required and the address adder is busy.
2. A general register is needed and is unavailable.
3. No queue register is available.
4. Operand boundary alignment is required and the necessary queue registers are not available.
5. An SS instruction* is currently being executed by the execution unit

*The instruction unit processes an SS-type instruction as two or three separate instructions.

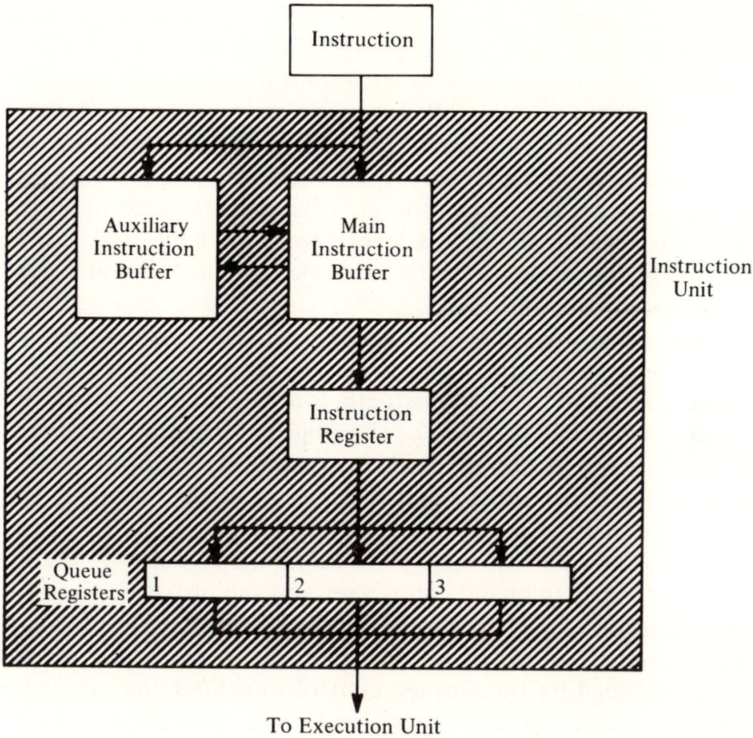

Figure 8.3 Working storage in the instruction unit.

and the instruction being decoded is not an RR-type instruction or a branch instruction.

6. The instruction being decoded prohibits overlap.
7. The instruction being executed and the instruction being decoded are both branches.

After an instruction is successfully decoded, the 24-bit three-input adder is used to compute an effective address (if necessary) from the contents of base and index registers and the value contained in the displacement field of the instruction. The address computed is used as a source data address, a destination data address, or a numerical value used for shift operations or an IO device address. Operands are prefetched and made available to the execution unit in two 8-byte data buffers.

For a branch instruction, the effective address calculated is the location of a series of instructions. It is here that the auxiliary instruction buffer is used. Instructions are prefetched down both paths. If the branch is estimated to be unsuccessful, instructions from the current stream (of instructions) are fetched into the main instruction buffer and instructions from the target stream are fetched into the auxiliary instruction buffer. Then, if the branch is successful, the contents of the buffers are swapped. Recall here that the instruction register is always filled from the main instruction buffer. On the other hand, if the branch is estimated to be successful, then the main instruction buffer is filled from target stream and the auxiliary instruction buffer is filled from the current instruction stream. If the branch is unsuccessful, in this case, the buffers are swapped. The process is depicted in Figure 8.3. The estimate of success is based upon the type of branch instruction, the contents of the mask field, and the general register specifications. As a trivial example, an unconditional branch is always estimated to be successful.

The decoding and execution of an execute (EX) instruction are processed in the instruction unit. The object instruction is placed in the main instruction buffer and the current stream is moved to the auxiliary instruction buffer. After the execution of the object instruction has been completed, the contents of the auxiliary instruction buffer are moved to the main instruction buffer and normal execution continues.

During the execution of a store operation, a check is made to determine if the execution of that instruction will affect the contents of the instruction buffers. If so, then an indicator is set and the instruction unit is reset after the execution of the store operation has been completed. An illegal store operation to a protected address or invalid location is handled differently. It is detected by the storage control unit after the instruction requesting the store operation has been completed and a subsequent instruction is being executed. Since the exact instruction is not known, an *imprecise interruption* is generated and the instruction length code in the old program interruption PSW is set to zero. Imprecise interruptions are not uncommon to high-performance computers that concurrently execute several internal operations.

An illegal storage fetch, however, is detected by the instruction unit during the prefetching of that operand. The condition is saved until the exact instruction causing the problem is sent to the execution unit. Then a *precise interruption* is initiated.

Execution Unit

The execution unit in the Model 165 is microprogram controlled except in cases where the execution sequence is dependent upon the data results of previous micro-operations. Working storage and functional components include: two 8-byte data buffers for prefetched operands, an 8-byte result register, a 64-bit parallel adder, a 32-bit logical unit, a 64-bit shifter, and an 8-bite serial adder. Fixed-point and floating-point arithmetic are performed in the 64-bit parallel adder. Decimal arithmetic is performed in the 8-bit serial adder.

CPU organization and data flow are depicted in Figure 8.4. All data paths are 8 bytes wide and are parity checked.

The execution unit can process a new instruction each machine cycle—

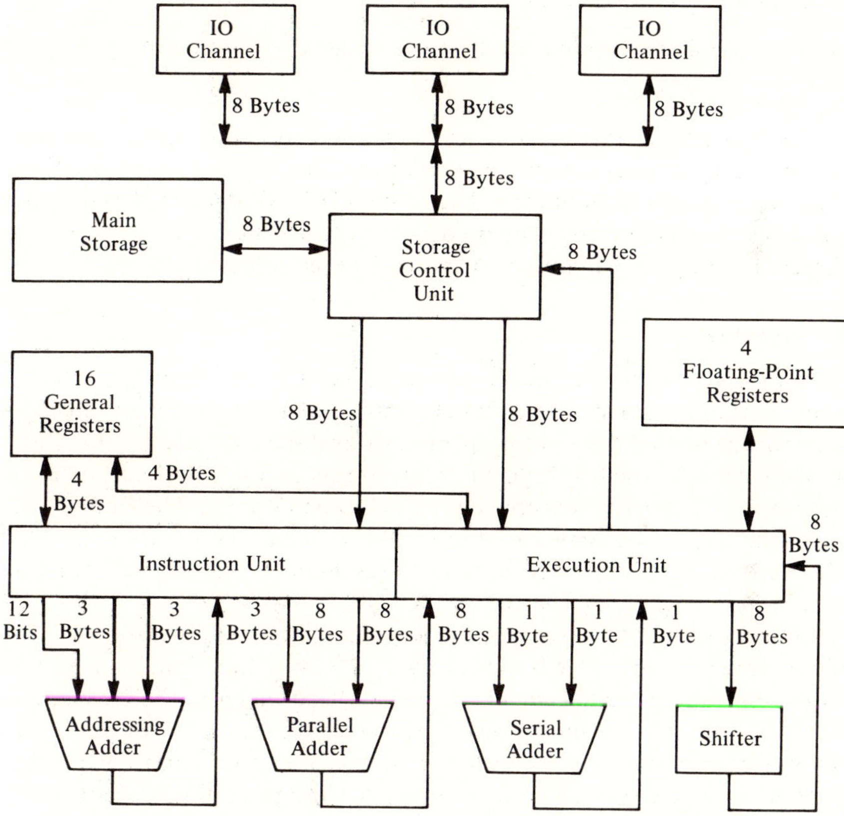

Figure 8.4 Model 165 CPU organization and data flow.

i.e., if the previous one has been completed—however, only one instruction is processed at a time.

Registers

CPU registers include the sixteen 4-byte general registers, four 8-byte floating-point registers, and four 32-bit control registers.

The general registers are designed to support the overlapped execution of the instruction unit and the execution unit. It is possible to fetch from four general registers and store into the fifth—all in one machine cycle. This implementation permits the following concurrent operations:

1. storing the result of one instruction,
2. execution of the next instruction,
3. calculation of an effective address in the instruction unit.

Similarly, two floating-point registers can be accessed simultaneously.

CPU Features

Many of the other CPU features are implemented in the CPU: extended floating-point arithmetic, high-speed multiply, the interval timer, the time-of-day clock, and direct control. The System/370 Model 165 also includes several new instructions over its predecessor, the System/360. The reader is directed to reference manuals for more detailed information.

8.3 STORAGE

The storage system in the Model 165 consists of control storage, a buffer storage unit and control, IO channel control facilities, and main storage. Main storage is used for holding programs and data for use by the CPU. Control storage is used to hold microprograms and is composed of read-only storage (ROS) and writable control storage (WCS). The buffer storage system serves as a high-speed interface between main storage and the CPU, and the IO channel control facilities manage the use of four-way interleaved storage by the channels.

This section mainly describes the organization and operation of the buffer storage system. The buffer storage system is functionally a part of a larger unit, the *storage control unit*, which also includes the IO channel control facilities, and main storage control (see Figure 8.5). All references to main storage from the CPU or the channels are processed by one of the components of the storage control unit. A storage request can be made by the SCU each machine cycle (80 nanoseconds) until all four main storage units are busy.

This section also covers control storage, the IO channel control facilities, and the main storage control. First, some general comments on main storage are required.

The byte-oriented operand feature is supported and allows operands for nonprivileged instructions to reside on byte boundaries without causing a specification program interruption. The feature does not apply to CPU instructions (which must be aligned on a half word boundary), CCWs (which must be aligned on a double word boundary), and the operands of privileged instructions. Main storage is normally four-way interleaved

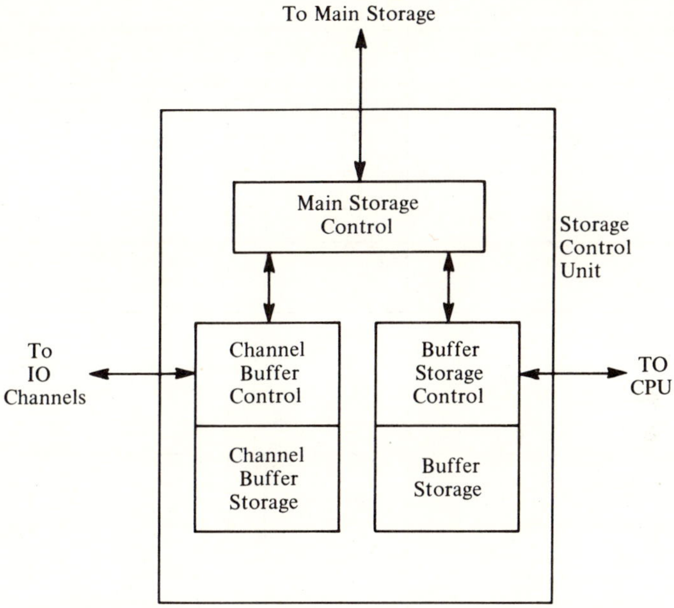

Figure 8.5 Organization of the storage control unit.

and error checking and correction (ECC) circuitry applies to all stores and fetches to main storage; it is considered, along with permanent storage assignments, in the section on reliability.

Control Storage

Control storage in the Model 165 consists of 108-bit control words: 2K are provided in read-only storage (ROS) and 512 are provided in writable control storage (WCS). When the compatibility feature is installed, 1024 additional control words are contained in WCS. WCS is loaded from a console file, when electrical power is applied to the computer, by depressing a console key, or under microprogram control.

The Model 165 microprogram, stored in control storage, enables the Model 165 computer to operate as a System/370. One control word is accessed, decoded, and used to control the CPU during each machine cycle.

Operation, Organization, and Maintenance of the Buffer Storage System

The objective of the buffer storage system is to increase the frequency with which main storage requests can be satisfied from the higher-speed unit. When a request for data is made by the CPU, the buffer control unit determines if the requested data are in the buffer. If the data are in the

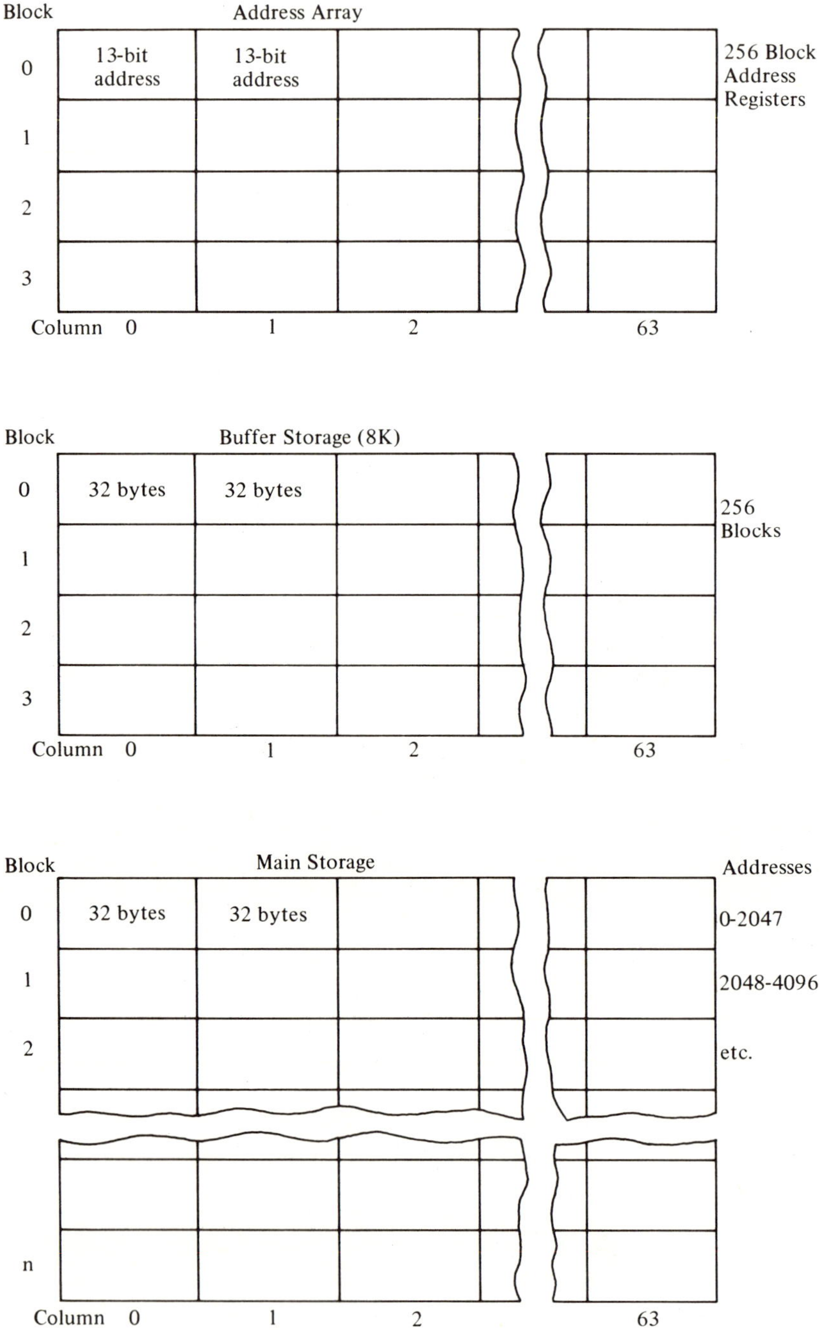

Figure 8.6 Buffer storage organization (8K).

buffer, they are transmitted to the CPU without a main storage access. If the requested data are not in the buffer, a main storage fetch is initiated and the data are sent directly to the CPU. A buffer location is also determined and the data are stored there for subsequent references. The buffer storage is maintained dynamically by the CPU and is transparent to the programmer. When data are stored by the CPU, both the buffer and main storage are updated if the corresponding location contains data that are currently in the buffer. The IO channels always reference main storage. However, if an IO channel stores data in a main storage location that contains data held in the buffer, then the buffer is also updated accordingly.

The buffer and main storage are both divided into blocks of 32 bytes, as shown in Figure 8.6. The 8K buffer contains 64 columns, each containing 4 blocks—a total of 256 distinct blocks of information. (The 16K buffer contains 128 columns and 4 rows for a total of 512 blocks.) Each buffer block contains 32 *consecutive* bytes from main storage, which is also regarded (logically) as containing 64 (or 128) columns with the number of blocks in each column being dependent upon the size of the main storage. Any of the blocks in a main storage column can be placed in one of the four blocks in the corresponding buffer column.

The buffer storage is managed with an address array (Figure 8.6) and a replacement array, which is described later. An element of the address array consists of the 13 high-order bits of the main storage address of the 32 bytes of data contained in the corresponding position in buffer storage. When the CPU references main storage, the address array is used to determine if the requested data are in the buffer.

The System/370 computer computes a 32-bit effective address* but uses only the low-order 24 bits of it, denoted by bits 8–31 in Figure 8.7. Bits

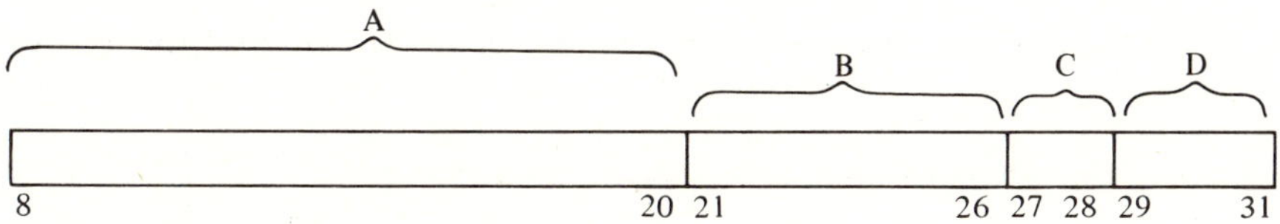

A - Address Compare (bits 8-19 with a 16K buffer)
B - Reference Buffer Column (bits 20-26 with a 16K buffer)
C - Reference Double Word
D - Reference Byte Within Double Word

Figure 8.7 Main storage address.

*See Chapter 3.

8–20 are used for comparison with address array entries (8–19 with a 16K buffer); bits 21–26 (20–26 with a 16K buffer) are used to select a column of the address array; bits 27 and 28 are used to address a double word within a block; and bits 29–31 are used for displacement within a double word. Thus, an effective address is compared with at most four address array entries; therefore, a column (of 32-byte blocks) of main storage contends for a position in a four-row column of the buffer.

Each column in the buffer is associated with a four-entry replacement array which controls buffer replacement activity. When a buffer block is referenced, it is put at the top of the list for its particular column. When a block must be reassigned, the entry at the bottom of the list is selected for replacement.

The 8K buffer storage system operates as follows:

1. When the CPU requests a unit of data, bits 21–26 (bits 20–26 with a 16K buffer) of the effective address are used to select a (buffer) column of the address array.
2. Bits 8–20 (bits 8–19 with a 16K buffer) of the effective address are compared with each of the four entries in that column of the address array.
3. If an equal compare is made, a buffer address (Figure 8.8) is calculated from the address compare and selected bits of the effective address; the double word indicated by bits 27 and 28 of the effective address is sent to the CPU. Main storage is not referenced and the referenced buffer block is put at the top of its column activity list in the replacement array.
4. If the block addressed is not found in the corresponding column of the address array, then the data unit is fetched from main storage, sent to the CPU, and stored in the buffer for future data requests. The buffer block on the bottom of the replacement array activity list for that column is assigned the new block of data and the address

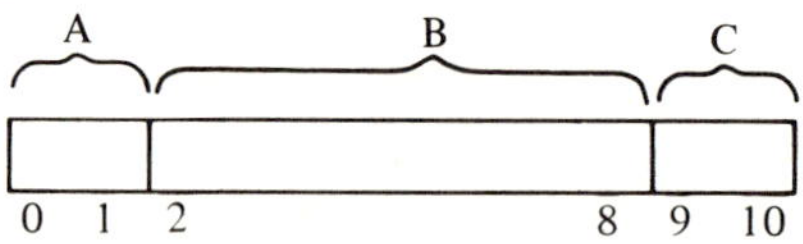

A - Row in Buffer Column (results from address compare)
B - Buffer Column (with an 8K buffer, bits 21-26 of storage address are used as bits 3-8 of buffer storage address; with a 16K buffer, bits 20-26 of storage address are used as bits 2-8 of buffer storage address)
C - Reference Double Word (storage address bits 27-28)

Figure 8.8 Buffer storage address.

array is updated accordingly. The double word required by the CPU is the first one that is fetched from main storage. It is sent to the CPU first and then to the buffer so that processing can be initiated as soon as possible. It is followed by three consecutive storage references, one cycle apart, to fill the remainder of that data block.

The procedure emphasizes an important point. All data paths in the CPU are 8 bytes wide, and whenever the CPU requests data, it always gets 8 bytes. Thus, the *physical word size* of the Model 165 is said to be 8 bytes. However, this physical word size should be distinguished from the 4-byte word defined in System/370 architecture.

IO Channel Control

Storage requests by an IO channel are received and processed by the IO channel control facilities in the storage control unit (SCU). Each channel attached to the CPU is assigned 8-byte buffers—for inbound data and for outbound data—called a *buffer group*. The buffers, depicted in Figure 8.9, are used to free the channel and storage data buses for use by other operations.

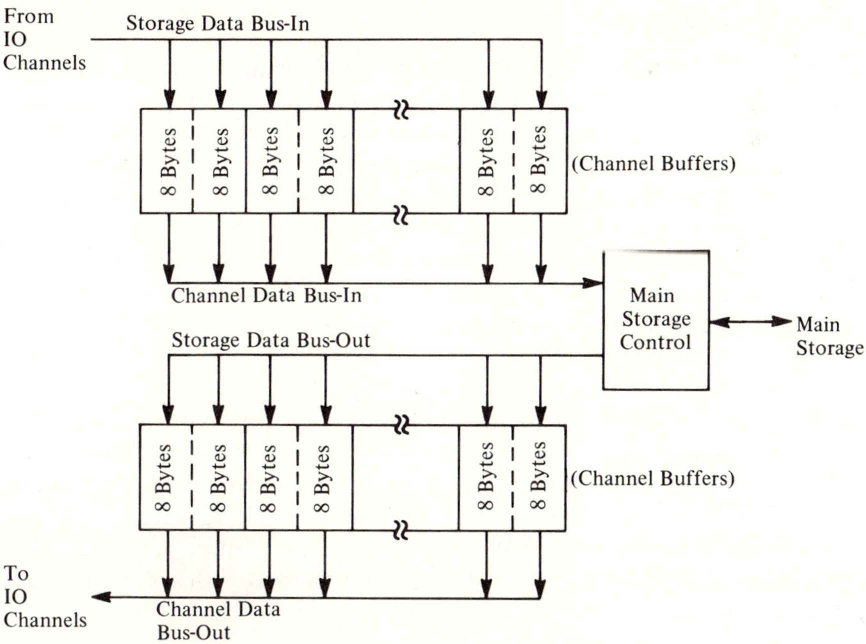

Figure 8.9 IO channel buffers. (Courtesy of International Business Machines Corporation.)

Processor Storage Control

The last major component of the storage control unit is the processor storage control (also referred to as main storage control) which processes main storage requests for the buffer control unit and the IO channel control. The processor storage control resolves contention problems, allows interleaved storage to be accessed concurrently by channels in the CPU, and passes error checking and interruption information (as well as data) to the requesting unit.

Reconfiguration

The configuration panel on the system console allows the installation to remove one or more main storage units from the system configuration and to reconfigure the address of the remaining units to obtain consecutive addressing. Four-way interleaving requires an even number of storage units. A Model 165 usually has an even number of storage units, regardless of the size of main storage, so that the removal of one unit reduces the interleaving to two-way. If two storage units are removed, four-way interleaving is maintained.

8.4 IO CHANNELS

The Model 165 IO channels are physically independent functional components and compete with the CPU for access to main storage. The number of concurrent IO operations that can be sustained is dependent upon the number and type of channels and the data rates of the IO devices attached to these channels. The standard interface between a control unit and a channel is one 8-bit byte. A 2-byte interface can be used with the block multiplexer channels and allows IO devices with very high data rates to be attached. The data path between the storage control unit (SCU) and an IO channel is 8 bytes.

Selector Channels

The 2860 selector channel can control a single operation on a single data path, even though eight control units can be attached to each selector channel and each control unit can have several devices attached to it. CPU processing is overlapped with IO operations and several selector channels can be operating concurrently. The maximum data rate of a single selector channel is 1.3 megabytes per second. Selector channels may be assigned to channel addresses 1–6.

Block Multiplexer Channels

A 2880 block multiplexer channel may be assigned to channel addresses 1–6 and, if the extended channel feature is installed, channel addresses

1-11. The 2880 can operate in the selector mode or the block multiplex mode, depending upon the setting of bit 0 in control register 0, when the start IO instruction for that channel is issued.

A block multiplexer channel operating in the selector mode is busy during the entire execution of a channel program. When operating in the block multiplex mode, the channel can disconnect for non-data operations during the operation of one channel program so that a data transfer operation can be executed for another channel program. During the execution of a channel program with multiple command chained CCWs, the channel disconnects from that program when a channel end is received without a concurrent device end. The channel is then available for another IO operation and the status of the disconnected operation is saved. When the disconnected operation is again ready to use the channel, the control unit attempts to regain the channel facilities. If the channel is free, the channel registers are reloaded and execution of that channel program is resumed. If the channel is busy at that time, the device must wait. Block multiplex operations are controlled by channel and control unit hardware.

Eight control units can be attached to a 2880 and each control unit can have several devices attached to it. Even though only one device per channel may be executing a data transfer operation at one time, as many as 64 channel programs may be in concurrent execution in the block multiplex mode.

The 2880 block multiplexer channel incorporates a high-speed data transfer mode that provides a data rate of 1.5 megabytes per second. If the 2-byte interface is used along with additional channel buffering, a data rate of 3 megabytes per second is possible.

Byte Multiplexer Channels

The 2870 byte multiplexer channel is designed to control multiple low-speed IO devices and operates in either the byte interleaved mode or the burst mode, depending upon the needs of a particular IO device. In the byte interleaved mode, several low-speed devices operate concurrently and share channel facilities. In the burst mode, only one medium- to high-speed device operates at one time.

The 2870 byte multiplexer channel permits eight control units to be attached and 192 byte multiplexer subchannels to be used—provided the aggregate data rate does not exceed the range of the channel. The first 2870 attached also provides four additional selector subchannels. The second 2870, which may be assigned any address between 1 and 6, provides 192 byte multiplexer subchannels and two additional selector subchannels. The maximum data rate for any subchannel is 180,000 bytes per second (180KB).

8.5 SYSTEM RELIABILITY AND AVAILABILITY

The System/370 Model 165 contains repair and recovery facilities that allow the system, with appropriate software, to operate in an environment where high availability is required. The facilities enable the buffer storage to be disabled or main storage to be reconfigured in response to equipment malfunction without forcing the system into an inoperable state. Checking and retry facilities include storage error checking and correction (ECC), CPU instruction retry, and IO retry. The machine check interruption system allows equipment and programming errors to be detected, recorded, and recovery procedures to be initiated—all under program control.

Reconfiguration and Storage Control

Reconfiguration has been discussed previously and allows operation of the system to continue after a failure of a system storage unit. The Model 165 also includes a storage ripple feature for use during maintenance and repair. A *storage ripple* is a hardware function that performs a read or write of zeros or ones through available storage locations to locate a malfunctioning storage unit. Ordinarily, a storage ripple is used during maintenance periods. An *inline* storage ripple feature is also implemented for use on storage facilities during normal computer processing. The inline storage ripple function applies only to a storage unit that has been reconfigured out of the system and is assigned to the highest addressing position.

The buffer storage system can be made inoperative with a console switch or by the execution of the CPU diagnose instruction. When the buffer is not operating, system performance is degraded and all storage references are made to main storage. The process of disabling the buffer storage system does not affect the validity of computed results.

CPU Retry

A CPU hardware error detected during the execution of an instruction normally causes that instruction to be retried up to seven times before the error is classified as uncorrectable. Instruction retry is performed with additional circuitry and microprogrammed routines. If the hardware error is caused by a buffer storage malfunction, the buffer is bypassed when the retry is attempted. The occurrence of hardware errors is always accompanied by either a "hard" or "soft" machine check interruption so that error recovery or error recording can be performed by the operating system.

Storage Error Checking and Correction

Eight bits of error checking and correction (ECC) are maintained with each double word of main and control storage. Checking on an 8-byte basis, rather than a single-byte basis, allows single-bit errors to be corrected and all double-bit and most multiple-bit errors to be detected. Internally to the CPU, a parity bit is maintained with each byte. A conversion between byte parity and ECC code is made by a *storage adapter unit* as each double word enters and leaves control or main storage.

After a single-bit error is corrected by the *correcter unit* in the storage adapter unit, it is sent back to storage and then to the CPU to continue the operation. An *ECC mode bit* is available that determines whether a

Decimal locations	Assignment		Area
0	IPL PSW		Fixed Area 0-127 • Model independent among System/360 and System/370 models except for PSW bit 12 • Processed by the control program
8	IPL CCW 1		
16	IPL CCW 2		
24	External old PSW		
32	SVC old PSW		
40	Program old PSW		
48	Machine check old PSW		
56	IO old PSW		
64	Channel status word – CSW		
72	Channel address word – CAW	76 Unused	
80	Interval timer	84 Unused	
88	External new PSW		
96	SVC new PSW		
104	Program new PSW		
112	Machine check new PSW		
120	IO new PSW		
128	128 – 167 Unused		
168	Channel ID	172 IO extended log pointer	
176	176 – 231 Unused		Fixed Logout Area 176-511 • Layout is model independent among System/370 models • Fields and bits used vary slightly by model • Always logged on a machine check interrupt • Processed by RMS
232	Machine check code		
240	240 – 255 Unused		
256	Used to store status data for CPU retry operations		
352	Floating point register save area		
384	General purpose register save area		
448	Control register save area		
512	CPU Extended logout – 1000 bytes (Pointer in control register 15 set to 512 at IPL or system reset)		CPU Extended Logout Area • Model dependent • Logged on all hard machine checks and first and seventh CPU retry if not disabled • Processed by Logout Analysis Program
1511			

Figure 8.10 Model 165 permanent storage assignments. (Reprinted by permission from "A Guide to the IBM System/370 Model 165," Form GC20-1730-0. Copyright 1970 by International Business Machines Corporation.)

soft machine check should be initiated for a corrected single-bit error. Double-bit and multiple-bit errors always initiate hard machine check interruptions.

IO Errors

IO channel errors and CPU errors associated with channel operations are accompanied by an IO interruption during which the channel status word (CSW) and channel logout are stored (see Figure 8.10). The channel logout data unit, which consists of 28 words, is stored starting with the address given in location 172—the IO extended logout pointer. The IO extended logout mask (bit 2 of control register 14) governs whether an IO extended logout should be performed.

IO command retry is provided automatically with certain control units and IO devices without requiring an IO interruption or a programmed error recovery procedure.

Machine Check Interruptions

Four classes of machine check interruptions are defined in the Model 165. They are listed in Table 8.1 and classified by whether they are hard or soft. A *hard machine check* interruption follows an unsuccessful retry attempt. A *soft machine check* interruption follows a successful retry effort and is initiated so that the occurrence of an error condition can be recorded.

TABLE 8.1 MODEL 165 MACHINE CHECK INTERRUPTIONS

Mask Bits	*Interruption Type*	*Machine Check*
PSW bit 13 CR[a] 14 bit 4	System recovery	Soft
PSW bit 13 CR 14 bit 6	Time-of-day clock damage	Soft
PSW bit 13 CR 14 bit 6	External damage (error not affecting CPU)	Soft
PSW bit 13	System damage (irreparable hardware malfunction)	Hard

[a]CR stands for control register.

A machine check interruption, accepted by the CPU, is accompanied by a logout to the fixed area (176–511). Model 165 fixed storage assignments are depicted in Figure 8.10. Machine check codes (locations 232–239 of the fixed logout area) are depicted in Figure 8.11. A model-dependent machine check extended logout (MCEL) of 1000 bytes occurs in locations 512–1511 (unless changed by programming) when a hard

Fixed Logout Area Locations 232-239

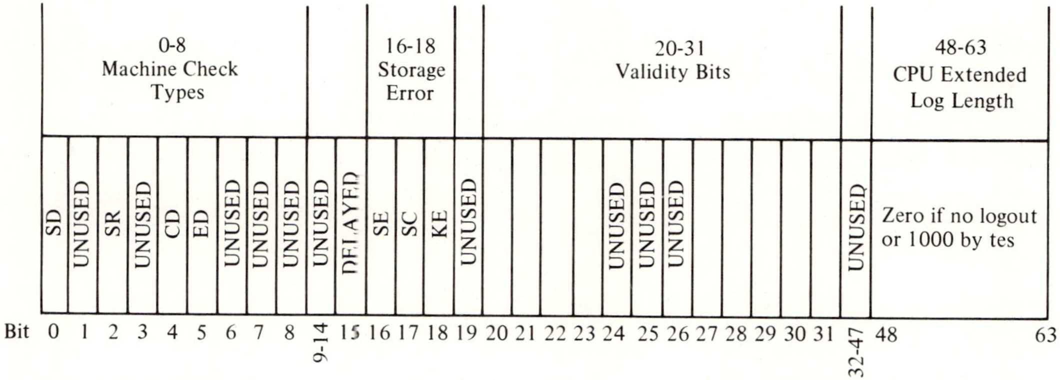

Bit	Interrupt Type
0	SD – System Damage
2	SR – System Recovery
4	CD – Time of Day Clock Damage
5	ED – External Damage

Bit	Error
15	Delayed Interrupt
16	Storage Error Uncorrected
17	Storage Error Corrected
18	Protection Key Error

Bit	Valid Fixed Area Data
20-23	Machine Check Old PSW (48-55)
	20 AMWP
	21 Masks and Protect Key
	22 Program Mask and Condition Code
	23 Instruction Address
27	Floating Point Registers (352-383)
28	General Purpose Registers (384-447)
29	Control Registers (448-511)
30	CPU Extended Logout
31	Storage (Validity of storage being processed by instructions when interrupt occurred)

Figure 8.11 Model 165 machine check codes. (Reprinted by permission from "A Guide to the IBM System/370 Model 165," Form GC20-1730-0. Copyright 1970 by International Business Machines Corporation.)

machine check interruption is accepted. The MCEL is controlled by two extended logout mask bits (1 and 8)* in control register 14. The CPU extended logout is intended for use by operating system recovery management routines.

8.6 SUPPORT FACILITIES

The System/370 Model 165 is supported by programming systems and advanced hardware facilities.

The Model 165 supports the IBM 2305 Fixed Head Storage Facility Models 1 and 2, which have data rates of 3 megabytes per second and 1.5 megabytes per second, respectively, the IBM 3330 Disk Storage Facility, with a storage capacity of 800,000,000 bytes, the IBM 3211 line printer, which prints at speeds of 2000 lines per minute, and the remote system console, with a CRT display and microfiche viewer.

The Model 165 supports OS/360, a multiprogramming operating system, and integrated emulators for the 7070/7074, 7080, and 709/7040/7094/7094II computers, which operate under OS control.

The IO devices are presented in Chapters 9 and 10; programming systems and emulators are introduced in the appendices.

REFERENCES

1. IBM System/370 publications: "Principles of Operation," Form GA22-7000. "Model 165 Functional Characteristics," Form GA22-6935. "Guide to the IBM System/370 Model 165," Form GC20-1730; "System Summary," Form GA22-7001. IBM Corporation, Data Processing Division, White Plains, N.Y., 1970.

*Bits 1 and 8 refer to synchronous and asychronous masks, respectively.

9 DIRECT-ACCESS DEVICES

9.1 INTRODUCTION

Most input/output and mass storage devices have physical characteristics that determine how they can be used and the manner in which information is recorded. Punched cards and magnetic tape, for example, are considered to be serial devices since the relative position of a unit of information is determined by the information that precedes it on that medium. Disk storage, on the other hand, is classified as a direct-access device since each unit of information has a physical location on the storage medium and that information can be referenced directly without sequential searching through previous information. This chapter is concerned with the nature of direct-access devices and describes the manner in which they are used.

The vehicle used here for introducing direct-access storage devices is disk storage. It is the most widely used direct-access storage medium and has been selected as the recording medium for IBM 3330 and the IBM 2305 storage devices, discussed in the next chapter.

Basic Concepts

Disk storage is similar in concept to a stack of phonograph records; information is recorded on the disk surfaces and is read or written as the disks rotate.

A disk storage unit has three major components; the recording surfaces, access arms and read-write heads, and the disk mechanism. In general, very little is said about the disk mechanism except that it causes the recording surfaces to rotate and that it works in conjunction with the access arms and read-write head to record and retrieve information. Figure 9.1 depicts a typical disk storage assembly. Several disks are used

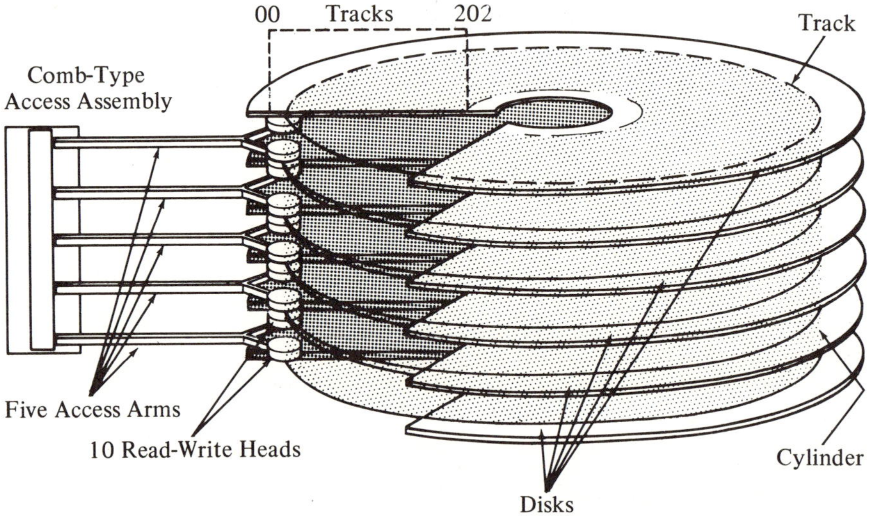

Figure 9.1 Typical disk storage assembly. (Courtesy of International Business Machines Corporation.)

together and are called a disk volume—or, if the volume is removable, a disk pack. Both surfaces of a disk are used for recording information except the top surface and the bottom surfaces of a volume, which provide protection. Therefore, a disk pack with six disks would have ten recording surfaces.

Each surface has discrete tracks upon which information is recorded. The various tracks are concentric and not continuous as on a phonograph record. Information is recorded serially by bit so that one 8-bit byte occupies 8 bit positions on a recording track (see Figure 9.2). The disk storage unit is designed so that each track holds the same amount of information.

The access mechanism and read-write heads are a comb-type assembly with two read-write heads per access arm—one for the upper surface and the other for the lower surface. Each read-write head is used to access one surface. All access arms and read-write heads move in and out together. Because all read-write heads are always positioned in the same vertical position, several tracks (one on each recording surface) are available for reading or writing purposes without moving the access mecha-

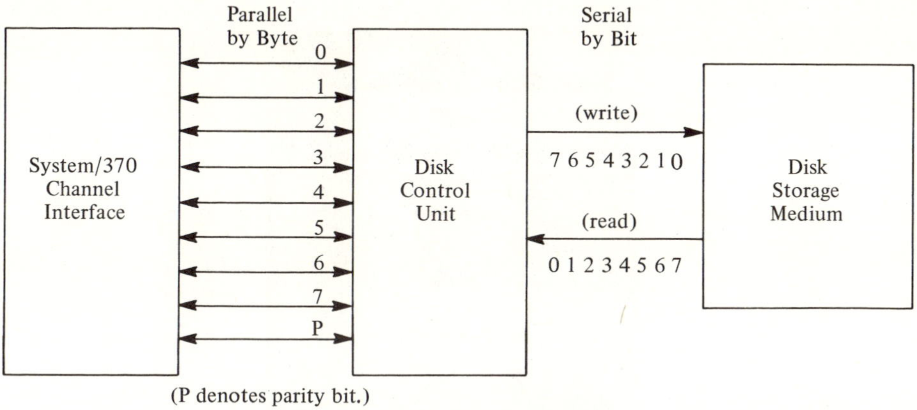

Figure 9.2 Data transfer methods.

nism. Therefore, the positioning of the read-write heads at any track location provides access to a *cylinder* of information. Thus, there are as many cylinders per volume as there are tracks per surface. The cylinder concept is used by programming systems to facilitate access to data on disk storage.

Disk Storage Organization

Collectively, the components* of a disk unit are referred to as a *module* although the term is frequently used for the disk surfaces alone. A convenient means of classifying disk storage units is on the basis of the number of modules they contain. Figure 9.3 shows the IBM 2311 Disk Storage Drive that supports one disk module. Figure 9.4 shows the IBM 2314 Disk Storage Facility that contains eight usable disk modules plus a spare module. Both units utilize removable disk packs that allow large quantities† of information to be removed from the system for storage. Figure 9.5 depicts the IBM 2316 removable disk pack used with the IBM 2314 Disk Storage Facility. The 2316 is composed of 11 disks (20 recording surfaces); the disks are 14 inches in diameter and mounted 1 inch apart on a vertical shaft. The cover is 15 inches in diameter and the complete assembly weighs approximately 13 pounds. The cover is used for protection and is removed when the disk pack is mounted as a disk storage module. The 2316 disk pack is very similar to the 3336 disk pack used with the IBM 3330, discussed later.

*That is, the access arms and read-write heads, the recording surfaces, and the disk mechanism.

†The IBM 1316 disk pack used with the IBM 2311 Disk Drive can hold 7.25 million bytes. The IBM 2316 disk pack used with the IBM 2314 Disk Storage Facility can hold 29.17 million bytes.

Figure 9.3 IBM 2311 Disk Storage (1 module per unit). (Courtesy of International Business Machines Corporation.)

Figure 9.4 IBM 2314 Disk Storage Facility (9 modules per unit). (Courtesy of International Business Machines Corporation.)

Disk Storage Operational Considerations

A disk storage unit is attached to an IO channel via an IO control unit that performs a variety of useful functions including the positioning and selecting of read-write heads and the searching for specific data records.

The effectiveness of a disk storage facility is a function of the time necessary to retrieve information. Two factors influence this time: rotational speed of the disks and the time necessary to position a read-write head. The latter is referred to as *seek time*. The seek time for a particular cylinder and head position is dependent upon the current position; the time necessary to select another read-write head within the same cylinder

Figure 9.5 IBM 2316 removable disk pack. (Courtesy of International Business Machines Corporation.)

is negligible and is called *switch time*. The rotational speed of the disks determines the time for the disk to rotate to the desired record (called *latency time*) and the data rate after the desired record is found.

As mentioned earlier, the control unit plays an important role in the operation of a disk unit. In disk facilities with more than one module, the control unit frequently allows more than one module to be concurrently engaged in IO operations. Many other disk functions, such as seek (to a cylinder and head position) and search (for a specific record), are handled completely by the control and disk units and do not require IO channel facilities.

9.2 DATA ORGANIZATION

Effective disk utilization is a function of hardware facilities and programming systems support. For example, many disk hardware operations are designed to facilitate disk programming and others automatically use information recorded on a track of a disk without requiring the use of a computer program. Another important function is the use of spare tracks as a substitute for those flagged as defective.

Track Format

Each track on a disk surface is closed, as depicted in Figure 9.6. The beginning of each track is also the end of that track and is denoted by an

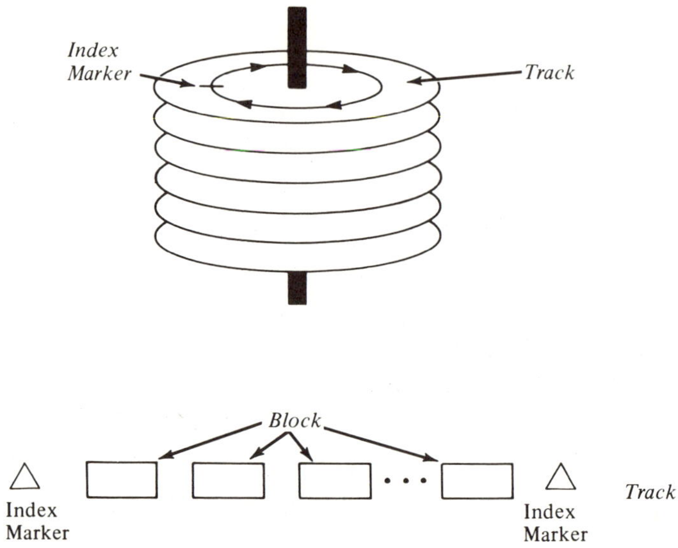

Figure 9.6 Track format for disk storage.

index marker (index point). The index point is a property of the disk volume, as a whole, and all tracks are synchronized to the same point. No index marker appears on individual tracks and the detection of the index point does not require an operation of the read-write heads. The index point is recognized by a special sensing device within the disk mechanism.

Information is recorded on a track as a series of consecutive bytes called a *block*; each block is delimited by a gap that contains no data and is used by the control unit for orientation and for control. There are several types of gaps and each varies in size according to the purpose it serves. Each gap contains one or more control bytes that denote the beginning of the next block and indicate the type of the recorded area that follows. All blocks contain 4 bytes used for data checking. When data are transferred from main storage to a disk volume, the parity bit from each byte is stripped off and a 2-byte *cyclic check* (CC) and a 2-byte *bit count appendage* (BCA) are added. During a write operation, the cyclic check and bit count appendages are computed and are appended to the block. On a subsequent read, the check bytes are recalculated and compared with the check bytes read with the associated data. The bit count appendage is also used to identify the physical drive on which the block was written and to indicate the presence of BCA for that block. The BCA is 2 bytes long; the first byte serves as an indicator to denote the presence of BCA. It is used for compatibility with earlier systems that did not use bit count checking.

If the BCA indicator is not present, then no comparison of bit count is made by the control unit. Data checking is strictly a hardware function.

Data records are written on a disk track by a combination of hardware and software facilities. In general, a data record is recorded as three blocks: a count area, a key area, and a data area (see Figure 9.7). The key

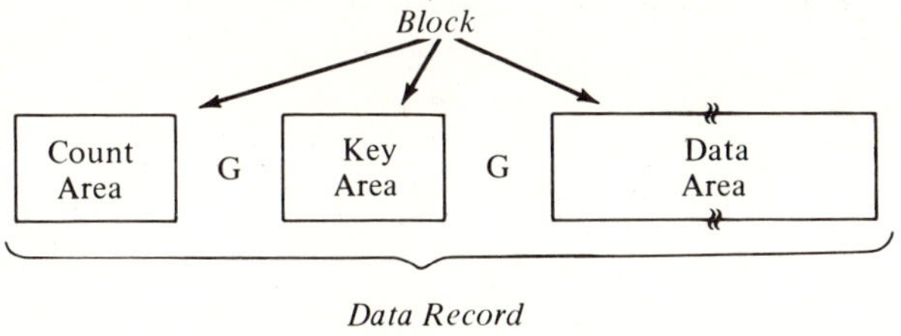

Figure 9.7 Block format of a disk record.

area may be omitted but the count and data areas are always present. The *count block* (Figure 9.8) denotes the beginning of a record and gives the lengths of the key and data blocks. The flag area is discussed later as are the cylinder and head numbers used to identify the track containing the record. The *record number* identifies a record and is used with a search command to locate a given unit of information. The *key length* (KL) and *data length* (DL) fields specify the number of bytes in the key and data areas, respectively. If the key length is zero, no key area is

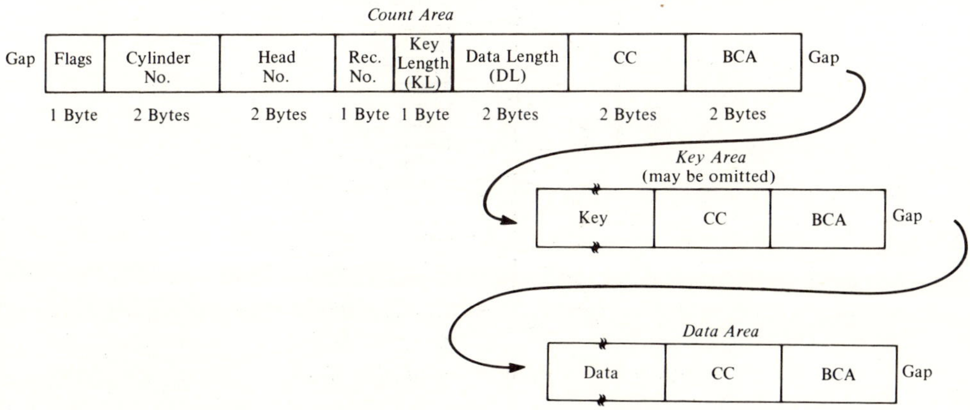

Figure 9.8 Fields in a disk record.

present. A data length of zero denotes an end of data (EOD) record and only four data check bytes are written. An EOD record may contain a key field.

Data Formats

Track and data formats are given in Figure 9.9.* The only record that does not conform to the above requirement (of at least two blocks) is the

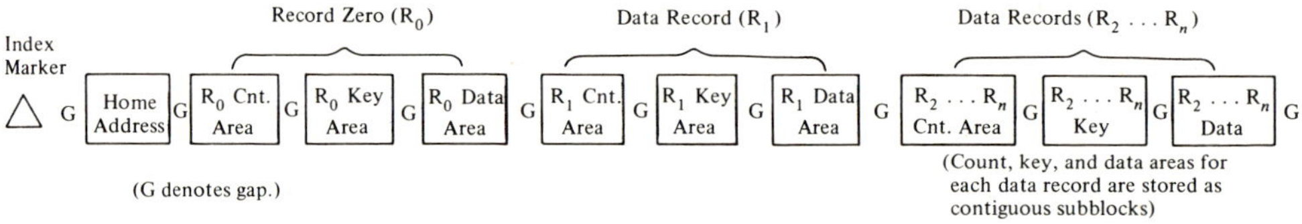

Figure 9.9 Track and data formats.

home address record. The *home address* gives each track a unique identity that is not affected by normal programming procedures. There is only one home address area per track and that area follows the index marker (index point). The cylinder and head numbers in the home address must agree

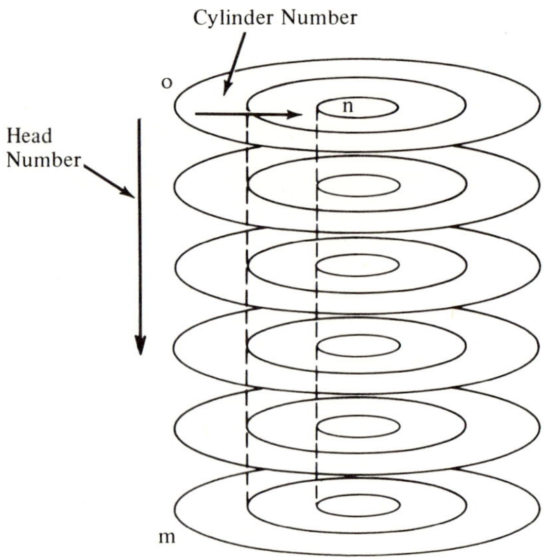

Figure 9.10 Cylinder and head numbers.

*Track formats and operating conventions are patterned after the IBM 2314 Disk Storage Facility; see reference 3.

with the seek address for that track; cylinder and head numbers are depicted in Figure 9.10. Two channel commands, read home address and write home address, are available for transferring information between the home address area and main storage. The home address area is 9 bytes in length and depicted in Figure 9.11. The first byte of the home

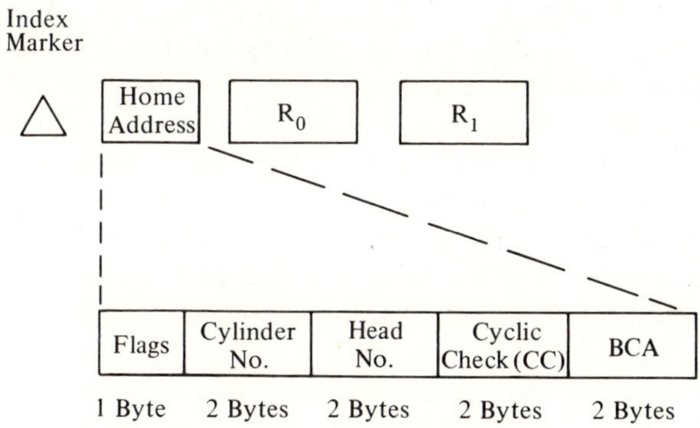

Figure 9.11 Home address.

address contains flag bits that are automatically propagated to each record on the track; the bits are defined as follows:

Flag Byte Bit	*Meaning*
0	Zero
1	Zero
2	Zero
3	Zero
4	Zero
5	Zero
6	Track condition: 0—operative track 1—defective track
7	Track use: 0—primary track 1—alternate track

The use of the track condition and track use bits is described under *Programming and Operating Procedures.* Cylinder and head numbers denote the track position and the cyclic check and BCA (bit count appendage) provide means of data checking.

The first record that follows the home address is the track descriptor record (R_0). The format of the R_0 record adheres to the count-key-data concept used with all disk records. The R_0 record is used by IBM programming systems to denote the location of an alternate track. When a disk volume is initialized,* defective tracks are flagged in the home ad-

*Disk pack initialization involves writing home addresses and the R_0 record on each track.

dress area and an alternate track is assigned. The location of the alternate track is recorded in the cylinder and head fields of the R_0 count area. Several tracks are reserved on each surface as alternate tracks. The R_0 record is read and written with special channel commands and is preceded by a distinctive gap—one without an address marker that is used to denote that a data record follows. The record number of an R_0 record is zero and the key length (KL) is normally zero, as well. With IBM programming systems, the data length (DL) is set to eight so that an R_0 record cannot be used as an end of data (EOD) indicator. IBM programming systems use the data area (block) of an R_0 record to record the identifier (i.e., the record number) of the last data record on the track and the number of bytes still available for writing records.

One or more data records normally follow the track descriptor record (R_0). All data records must adhere to the count-key-data format and vary in specific content depending upon the needs of a particular application. A data record is preceded with a special gap containing *address marker* bytes—used to denote the beginning of a data record.

The end of a logical file is denoted by a data record with a data length of zero. The disk control unit normally sends a unit exception status to the CPU when an end-of-file record is written or read.

9.3 PROGRAMMING AND OPERATING CONCEPTS

Data stored on direct-access devices can be accessed sequentially or directly, depending upon the IO system and the needs of a particular application. The disk IO operations are generally the same in either case and the IO program controls the manner in which they are used.

Basic Concepts

Input/output programming was introduced in Chapter 4 and applies to disk programming as well as to other devices. IO operations are initiated with a start IO instruction in the CPU and are controlled by a channel program that is executed in an IO channel. Device addressing is also the same. The essential difference between disk programming and the programming of other IO devices is in the manner that the read, write, control, and sense commands are used.

Command chaining was introduced as a means of executing successive channel command words (CCWs) under control of an IO channel, without intervention by the CPU. In IO programming for tape or card equipment, command chaining is the exception and is used only under special circumstances. In disk IO programming, practically every series of IO operations uses command chaining.

The basic principle behind disk utilization is that information must be located before it can be referenced. With serial equipment, IO operations apply to the current state of the IO device or to the next physical record. With disk equipment, the read-write heads must first be positioned.

Disk Programming Fundamentals

Disk programming involves well-defined steps that are summarized as follows:

1. *Set the file mask.* This control command sets a mask in the control unit and prevents commands from being executed that should not access the specified file area.
2. *Locate the proper disk area.* This function is performed with the seek control commands. A specific cylinder, head within a cylinder, or a cylinder and head may be specified.
3. *Find the desired record.* This function is performed with the search command that searches for a particular record number in the count area of a data record.
4. *Perform the required operation.* Either a read or write operation is usually executed after the desired record is found.

Usually, the information on a track is recorded so that enough time exists for a record to be located and then read or written in the same revolution.

Not all IO operations require all of the preceding steps. For example, a channel program to write or read a home address would not require a search operation.

Most disk commands require data from main storage. For example, a seek command requires information on the cylinder and head numbers that must be located. Similarly, a search command requires a record number to match the record number found in the count area of a data record. This information is provided through the data address and count fields in the CCW.

Even in a System/370 environment, disk devices respond differently to some commands and provide different sense information under varying circumstances. Nevertheless, a representative set of disk commands are given in the following list (They are provided with the IBM 2314 series devices):

Write Commands	*Search Commands*
Write data.	Search equal ID.
Write key, data.	Search equal key.
Write count, key, data.	Search equal home address.
Write home address.	Search hi ID.
Write record zero.	Search hi key.
Write special CKD.	Search hi equal ID.
Erase.	Search hi equal key.

Control Commands	*Read Commands*
Control seek (BBCCHH).	Read data.
Control recalibrate.	Read key, data.
Control restore.	Read count, key, data.
Control no op.	Read home address.
Control cylinder seek (CCHH).	Read record zero.
Control head seek (HH).	Read count.
Control set file mask.	Read IPL.

A precise description of each command is beyond the scope of this chapter. However, some typical channel programs are appropriate.

The first example involves updating a record from a file organized by ID (record number) with no key access. The cylinder, head, and record numbers are calculated (or retrieved from a table) and the following channel program is used:

Command	*Function*
Seek	Locate cylinder and head.
Search ID equal	Search for record number; if found skip next CCW.
TIC *-8	Transfer in channel to preceding CCW.
Write data	Write data and terminate channel program.

The next example involves reading a record from a file organized by key. Again, the cylinder and head are calculated (or retrieved from a table) and the following channel program is used:

Command	*Function*
Seek	Locate cylinder and head.
Search key equal	Search for matching key area. If found, skip next CCW.
TIC *-8	Transfer in channel to preceding CCW.
Read data	Read data and terminate.

Unusual conditions (such as when a record is not found) are recorded in the CSW (channel status word) that is stored with an IO interrupt. Other detailed information is available from appropriate reference manuals.

Multiple Track Operation and Record Overflow

Most modern disk devices have the capability to select the next head (numbered sequentially) in a cylinder when requested by a particular bit setting.* This facility allows an entire cylinder to be searched for a particular key or record number before a no-record-found indication is generated.

Record overflow allows a data record to exceed the capacity of a track, and the size of a cylinder becomes the limiting factor in the length of a

*Usually, a multiple track operation is specified by bit zero of the operation code in the CCW.

record. Overflow records are formatted differently from standard records and use the "write special CKD" CCW. Another method of storing records that exceed the size of a track is to use *spanned records* (see Chapter 2).

IO Channel Utilization

Ordinarily, a non-data channel command frees channel facilities after the command is accepted by the control unit. However, when a channel program containing a control command is command chained, then the channel is busy during the entire time the channel program is in operation—regardless if data transfer is occurring or not.

In the past, two channel programs were required for each record read or written so that different seek operations could be overlapped on the same channel. The first channel program is a standalone seek that frees the channel as soon as the seek is accepted. After the seek is completed, a search and read (or write) channel program is initiated to access the desired record.

Rotational position sensing together with block multiplexing (Chapter 4) eliminates the need for special channel programming procedures and frees the channel during non-data operations, even though they may be command chained.

Rotational position sensing (RPS) is available with two new disk facilities: the IBM 3330 and the IBM 2305. They are presented in Chapter 10.

RPS and multiple requesting are introduced in the next section of this chapter.

9.4 ROTATIONAL POSITION SENSING AND MULTIPLE REQUESTING

The purpose of rotational position sensing (RPS) and multiple requesting is to decrease the amount of time that the channel is busy with non-data operations. Not only are rotational delays overlapped but seeks and subsequent reads can be initiated sooner. The two facilities operate in conjunction with block multiplexing and are designed to support each other in a complex operating environment.

Rotational Position Sensing

Rotational position sensing reduces the time that the channel spends searching for a disk record. Without rotational position sensing, a search operation is executed as follows:

1. A number of bytes (the search argument) is transferred from main storage to the control unit via the IO channel. Thus, the channel operates as though a write operation were taking place.

2. A number of bytes is read from the disk into the control unit; the disk operates as though a read were being executed.
3. The arguments are compared in the control unit to determine if the search condition is met.

It follows that the IO channel is busy during the entire search operation and part of this time can be eliminated by initiating the search just before the desired record is to come under the read-write heads. Toward this end, disk tracks are divided into equally spaced sectors so that each record has a sector location as well as a record address. The sector concept is implemented through a timing mechanism and the sectors are not physically indicated on the disk tracks. A *sector* is defined as the length of the track that passes under the read-write heads in one sector time. For the 3330, a sector time is defined as 130 microseconds so that a single track contains 128 sectors. Similarly, a 2305 Model 1 track contains 90 sectors and a 2305 Model 2 track contains 180 sectors.

Two new disk commands are provided for use with rotational position sensing: SET SECTOR and READ SECTOR. When the sector number of a particular record is known, the SET SECTOR command orders the control unit to look for the specified sector and allows it to disconnect (with a channel end) from the block multiplexer channel. When the desired angular position is reached, the control unit signals (with a device end) that it is ready to reconnect. If the channel is free, the control unit is connected to the block multiplexer channel and execution of the channel program is resumed. If the channel is busy, the reconnection is attempted on subsequent revolutions. The READ SECTOR command provides the sector number required to access the record processed by the previous channel command word (CCW); usually, that sector number is used with a subsequent SET SECTOR command. The read sector command can be command chained from a read, write, or search command. A sector number can also be calculated if the necessary parameters are available. Thus, a simple channel program to read a disk record, when the sector number is known, would look somewhat as follows:

Command	*Comment*
Seek	Channel is free during arm motion.
Set sector	Channel is free until sector is found.
Search ID	Channel is busy.
TIC *-8	Usually, TIC is not executed since first ID inspected is the desired record.
Read data	Channel is busy.

Rotational position sensing also applies to the 2305 Fixed Head Storage Module even though multiple read-write heads are used.

Multiple Requesting

Multiple requesting is a control unit/device function that permits multiple command sequences to be active in a single storage facility. With the 3330, multiple requesting applies to the entire facility (several disk modules) and up to eight concurrent command sequences are monitored by the control unit. With the 2305, up to eight set sector commands can be issued to a single device (i.e., module). The control unit constantly monitors angular position counters, in the 2305, and presents a device end status to the channel when the counter is equal to one of the stored set sector arguments.

9.5 SUMMARY

Direct-access devices provide a means of accessing data directly without requiring that preceding data be passed over. The most widely used direct-access device is disk storage, which has three major components: recording surfaces, access arms and read-write heads, and a disk mechanism. Recording surfaces are composed of tracks upon which data are recorded serially by bit. A disk volume is composed of a stack of disks mounted on a vertical shaft. Each vertical position of the access mechanism provides access to a cylinder of data without movement of the mechanism. All surfaces contain the same number of tracks and a specific track is located by cylinder and head numbers. Records on a track are also numbered so that a particular data record is located by its cylinder, head, and record numbers.

Track and data formats support disk utilization by including identification and control information on each track and by providing a data record format that includes three areas; count, key, and data. Data can be accessed by record number (contained in the count area) or by key.

Disk storage programming utilizes the concept of command chaining in a channel program and involves locating a specific track, finding the desired record, and performing the requested IO operation.

Disk storage programming is facilitated by effective programming systems.

REFERENCES

1. Flores, I., "Data Structure and Management," Prentice-Hall, Inc., Englewood Cliffs, N.J., 1970.
2. "Introduction to IBM System/360 Direct Access Storage Devices and Organization Methods," Form C20-1649, IBM Corporation, Endicott, N.Y., 1969.
3. IBM System/360 Component Descriptions, "2314 Direct Access Storage Facility and 2844 Auxiliary Storage Control," Form A26-3599, IBM Corporation, San Jose, California, 1969.

4. IBM System/360 Component Descriptions, "2841 and Associated DASD," Form GA26-5988, IBM Corporation, San Jose, California, 1969.
5. IBM System/370 publications: "Guide to the IBM System/370 Model 145," Form GC20-1734; "Guide to the IBM System/370 Model 155," Form GC20-1729; "Guide to the IBM System/370 Model 165," Form GC20-1730. IBM Corporation, Data Processing Division, White Plains, N.Y., 1970.

10 INPUT/OUTPUT DEVICES

10.1 INTRODUCTION

System/370 input/output devices are classified into nine categories:

Direct-access devices
Display devices
Magnetic ink devices
Magnetic tape devices
Manual controls
Optical readers
Printers
Punched card devices
Punched tape devices

Most devices in these categories are not new to the System/370 and are available for its predecessor, the System/360. Three devices are of particular interest since they represent state-of-the-art advances in computer technology.

The IBM 3330 Disk Storage Facility is a modular high-performance mass storage facility that uses removable disk packs. The 3330 has a data rate of 806,000 bytes per second and a maximum capacity of 800,000,000 bytes.

The IBM 2305 Fixed Head Storage Module combines the advantages of disk and drum storage. The storage medium is magnetic disk using either one or two fixed heads per track. The device has a maximum capacity of

10.8 megabytes at a data rate of 3 megabytes per second and a maximum capacity of 22.4 megabytes at a data rate of 1.5 megabytes per second.

The IBM 3211 Printer prints lines at 2000 lines per minute and uses a program-controlled carriage. The use of a program-controlled carriage instead of a paper tape-controlled carriage is designed to reduce the amount of operator intervention.

10.2 3330 DISK STORAGE FACILITY

The IBM 3330 Disk Storage Facility (Figure 10.1) is composed of from one to four 3330 Disk Storage units and the 3830 Storage Control. Each

Figure 10.1 IBM 3330 Disk Storage Facility. (Courtesy of International Business Machines Corporation.)

3330 disk storage unit contains two independent modules, each using the IBM 3336 Disk Pack (Figure 10.2) with a capacity of 100,000,000 bytes. The 3330 utilizes moving access arms and read-write heads.

Figure 10.2 IBM 3336 removable disk pack. (Courtesy of International Business Machines Corporation.)

Features

A 3330 Disk Storage Facility must be attached to a block multiplexer channel and provides the following features discussed earlier:

rotational position sensing,
multiple requestings,
command retry,
overflow records,
multitrack operation,
error correction capability, and
a two-channel switch.

The *two-channel switch* allows the 3830 control unit to be attached to two different IO channels.

Specifications

Design specifications for the 3330 Disk Storage Facility are listed in this section. Track capacities assume full track records and utilize self-formatting records as introduced in Chapter 9.

Hardware Characteristics
Capacity:
2 drives—200,036,000 bytes
4 drives—400,073,000 bytes
6 drives—600,109,000 bytes
8 drives—800,146,000 bytes
Access time:
maximum—55 milliseconds
average—30 milliseconds
cylinder-to-cylinder—10 milliseconds
Rotation speed—3600 RPM
Rotation time—16.7 milliseconds
Data rate—806 kilobytes per second

Storage Characteristics
Disks per pack—12
Recording disks—10
Recording surfaces—19
Cylinders—404 plus 7 alternates
Tracks per cylinder—19
Tracks per pack—7,676
Track capacity—13,030 bytes
Cylinder capacity—247,570

Commands

The 3330 provides a complete set of channel commands. The facility has a unique device address defined as follows:

Address Byte	*Function*
Bits 0–4	Storage control unit
Bits 5–7	Drive number (0–7 are valid)

The 3330 channel commands support System/370 architecture with regard to sense data and operational characteristics. The following commands are provided:

Sense

Sense IO
Read-and-reset-buffer-log

Control

No operation
Seek
Seek cylinder
Seek head
Recalibrate
Restore
Set file mask
Space count
Set sector

Search

Search identifier equal
Search key equal
Search home address equal
Search identifier high
Search key high
Search identifier equal or high
Search key equal or high

Read

Read data
Read key and data
Read count, key, and data
Read home address
Read record zero (R_0)
Read count
Read initial program load
Read sector

Write

Write home address
Write record zero (R_0)
Write count, key, and data
Write special count, key, and data
Write data
Write key and data
Erase

Data Checking

The cyclic check provided with earlier disk storage units is replaced by error checking and correction (ECC) code in the 3330. The use of ECC code by the 3830 control unit allows the correction of single-bit errors in the data area of a record. Information on the nature of errors corrected is provided with the sense command.

10.3 2305 FIXED HEAD STORAGE

The IBM 2305 Fixed Head Storage Model 1 or 2 (Figure 9.3) is composed of one or two 2305 Storage Modules and the 2835 Storage Control

Figure 10.3 IBM 2305 Fixed Head Storage and 2855 Storage Control. (Courtesy of International Business Machines Corporation.)

unit. The 2305 uses nonremovable magnetic disks, as the storage medium, and fixed-position read-write heads. The 2305 must be attached to a block multiplexer channel.

Each storage volume contains 6 recording disks and 12 recording surfaces. Alternate tracks are hardwired and are accessed automatically by the hardware. However, one spare track is available for assignment, dynamically, during computer processing.

Information is recorded serially by bit, and tracks are formatted in the same manner as with other direct-access devices. Home addresses are not needed and are not used. The 2505 Model 1 also requires two R_0 records, as described later.

The Model 2 is presented first since it provides introductory information for the Model 1.

2305 Model 2

The IBM 2305 Model 1 is available with one disk module or two disk modules. Each Model 1 module has the following characteristics:

Characteristics

Tracks per surface—64 plus 8 spare
Tracks per module—768 plus 96 spare
Bytes per track—14,660 (R_0 plus 1 data record)
Bytes per module—11,258,880
Rotation time—10 milliseconds
Access time:
  maximum—10.25 milliseconds
  average—5.0 milliseconds
Data rate—1.5 megabytes per second
Number of read-write elements per module—768 plus 96 spare

The Model 2 is depicted in Figure 10.4. Four access mechanisms are positioned around each surface. Each access mechanism contains two groups of nine recording elements (read-write heads) that access eight addressable tracks plus one spare. The spare tracks are interspersed among the 72 tracks on each surface so that every ninth track is a spare. The four access mechanisms are positioned so that each accesses one-fourth of the tracks on that surface. A Model 2 recording track contains 180 sectors for rotational position sensing (RPS). When RPS is used, channel search time with the Model 2 is reduced to between 114 and 198 microseconds.

2305 Model 1

The IBM 2305 Model 1 uses a unique design philosophy for increasing the data rate and reducing the average access time. The physical hardware is the same as for the Model 2 and the 2305 disk drive is available with either one or two storage modules.

To increase the effective data rate, a single data record is recorded on two surfaces of a 2305 disk. The odd bytes of that record are recorded on the top side of a disk and the even bytes are recorded on the bottom side of the same disk. The top and bottom track segments are recorded and read in parallel—thus doubling the effective data rate. Data are recorded on a 180 degree arc of a track; thus, one full track of data is recorded or read in one-half of a disk revolution. The read-write elements are paired so that there are 36 paired elements per disk (i.e., two surfaces) for each of two access arms—180 degrees apart. As depicted in Figure

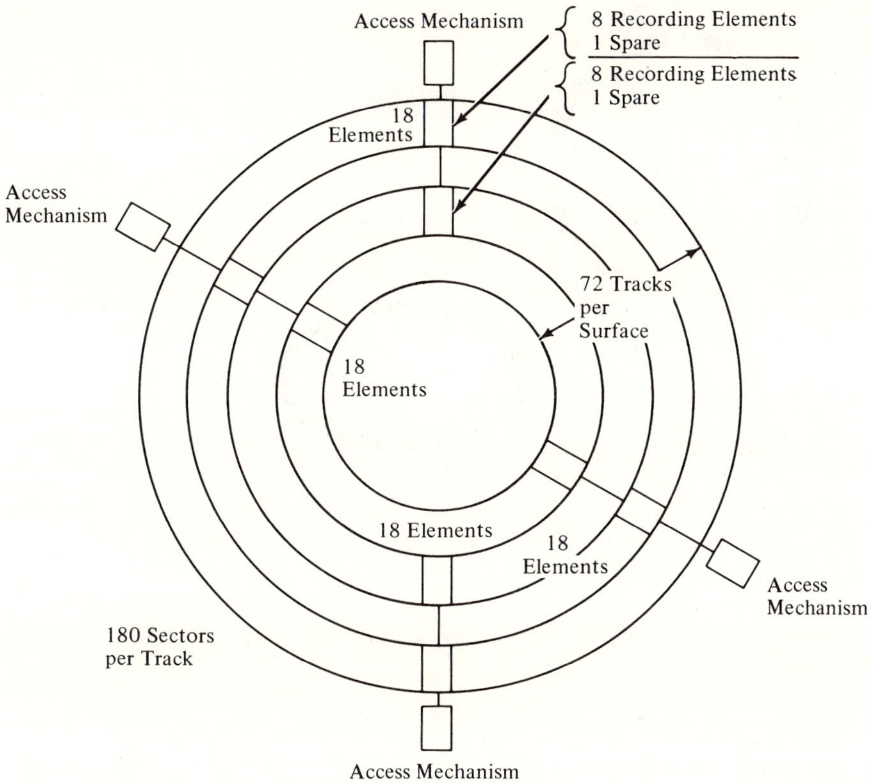

64 recording tracks/surface x 12 = 768 recording tracks/module
8 spare tracks/surface x 12 = 96 spare tracks/module
216 recording elements (read/write heads)/access mechanism x 4 = 864 recording elements

Figure 10.4 2305 Model 2 disk surface. (Courtesy of International Business Machines Corporation.)

10.5, all odd track addresses occupy the same half of the disk module and all even addresses occupy the other half.

The split track organization of the Model 1 design requires that two R_0 records are recorded on each track so that storage capacity is less than one-half of a Model 2. Other characteristics are given as follows:

Characteristic

Tracks per disk—64 plus 8 spare
Tracks per module—384 plus 48 spare
Bytes per track—14,136 (R_0 plus 1 data record)

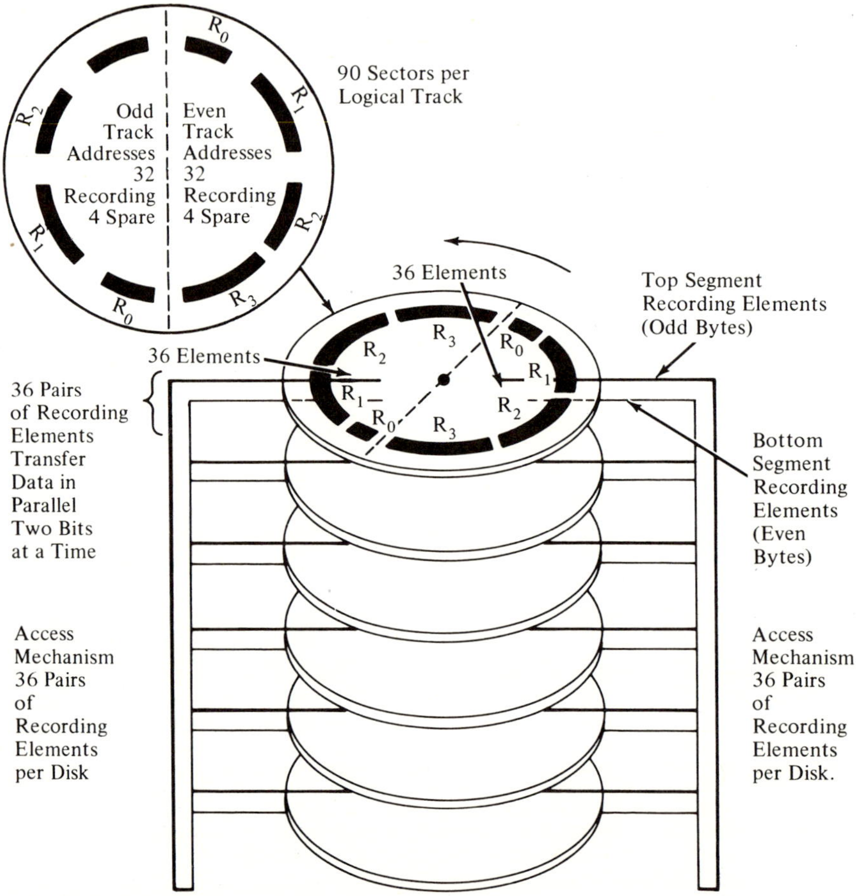

64 recording tracks/disk x 6 = 384 recording tracks/module
8 spare tracks/disk x 6 = 48 spare tracks/module
216 pairs of recording elements (read/write heads)/access mechanism

Figure 10.5 2305 Model 1 module. (Courtesy of International Business Machines Corporation.)

Bytes per module—5,428,224
Rotation time—10 milliseconds
Access time:
  maximum—5.1 milliseconds
  average—2.5 milliseconds
Data rate—3.0 megabytes per second
Number of read-write elements per track—2

Since a track of data is recorded on an 180 degree arc of a Model 1 disk, the number of sectors for rotational position sensing is halved to 90. With RPS, channel search time remains the same as with the Model 2.

Features

Both models of the 2305 provide the following direct-access features:

multiple track operation,
overflow records,
rotational position sensing,
multiple requesting,
command retry,
error correction, and
a two-channel switch.

The *two-channel switch* allows the 2835 storage control unit to be attached to two IO channels, connected to the same or different CPUs.

Commands

The IO unit address for the 2305 is determined as follows:

Address byte	*Function*
Bits 0–3	Control unit number (wired at installation)
Bits 4–7	Module number (may be 0 or 8)

In support of multiple requesting, devices 0–7 cause module 0 to be selected and devices 8–15 cause module 8 to be selected.

A seek address of 6 bytes must be used to select a particular track. The first 3 bytes and the fifth must be zero. Bytes 4 and 6 must contain binary numbers that denote the pseudo-cylinder and head, respectively. Any number between 0 and 47 (Model 1) or 0 and 95 (Model 2) is a valid cylinder address. Any number between 0 and 7 is a valid head address.

The following channel commands are provided:

Sense

Sense IO
Read buffered log

Control

No operation
Seek
Seek head
Seek cylinder
Recalibrate
Restore
Set file mask
Set sector

Search

Search home address equal
Search identifier-equal
Search identifier-high
Search identifier-equal or high
Search key equal
Search key high
Search key equal or high

Read

Read data
Read key and data
Read count, key, and data
Read home address
Read record zero (R_0)
Read count
Read initial program load (IPL)
Read sector

Write

Write home address
Write record zero (R_0)
Write count, key, and data
Write special count, key, and data
Write data
Write key and data
Erase

Several commands do not perform any operation in the 2305 facility and are maintained for compatibility with other direct-access storage devices.

Data Checking

The 2-byte cyclic check code provided with earlier disk storage units is replaced with new error correction code in the 2305. The Model 1 has 16 correction code bytes appended to each data area of a self-formatting record and the Model 2 appends 10 correction code bytes. The correction codes are used by the 2835 control unit for error correction and detection.

10.4 3211 PRINTER

The IBM 3211 Printer and 3811 Control Unit are depicted in Figure 10.6. The line printer operates at 2000 lines per minute with a 48-character set and incorporates the following features: interchangeable train cartridge, universal character set, program-controlled carriage, power stacker, automatic forms thickness control, and a motorized cover. The program-controlled carriage is of interest here.

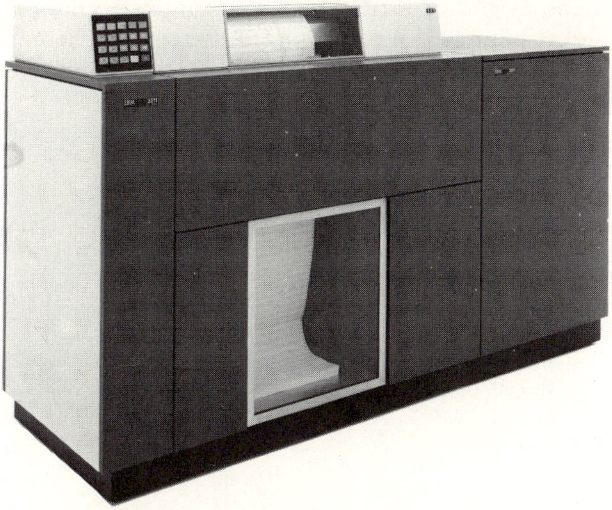

Figure 10.6 IBM 3211 Printer and 3811 Control Unit. (Courtesy of International Business Machines Corporation.)

Program-Controlled Carriage

The 3811 contains a forms control buffer (FCB) used in conjunction with write and control commands (CCWs) to control the position of the printer carriage. The FCB contain 180 positions,* each coordinates with a position on the printed page. For example, buffer position 1 corresponds to the first line of a printed page and buffer position 34 corresponds to the 34th line of the same page. Each buffer position holds one byte (or two hexadecimal digits).

The carriage is controlled by a *carriage control register* that is used to address the forms control buffer. When the value in the carriage control register is incremented by one, the carriage is spaced one line so that a correct line position is maintained with respect to the form. A CCW that specifies a channel number† along with a write or as a control command causes the carriage control register to be incremented until the indicated channel number is found in one of the buffer positions. In this way, the programmer can order the printer to space to a given position on the page. The bits in a buffer position are numbered 0–7. Bits 4–7 specify channel

*Thus, the maximum forms size is 22.5 inches (in length) at 8 lines per inch and 30 inches at 6 lines per inch.

†Earlier printers utilized a carriage control tape wherein a hole punched in a given channel (longitudinal row) and at a specific position on the tape allowed the carriage to space to that position. The same functional capability is achieved in the 3211 printer by placing a channel number (two hex digits) in a given position in the forms control buffer (FCB).

codes; bit 3 denotes end of form; and bit 0 denotes 8 lines per inch spacing, if set, and 6 lines per inch spacing, otherwise. The end-of-form is specified as a hexadecimal 10 and resets the carriage control register. The channel codes are given in Table 10.1.

TABLE 10.1 3211 FCB CHANNEL CODES

Binary Position 0 1 2 3 4 5 6 7	*Hex*	*Channel*
0 0 0 0 0 0 0 0	00	Space (null)
0 0 0 0 0 0 0 1	01	Channel 1
0 0 0 0 0 0 1 0	02	Channel 2
0 0 0 0 0 0 1 1	03	Channel 3
0 0 0 0 0 1 0 0	04	Channel 4
0 0 0 0 0 1 0 1	05	Channel 5
0 0 0 0 0 1 1 0	06	Channel 6
0 0 0 0 0 1 1 1	07	Channel 7
0 0 0 0 1 0 0 0	08	Channel 8
0 0 0 0 1 0 0 1	09	Channel 9
0 0 0 0 1 0 1 0	0A	Channel 10
0 0 0 0 1 0 1 1	0B	Channel 11
0 0 0 0 1 1 0 0	0C	Channel 12

Programming

The carriage control mechanism is activated by a write or control CCW, executed in an IO channel, and sent to the attached 3811 control unit. The write and control commands, provided by the 3211 Printer and 3811 Control Unit, are given in the following lists:

Write Commands	*Control Commands*
Write without spacing	Space 1 immediate
Write and space 1	2
Write and space 2	3
Write and space 3	Skip immediate to channel 0
Write and skip to channel 1	Skip immediate to channel 1
Write and skip to channel 2	Skip immediate to channel 2
Write and skip to channel 3	Skip immediate to channel 3
Write and skip to channel 4	Skip immediate to channel 4
Write and skip to channel 5	Skip immediate to channel 5
Write and skip to channel 6	Skip immediate to channel 6
Write and skip to channel 7	Skip immediate to channel 7
Write and skip to channel 8	Skip immediate to channel 8
Write and skip to channel 9	Skip immediate to channel 9
Write and skip to channel 10	Skip immediate to channel 10
Write and skip to channel 11	Skip immediate to channel 11
Write and skip to channel 12	Skip immediate to channel 12

Detailed programming procedures are supplied in appropriate reference manuals.

Loading the FCB

The most significant aspect of the forms control buffer (FCB) is that it can be loaded under program control. The CCW command code byte of the *load FCB* command is a hexadecimal 63. The data address field of the CCW specifies the main storage location of a FCB image; the count field specifies the number of lines in the printed form. The last FCB position used must contain the end-of-form flag byte.

The program-controlled carriage feature of the 3211 Printer replaces the *carriage control tape* used with earlier line printers. The feature provides more effective utilization of the printer's facilities by reducing operator intervention.

REFERENCES

1. IBM Component Summaries: "3830 Storage Control and 3330 Disk Storage," Form GA26-1592; "2835 Storage Control and 2305 Fixed Head Storage," Form GA26-1589; "3211 Printer and 3811 Control Unit," Form GA24-3543. IBM Corporation, Data Processing Division, White Plains, N.Y., 1970.
2. "A Guide to the IBM System/370 Model 165," Form GC20-1730, IBM Corporation, White Plains, N.Y., 1970.

APPENDICES

APPENDIX A
MICROPROGRAMMING, EMULATION, AND COMPATIBILITY

A.1 INTRODUCTION

A computer can be viewed as being composed of two kinds of circuits: data flow circuits and control circuits. Data flow circuits include the wires and storage elements through which flow the electrical pulses that represent data. Ordinarily, data flow circuits include a great many branches and paths and data are transformed as they pass through arithmetic and logical components. Control circuits interpret computer instructions and establish appropriate data paths among the maze of data flow circuits. The design of the computer, as seen by the programmer, is reflected in both data flow and control circuits. In conventional computers, both kinds of circuits are implemented as hardwired components, so that the architecture of the computer is established when the hardware components are assembled.

The Concept of Microprogramming

Professor M. V. Wilkes of the Cambridge University Mathematical Laboratory recognized in the early 1950s[1] that the control circuits operate as a series of discrete steps, much like an ordinary computer program, and proposed a concept termed *microprogramming* whereby the control unit of a computer could be programmed to use the other components in the system in a prescribed fashion. The concept was indeed revolutionary but not practical on a large-scale basis until the mid-1960s when read-only storage (ROS) became available for widespread use.* Originally, the utilization of a microprogram involves placing that microprogram in a form of ROS for use by the control unit of the computer. A loaded ROS, usually

*See reference 2.

provided by the computer manufacturer, is not accessible to a computer program and is usually fixed for a given ROS unit. A more recent development known as *writable control storage* permits a microprogram to be loaded from the computer console or from main storage by using a computer instruction. Read-only storage (ROS) and writable control storage (WCS) are referred to as *control storage*—obviously implying storage used by the control circuits of the computer. Computers that operate under microprogram control frequently use a combination of ROS and WCS.

The term microprogramming implies a program composed of microinstructions. In general, a microinstruction is a primitive hardware-oriented function such as one of the following:

1. Moving a word of data from the storage buffer register to the accumulator.
2. Clearing the adders.
3. Increasing the instruction address register by a fixed value (such as one).
4. Moving the contents of the adders to the accumulator.

Each function performed by the control unit requires a microprogram composed of microinstructions such as those given above. It follows that the execution of a single computer machine language instruction would involve several control unit functions. For example, a simple *ADD* instruction would require a microprogram routine for fetching the instruction from main storage and for performing miscellaneous housekeeping chores; the execution of that operation by the arithmetic and logical units also would be controlled by a similar routine.

Benefits of Microprogramming

The use of the microprogramming concept in the design and construction of computers has several distinct advantages and disadvantages. Husson[3] lists the advantages from the manufacturer's point of view as: (1) flexibility and tailorability; (2) changeability; (3) ease of designing, maintaining, and checking; (4) uniformity of design; (5) ease of education; (6) useful life of the system; and (7) economy. He also gives the disadvantages as: (1) operational loss of efficiency; (2) performance loss; and (3) cost.

For the user, the major benefits of microprogramming are twofold:

1. More than one model of computer per instruction set.
2. More than one instruction set per computer.

In the first case, it is feasible to develop a series of computers, differing in computing power, but with the same instruction set. Thus, the instruction set is independent of the engineering design of the computer. The user is provided a growth path, therefore, without reprogramming, and programs may be exchanged among a wide range of models. The second benefit facilitates conversion by allowing programs from earlier computers to be run without modification. The process, termed *emulation*, combines hardware and software features and new instructions (implemented in microcode) to facilitate the emulation process. One of two approaches to emulation is usually taken:

1. Use a macroprogram-assisted (i.e., machine language) microprogram.
2. Use a microprogram-assisted macroprogram.

When no macroprogram is required in the first approach, it is referred to as *compatibility mode.* The second approach is more closely akin to the software simulation of another computer. Both approaches are considered again later.

A.2 THE NATURE OF MICROPROGRAMMING

Microprogramming is indeed a complex process intended to be performed by one with expertise in both programming and basic hardware functions. This section is not intended as a definitive treatment of the subject but rather as a general introduction to the nature of microprogramming. The material is patterned after similar introductions contained in Rosin[2] and Husson[3]—both included for the same purpose. A hypothetical machine is given first, microspec functions are considered next, and some simple microprograms are presented last.

A Hypothetical Machine

A hypothetical machine is depicted in Figure A.1. It is intended to represent a simplified one-address computer with storage organized on a word basis. A single

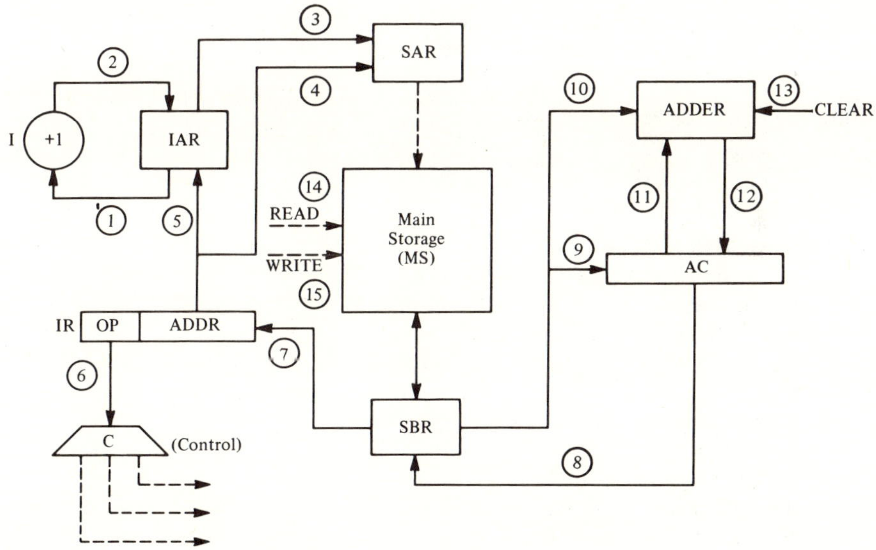

Figure A.1 A hypothetical machine.

accumulator is available for arithmetic operations. The functional components are listed as follows:

Instruction address register (IAR)—holds address of the next instruction to be executed.

Storage address register (SAR)—holds storage address for use by main storage read or write functions.

Incrementor (I)—used to increment the IAR by 1.

Adder—performs addition.
Instruction register (IR)—holds instruction during decoding.
Accumulator (AC)—holds results during computation.
Storage buffer register (SBR)—holds data during main storage read or write function.
Main storage (MS)—organized on a word basis.
Control (C)—causes a microprogram branch to a specified microprogram.

The control, incrementor, and adder components are of particular interest. Supplying control with an operation code or a microprogram address causes a microprogram branch to an appropriate microprogrammed routine. The control component is either hardwired or implemented through a transfer table held in control storage. The process of moving information from a source to either the incrementor or the adder causes the respective function to be executed. For example, the microspec function AC→ADDER (see the next section) causes the contents of the accumulator to be added to the adder component.

Microspec Functions

A *microspec function* is defined as a logical entity in the data flow of a system that performs a specific operation in one or more machine cycles.* The microspec functions of interest here are listed in Table A.1 and are denoted in Figure A.1 by

TABLE A.1 MICROSPEC FUNCTIONS

1	IAR→I
2	I→IAR
3	IAR→SAR
4	IR(ADDR)→SAR
5	IR(ADDR)→IAR
6	IR(OP)→C
7	SBR→IR
8	AC→SBR
9	SBR→AC
10	SBR→ADDER
11	AC→ADDER
12	ADDER→AC
13	0→ADDER
14	READ (MS(SAR)→SBR)
15	WRITE (SBR→MS(SAR))
16	(Unconditional branch)→C

numbers enclosed in small circles. Most microspec functions serve to move information within the machine. For example, the function IAR→SAR specifies a movement of information from the instruction address register (IAR) to the storage address register (SAR).

*Quoted from Husson,[3] page 4.

The read and write functions* permit main storage to be referenced. Both functions use the storage address register (SAR) and the storage buffer register (SBR). The read function causes the contents of the main storage location specified by the address in the SAR to be moved to the SBR. The write function causes the contents of the SBR to be moved to the location in main storage specified by the address in the SAR.

Microprogrammed Operations

This section presents some microprogrammed routines for use with the hypothetical machine given above. Collectively, they could be considered an emulator for a sample second generation computer. The routines are listed in Table A.2 and

TABLE A.2 SAMPLE MICROPROGRAMS

FETCH	IAR→SAR
	READ(MS(SAR)→SBR)
	SBR→IR
	IAR→I
	I→IAR
	IR(OP)→C
LOAD	IR(ADDR)→SAR
(Accumulator)	READ(MS(SAR)→SBR)
	SBR→AC
	(FETCH)→C
ADD	IR(ADDR)→SAR
(to Accumulator)	READ(MS(SAR)→SBR)
	0→ADDER
	AC→ADDER
	SBR→ADDER
	ADDER→AC
	(FETCH)→C
STORE	IR(ADDR)→SAR
(Accumulator)	AC→SBR
	WRITE(SBR→MS(SAR))
	(FETCH)→C

described in the following paragraph. The FETCH routine retrieves an instruction from main storage, moves it to the instruction register, increments the instruction address register (containing the current instruction address), and sends the operation code to the control component. Control will pass microprogram control to a microprogrammed routine to execute the operation specified by the operation code. The LOAD routine causes the contents of the main storage address specified in the instruction address field to be moved to the storage buffer register and then

*The read and write functions discussed here should not be confused with those used for input and output.

to the accumulator. Control is then passed to the control component to fetch and decode another machine language (macroprogram) instruction. The ADD routine clears the adder and then adds the contents of the accumulator and the contents of the main storage location specified in the instruction to it. The results are returned to the accumulator and control is passed to the control component, as in the LOAD routine. The STORE routine functions in a similar manner to the other routines and moves the contents of the accumulator to the specified locations in main storage.

Although the examples are unsophisticated and the hypothetical machine is lacking in many necessary functions, the reader can quickly grasp the "level" at which microprogramming is performed. It is also relatively easy to imagine how the System/370 instruction set can be incorporated into a family of computers, each with a different engineering design and differing in computing power. The emulation of one computer on another computer is similar in concept; the instruction set and hardware features of the emulated computer are programmed on the host computer using its microspec functions and hardware components.

A.3 CONVERSION

The main advantage of a compatible family of computers was mentioned previously—i.e., programs can be exchanged between members of the family without reprogramming, conversion, emulation, or simulation. In the event the source and target computers are not compatible by design, a well-defined hierarchy of methods for conversion exists. They are given by Husson[3] as: (1) reprogramming or recompiling; (2) code and data conversion; (3) simulation; (4) emulation; and (5) compatibility. *Reprogramming* is costly in terms of both programmer and computer time, but allows the user to take advantage of features of the target machine. *Recompiling* is a cost-effective alternative when programs are written in a standard programming language, such as FORTRAN or COBOL. *Code and data conversion* is the most infrequently used method of conversion and involves the development of a computer program to physically translate programs and data from the source to the target machine. Translation, in this case, is hampered by sequence and time-varying programs and by program segments that are not meaningful in the target computer. Simulation, emulation, and compatibility are of immediate concern here and are covered in more detail.

Simulation

Simulation involves the use of a computer program to interpret and execute the operations of the simulated computer. The simulated computer is mapped into the host computer and each operation is modeled as though it were being executed in real time.

In general, simulation requires two types of programs: a CPU simulator program and an input/output supervisor program. Although software simulator programs are relatively simple* to design and implement, they frequently operate too slowly to be used for a large volume of data processing.

*The simplicity of designing and implementing a simulator results from the fact that no hardware features are required.

Emulation

Emulation involves both hardware and software as introduced earlier. The instruction set of the host machine is augmented to recognize critical instructions and to implement registers, switches, and accumulators of the emulated computer. Special instructions are included to speed up software simulation and facilitate main storage and input/output mapping. Hardware interruptions and special conditions must also be incorporated into the host computer through microcode or specially designed hardware features. These hardware features are frequently a part of an optional emulation feature.*

The *operating environment* for emulation is also of concern since emulator microcode and emulator software programs imply a standalone machine. In most cases, a host machine can operate in normal mode or emulation mode—but cannot alternate between the two without operator intervention.† However, the System/370 operating systems and the System/370 compatibility features provide an operating concept known as *integrated emulation*, whereby emulation jobs can be intermixed with normal System/370 jobs in an input job stream.

Compatibility

The last method of conversion is known as *compatibility*, wherein 100% of the instructions of the emulated computer are microcoded in control storage of the host computer. Compatibility, in this sense, is rarely achieved‡ but provides good performance and ease of operation. Through the years, a *compatibility feature* has become known as a set of hardware facilities, microprograms, and emulator programs that allow a computer to be emulated on a host computer.

A.4 SYSTEM/370 COMPATIBILITY FEATURES

The System/370 provides compatibility features that facilitate conversion from earlier IBM computer systems. All compatibility features allow integrated emulation under control of an operating system. Integrated emulation has several distinct advantages:

1. System resources are better utilized since emulation jobs, which usually require only a portion of the system's hardware resources, can be multiprogrammed.
2. Standardized accounting is available and less operator intervention is required.
3. Operating system facilities can be utilized.
4. Emulator jobs can run concurrently in one or more partitions (or regions) of the operating system.
5. Device independence can be achieved for emulator-supported IO devices.

*Usually referred to as a compatibility feature.

†The IBM Disk Operating System (DOS) included a feature referred to as CS/30 and CS/40 whereby emulation jobs could operate under operating system control on the System/360 Models 30 and 40, respectively.

‡To the author's knowledge, the only compatibility feature to provide 100% compatibility in the IBM product line is the 1401/1460 compatibility feature for the IBM System/360 Model 30.

In general, the installation and use of an integrated emulator involves five related activities. They are listed here for reference:

1. Establishing minimum system requirements.
2. Determining auxiliary storage requirements.
3. Reformatting data files.
4. Generating an operating system that includes emulator routines.
5. Establishing operating and control procedures.

The installation of an emulator is usually considered to be a systems programming function. Detailed planning information is available from IBM reference manuals for each compatibility feature operating under the control of either of the operating systems.

The integrated emulators operate in conjunction with one of the System/370 operating systems. Job control language statements (i.e., control cards) are available for loading the emulator programs from the system residence device and for processing emulator control information. In all cases, emulator jobs can be intermixed with normal operating system jobs by using appropriate control information. The termination of an emulator job is processed as any other job. In addition, emulator job output tapes can be converted to run on the computer being emulated. Tape preprocessor and tape postprocessor programs can be run concurrently (multiprogrammed) with other operating programs.

Models 135, 145, and 155 Emulation

Two compatibility features are provided with the System/370 Models 135, 145, and 155:

1401/1440/1460 Compatibility Feature
1401/1440/1460, 14010/7010 Compatibility Feature

The appropriate feature is required for either of two emulator programs that operate under either DOS or OS control:

1401/1440/1460 Emulator Program
1410/7010 Emulator Program

OS emulator programs are relocatoable and are executed as any other OS job. DOS emulator programs can be used in a batch-only system or in the background and batched-foreground partitions of a system being multiprogrammed.

Also available for the Model 135, 145, and 155 is an OS/DOS compatibility feature that permits a DOS operating system to be run in an OS operating environment. The OS/DOS compatibility feature is considered in Appendix B, "System/370 Operating Systems."

Model 165 Emulation

Three mutually exclusive hardware compatibility features are provided with the System/370 Model 165:

7070/7074 Compatibility Feature
709/7090/7094/7094II Compatibility Feature
7080 Compatibility Feature

The appropriate feature is required for any of three emulator programs that operate under OS control:

7070/7074 Emulator Program
709/7090/7094/7094II Emulator Program
7080 Emulator Program

These OS emulator programs are relocatable and are executed as any other OS job. The minimum main storage requirement for any of the above emulator programs is 512K. If the 709/7090/7094/7094II and 7080 emulator programs are used in an OS/MVT environment, then 1024K of main storage is required. The minimum partition or region size for 7070/7074 emulation is 188K, for 709/7090/7094/7094II emulation is 374K, and for 7080 emulation is 232K. In general, storage requirements are dependent upon the configuration and main storage size of the emulated computer.

REFERENCES

1. Wilkes, M.V., "The growth of interest in microprogramming—a literature survey," *Computing Surveys*, **1,3,** 139–145, (Sept. 1969).
2. Rosin, R.F., "Contemporary concepts of microprogramming and emulation," *Computing Surveys*, **1,4,** 197–212, (Dec. 1969).
3. Husson, S., "Microprogramming: Principles and Practices," Prentice-Hall, Inc., Englewood Cliffs, N.J., 1970.
4. Tucker, S.G., "Microprogram Control for System/360," *IBM Systems Journal*, **6** (4)(1967).
5. IBM System/370 publications:
   "A Guide to the IBM System/370 Model 135," Form GC20-1738.
   "A Guide to the IBM System/370 Model 145," Form GC20-1734-0.
   "A Guide to the IBM System/370 Model 155," Form GC20-1729-0.
   "A Guide to the IBM System/370 Model 165," Form GC20-1730-0.
   "Emulating the IBM 1401, 1440, and 1460 on the IBM System/370 Models 145 and 155, using DOS/360," Form GC33-2004-0.
   "Emulating the IBM 1401, 1440, and 1460 on the IBM System/370 Models 145 and 155, using OS/360," Form GC27-6945-0.
   "Emulating the IBM 1410 and 7010 on the IBM System/370 Models 145 and 155, using DOS/360," Form GC33-2005-0.
   "Emulating the IBM 1410 and 7010 on the IBM System/370 Models 145 and 155, using OS/360," Form GC27-6946-0.
   "Emulating the IBM 7074 on the IBM System/370 Model 165 using OS/360," Form GC27-6948-0.
   "Emulating the IBM 7080 on the IBM System/370 Model 165 using OS/360," Form GC27-6952-0.
   "Emulating the IBM 709, 7090, 7094, 7094II on the IBM System/370 Model 165 using OS/360," Form GC27-6951-0.

IBM Corporation, Data Processing Division, White Plains, New York, 1970.

APPENDIX B
SYSTEM/370 OPERATING SYSTEMS

B.1 INTRODUCTION

An operating system was introduced earlier as a set of control programs designed to effectively utilize the resources of a computer system. An operating system also manages job scheduling and provides functions that facilitate programming. The IBM Corporation provides two operating systems that support the System/370:

Disk Operating System/360
Operating System/360

Disk Operating System/360 (DOS) is a low-entry operating system and requires at least 16K of main storage. Operating System/360 (OS) is a comprehensive operating system and requires at least 64K of main storage. This appendix is not intended as a definitive treatment of DOS or OS but rather as an informal presentation of their respective capabilities. It is included to support the earlier chapters by providing general information on the subject.

B.2 DISK OPERATING SYSTEM/360

System Structure

DOS/360* consists of a control program and processing programs as depicted in Figure B.1. The control program consists of supervisor, job control, and IPL routines. The *supervisor* manages the entire system by fielding interruptions, scheduling work for the system, performing IO operations, performing error recovery, loading programs for execution, and processing program terminations. *Job control* reads the user's control cards and assigns IO devices, establishes

*DOS/360 is frequently abbreviated as DOS.

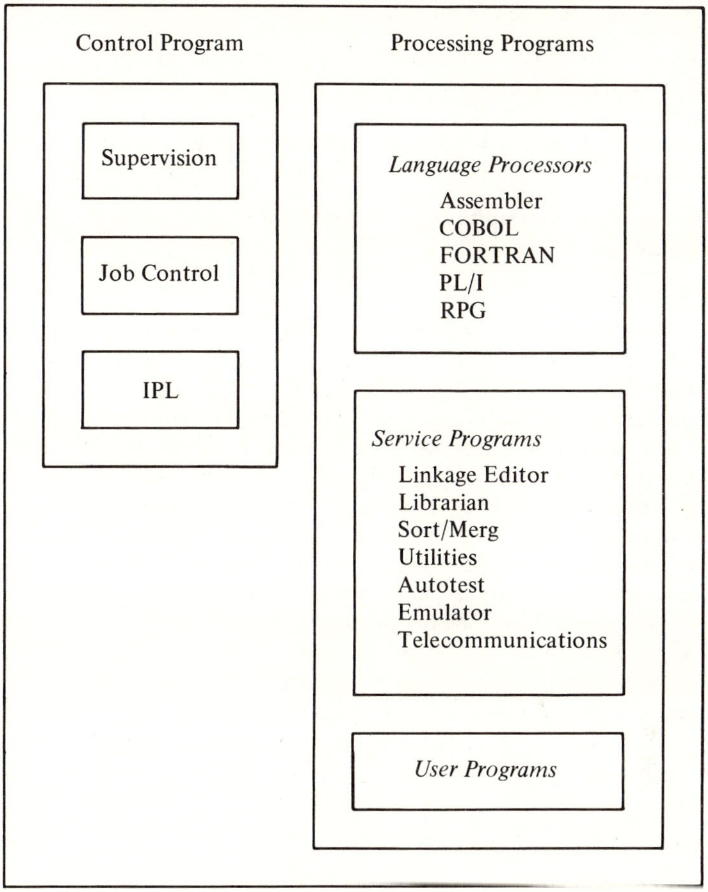

Figure B.1 DOS/360.

system options, and processes volume and file information. The *IPL* routines initialize the operation of the system.

Processing programs are classed into three general categories: language processors, service programs, and user-written problem programs. *Language processors* support Assembler, COBOL, FORTRAN, PL/I, and RPG languages. *Service programs* include a linkage editor (for combining object modules), a librarian (for core image, relocatable, source program, and private libraries), three sort/merge programs, utility programs, autotest (a debugging package), emulator programs, and a telecommunications package (BTAM and QTAM).

Multiprogramming

DOS/360 supports single-job and fixed-partition operating environments. In the latter case, the partitions are independent and are initiated asynchronously. Three types of partitions may be established:

Background—initiated by Job Control and operates at the lowest priority.
SPI Foreground—single program initiator mode initiated by the system operator.
BJF Foreground—batch job foreground mode initiated by Job Control or by the operator.

The three partitions are multiprogrammed using the following priority structure: SPI, BJF, and background.

Data Management

Data management facilities are referred to as IOCS (input/output control system) and include a Physical IOCS (PIOCS) and a Logical IOCS (LIOCS). PIOCS is part of the supervisor and includes facilities for scheduling and queuing IO operations, processing error conditions, and optimizing IO performance. LIOCS routines are part of a user's program and provide a logical interface between that program and PIOCS. LIOCS is designed to perform the following functions: initiating IO requests to PIOCS, opening and closing files, servicing end-of-file and end-of-volume conditions, processing label information, blocking and deblocking records, managing IO buffers, and controlling IO devices. LIOCS supports sequential file organization (for tape systems) and sequential, indexed sequential, and direct-access file organizations (for disk systems).

Job Control Language

Most computer jobs are composed of discrete steps that must be performed in a particular sequence. A typical series of steps might be the compiling of a program, linkage editing of the program to produce a program suitable for loading and

```
// JOB SAMPLE                )            )
// OPTION LINK               |            |
// EXEC PL/I                 } Job Step 1 |
   (PL/I Source Deck)        |            |
/*                           )            } Job
// EXEC LNKEDT               } Job Step 2 |
// EXEC                      )            |
   (Data)                    } Job Step 3 |
/*                           )            |
/&                                        )
```

Figure B.2 Sample DOS/360 job.

execution, and the loading and execution of that program. DOS/360 includes a *job control language* that facilitates use of the system and allows job step processing. Figure B.2 depicts a DOS/360 sample job.

B.3 OPERATING SYSTEM/360

System Structure

OS/360* consists of a control program and processing programs as depicted in Figure B.3. The control program consists of task management, job management, and data management routines. *Task management* routines are concerned with

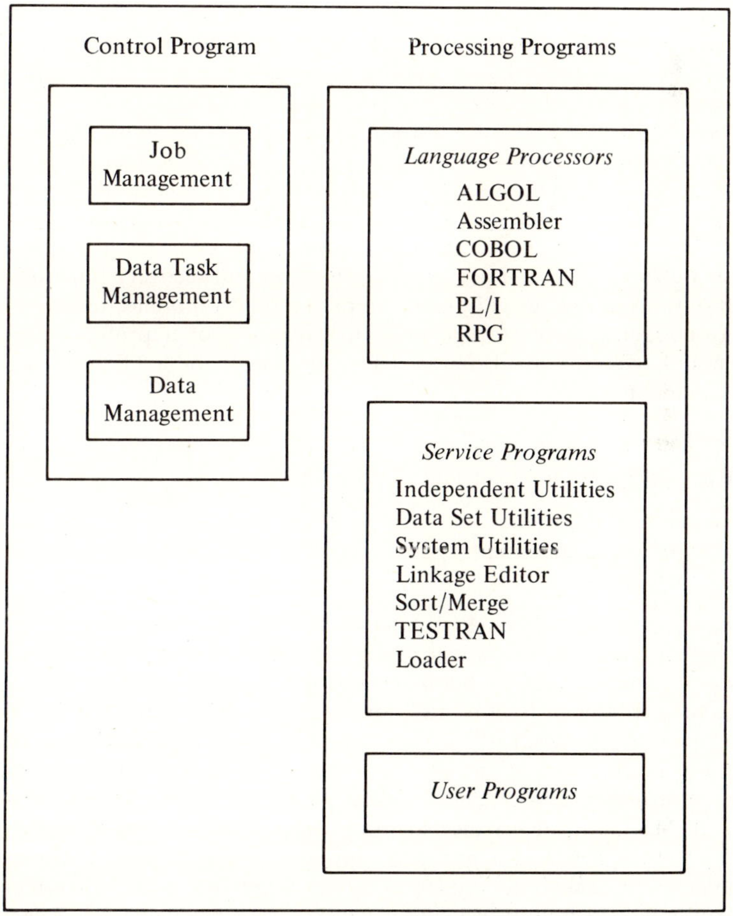

Figure B.3 OS/360.

*OS/360 is frequently abbreviated as OS.

the overall operation of the computing system and allocate system resources to satisfy installation requirements. Task management functions include scheduling CPU time (among several tasks in a multiprogramming environment), allocating main storage on a dynamic basis (providing program and data sharing), and managing efficient input/output processing. Task management also serves as an interface between the hardware and the software by processing interruptions and by performing reliability and serviceability functions. *Job management* routines allow continuous operation of the system by preparing jobs for execution and by scheduling their execution on either a priority or a sequential basis. Job management is responsible for reading and interpreting information from the input job stream, initiating and terminating job steps, communicating with the system operator for volume mounting and recognition, and controlling output writers (to printer and punch devices). *Data management* routines perform data access functions, manage input/output buffers, allow device independence, maintain catalogs and data set control information, supply program library facilities, and provide verification and retrieval services.

Processing programs fall into three general categories: language processors, service programs, and user-written problem programs. *Language processors* support Assembler, ALGOL, COBOL, FORTRAN, PL/I, and RPG languages. *Service programs* include system utilities (for managing system control information), data set utilities (executed under control of OS), independent utilities (executed outside of OS and perform initialization and recovery functions), sort/merge programs, a linkage editor (for preparing object modules for execution), a loader (for loading main storage prior to execution of a problem program—combines linkage editor and program fetch functions), and a TESTRAN package (used as an aid in debugging).

Multiprogramming

OS/360 provides three levels of control program structure:

Primary control program,
MFT control program, and
MVT control program.

The *primary control program* (PCP)* provides sequential scheduling of jobs and basic OS/360 functions; it is intended for systems that meet the minimum main storage requirements. *Multiprogramming with a Fixed Number of Tasks* (MFT) provides the facilities of PCP in addition to supporting concurrent operation of up to 15 problem programs—in fixed partitions. MFT supports multiple input readers and output writers and also provides graphics and telecommunications support. *Multiprogramming with a Variable Number of Tasks* (MVT) provides the facilities of MFT but allows the partition (region) size to vary dynamically depending upon the needs of a particular problem program. MVT also provides subtasking within each of the active problem programs along with shared modules, roll-in/roll-out, and multiprocessing capability. Additionally, MVT includes a

*The primary control program (PCP) is not supported on certain models of System/360 and System/370.

time-sharing option (TSO) that provides a general-purpose time-sharing capability in a compatible OS/360 environment. TSO facilities include a conversational command language and remote access to the entire OS/360 system—concurrently with normal background OS/360 operations.

Scheduling

PCP provides sequential scheduling of problem programs in an operating system environment. MFT and MVT provide priority scheduling in which problem programs are multiprogrammed within each priority class. The MFT and MVT control programs also provide a *time slicing* feature that can be used to prevent any task in a group from monopolizing CPU time.

Data Management

Data management facilities in OS/360 are provided through a data set control system and through data access methods. *Data set control* allows data files to be named and located through a central catalog. Also included among the data set control facilities are: labels and label checking, generations of data sets, direct-access space allocation, password protection, and the recording of error statistics. *Access methods* provide for device independence, reading and writing (directly or sequentially), blocking and deblocking records, overlapped input/output and processing, and the detection and correction of error conditions. The following options are available for data organization and input/output processing:

Sequential access methods (basic, queued, and partitioned).
Direct-access method (basic).
Indexed sequential access method (basic and queued).
Telecommunications access method (basic and queued).
Graphic access method.

Data management facilities also support shared direct-access devices (by two CPUs), multiple operator consoles, and device-independent display operator console support (DIDOCS). DIDOCS allows a variety of CRT-like display devices to be used as operator consoles.

Miscellaneous Facilities

In addition to the facilities mentioned previously, OS/360 also supports: remote job entry, a graphics job processor, satellite graphic job processor, recovery management, and checkpoint/restart. Additional software facilities include a variety of time-sharing systems (that operate under OS/360 control), a real time monitor, and a DOS emulator.

Job Control

OS/360 Job Control Language (JCL) supports jobs composed of discrete job steps and includes the following six types of job control statements:

1. Job statement (marks beginning of job).
2. Execute statement (marks beginning of a job step).
3. Data Definition statement (describes data sets).

4. Command statement (for entering operator commands).
5. Delimiter statement (separates data from control statements).
6. Null statement (marks end of job).
7. Comment statement (for entering comments not used by OS/360).
8. PROC statement (for defining cataloged procedures of JCL statements).

JCL statements are read and interpreted by Job Management routines that initiate appropriate OS/360 processing activities. A sample OS/360 job is given in Figure B.4.

```
//FLEPR JOB 1234,JONES
//STP1 EXEC PGM=CNVT                              } Job
//INPT DD DSNAME=A.B,DISP=(OLD,KEEP)              } Step 1
//SCRATCH DD UNIT=2400-2,LABEL=(,NL)
//STP2 EXEC PGM=PRINT
//INFLE DD DSNAME=*.STP1.SCRATCH,DISP=(OLD,DELETE)
//OUTFLE DD SYSOUT=A                                        } Job
//SYSIN DD *                                      } Job
                                                  } Step 2
  (data cards)

/*
//
```

Figure B.4 Sample OS/360 job.

B.4 DOS EMULATION

The DOS emulator feature allows a DOS operating system to run under control of the OS control program. Under control of OS, the DOS system is multiprogrammed as any other problem program; moreover, the DOS system, thus emulated, can also operate in a multiprogramming mode. The DOS emulator program requires dedicated devices (during execution) but can operate in as many OS partitions (or regions) as required. The DOS emulator program can operate under either the MFT or MVT control program. The DOS operating system need not be altered to operate under OS, and the emulator program provides the interface between the two systems. The DOS emulation feature uses both hardware features and programming (the emulator program) to provide the DOS operating environment.

System Structure and Operation

The DOS emulator program is scheduled for execution under OS along with other problem programs. When the DOS emulator program is given control of the system, it obtains the required main storage from the OS system and DOS location zero is established. IO devices are assigned, control blocks are built, and DOS processing is initiated. A main storage map for DOS emulation is given in Figure B.5.

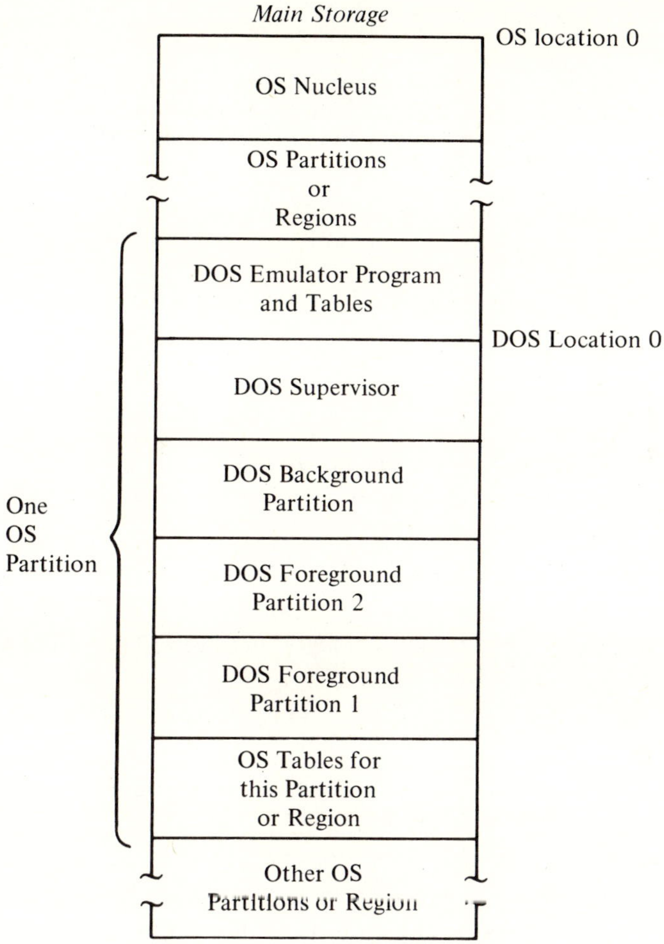

Figure B.5 Main storage map for DOS emulation.

The job management facilities of OS allow DOS emulator jobs and OS problem programs to be interspersed. A DOS emulator run can consist of a number of DOS stacked jobs and it is an economical practice to group DOS jobs that require a similar system configuration.

Input/output facilities for unit record devices are of special concern. This type of IO can be dedicated or staged. *Dedicated* IO involves assigning a particular device to a DOS emulator partition such that it is unavailable for use by other partitions. *Staged* IO does not require a dedicated device and uses standard OS IO facilities. However, when staged output is used, output for a DOS emulator partition is not available until the execution of the entire OS job (i.e., the set of stacked DOS jobs) has been completed.

```
(previous OS/360 job)

//EMJB JOB ...
//EM1  EXEC PGM=IIVEMU,PARM='...'
// (DDs for DOS device assignments)
// (DDs for input and output assignments)
//SYSEM00C DD DATA

  (DOS input job stream)

/*

  (next OS/360 job)
```

Figure B.6 Job control language statements for DOS emulation.

Job Control

Processing of the DOS emulator is initiated with standard OS job control language statements. The JOB statement does not require special attention. The EXEC statement initiates the DOS emulator program and passes parameters to it regard-

```
//EMULATE JOB [(acct#,acctg information),,CLASS=
//          jobclass,PRTY=nn]

//EMU1  EXEC PGM=IIVEMU,PARM=('DOSRES=190,DOSIPL=00C,
            DOSSYS=16K,DOSLOG=01F')

//SYSEM190 DD UNIT=(2311,,DEFER),DISP=OLD,VOLUME=
//          (PRIVATE,SER=111111)

//SYSEM191 DD UNIT=(2311,,DEFER),DISP=OLD,VOLUME=
            (PRIVATE,SER=111112)

//SYSEM192 DD UNIT=(2311,,DEFER),DISP=OLD,VOLUME=
            (PRIVATE,SER=111113)

//SYSEM180 DD UNIT=2400,DISP=(OLD,DELETE),LABEL=(BLP)

//SYSEM181 DD UNIT=2400,DISP=(NEW,PASS),LABEL=(,BLP)

//SYSEM00E DD UNIT=1403

//SYSEM00D DD UNIT=2540-2

//SYSEM00C DD UNIT=2540

//SYSUDUMP DD SYSOUT=A

//SYSSNAP DD SYSOUT=A

/*
```

Figure B.7 Sample job control language for a DOS emulation run with nonstaged IO. (Quoted from reference 6, p. 30.)

ing the DOS residence file, the DOS operator console, the DOS IPL input unit, and the size of the DOS configuration. The DD statements provide the emulator with DOS device assignments, information for input and output staging, and the attributes of tape or disk volumes. The general form of OS job control language for DOS emulation is given in Figure B.6. An example of JCL for a DOS emulation run with nonstaged IO is given in Figure B.7. When nonstaged input is used, DOS input is supplied through a card reader allocated by OS Job Management for that purpose.

B.5 SUMMARY

In general, programming systems for a System/370 computer include operating systems, programming languages, and service programs. System/370 operating systems include DOS/360, OS/360, and DOS emulation under OS. DOS supports Assembler, COBOL, FORTRAN, PL/I, and RPG languages. OS supports Assembler, ALGOL, COBOL, FORTRAN, PL/I, and RPG languages. Both systems provide a variety of service programs.

REFERENCES

1. G. Bender, D.N. Freeman, and J.D. Smith, "Function and Design of DOS/360 and TOS/360," *IBM Systems Journal*, **6** (1)(1967).
2. IBM System/360, "Disk and Tape Operating Systems, Concepts and Facilities," Form C24-5030-5, IBM Corporation, Data Processing Division, White Plains, N.Y., 1968.
3. G.H. Mealy, "The Funcational Structure of OS/360: Part I. Introductory Survey," *IBM Systems Journal*, **5** (1)(1966).
4. IBM System/360, "Operating System Introduction," Form C28-6534-2, IBM Corporation, Data Processing Division, White Plains, N.Y., 1969.
5. IBM System/360, "Operating System Concepts and Facilities," Form C28-6535-5, IBM Corporation, Data Processing Division, White Plains, N.Y., 1969.
6. IBM System/360, "OS Program Planning Guide For the DOS Emulator on IBM System/370 Models 145 and 155," Form GC24-5076-0, IBM Corporation, Data Processing Division, White Plains, N.Y., 1970.

APPENDIX C
A SURVEY OF STORAGE HIERARCHY SYSTEMS*

C.1 INTRODUCTION

The announcement by IBM on June 30, 1970 of System/370 Models 155 and 165 with buffer/core storage facilities revived an interest in storage hierarchy systems that was created initially by the System/360 Models 85 and 195. However, the notion of a storage hierarchy is not new and has been used previously with regard to storage management by an operating system[2] and for efficient use of mass storage devices. In fact, storage hierarchy, in one form or another, has been used in a variety of systems. The purpose of this appendix is to survey the various storage hierarchy systems. As such, it presents a state-of-the-art analysis of this important area of computer science and places many of the concepts mentioned earlier in the book in perspective.

The material is covered from three points of view. The first is *addressable storage* and includes main storage buffer systems and large capacity storage (LCS). Also included in the LCS discussion are storage management in an LCS environment and the special case where LCS is not directly addressable and must be accessed through a computer instruction or storage channel. The second topic involves *storage management* and relates to the manner in which addressable storage is managed by an operating system. Covered here are overlay schemes, relocation methods, and virtual memory. The concepts are applied to multiprogramming and time-sharing environments. The final section presents a brief discussion of *data organization and management.* Included here is a discussion of hierarchial data management, data base organization, and the migration of infrequently used information.

*This appendix is reproduced in part, with permission, from the *Proceedings of the 1971 Spring Joint Computer Conference* AFIPS Press, Vol. 38; see Katzan.[1]

C.2 STORAGE HIERARCHY CONCEPTS

The purpose of a storage system is to hold information, but the simplicity of the concept ends there. A variety of storage mechanisms exists ranging from high-speed circuitry to low-speed tape or cards. Each type, obviously, has a relative cost/performance index that is used to correlate a storage medium with the function it is to perform. In many cases, it is necessary to synthesize a storage system from two or more types of storage to meet cost objectives and functional requirements. The most simple example of the latter concept is the conventional computing system, depicted in Figure C.1, with a relatively small high-speed main

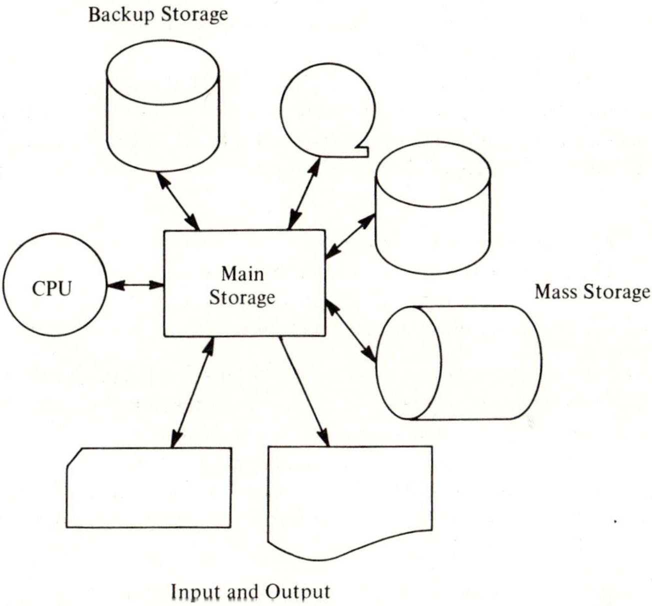

Figure C.1 Storage hierarchy of a conventional computing system (simplified).

storage for programs and data, and mass storage consisting of direct-access devices such as magnetic disk or magnetic drum for storing large amounts of information for relatively short periods of time and for use as an overflow device for high-speed main storage. In this case, back-up storage usually consists of tape or disk. The concepts have been extended, obviously, in the high-performance computing systems of today.

The notion of storage hierarchy is important for the following reasons:

1. It has been possible to speed up the functioning of the arithmetic and logical units of a computer to such an extent that performance is dependent upon storage speeds.
2. High-speed computer storage is particularly cost sensitive.

3. Programmers are frequently required to prepare programs for computers with storage that is considerably smaller in size than that which is actually needed. Thus, programs must be structured accordingly, a process that limits the functional effectiveness of the programmers and the computing system.
4. Most installations have accumulated and continue to accumulate large amounts of information.

The purpose of a storage hierarchy system is to increase the overall functional effectiveness of a computing system. In this context, functional effectiveness can take one of several forms:

1. Increasing the performance of the central processing unit.
2. Increasing total system throughput.
3. Providing the user with a functional capability that is otherwise not inherent in the individual components themselves. (For example, a virtual memory provides a single-level store larger than actual high-speed storage.)
4. Making large amounts of data available within reasonably short periods of time.

In all cases, the objective of a storage hierarchy system is to maximize the frequency with which the faster device is referenced so that access speeds approach those of the faster devices at a cost that approaches the slower devices. A storage hierarchy system is usually characterized as follows:

1. Fast and slow storage devices are organized into blocks (of information).
2. The first reference to a particular block requires that the entire block be fetched from the slow device and stored in the fast device. Subsequent fetches to that block require only that fast storage be accessed.
3. The fast storage (usually referred to as a buffer) is capable of storing several blocks which are replaced on a dynamic basis using an appropriate replacement algorithm.

Because storage devices have radically different characteristics and the expected pattern of storage references is difficult to determine beforehand, the methods for designing an optimum hierarchy are not well-defined and often require simulation and empirical analyses. Gecsei, Slutz, and Traiger[3] have described the evaluation of a variety of replacement algorithms for buffer/core storage hierarchy systems. Denning[27] surveys replacement techniques for virtual memory and paging.

C.3 ADDRESSABLE STORAGE

Historical Perspective

One of the problems in designing a high-speed computing system is that main storage is slower than the arithmetic and logical units because of the memory paradox, depicted in Figure C.2. Although attempts were made in the past to compensate for the difference in CPU and storage access time by overlap, local storage buffering, and interleaving, the results were only partially successful and demanded that changes be made to the architecture of the conventional computing

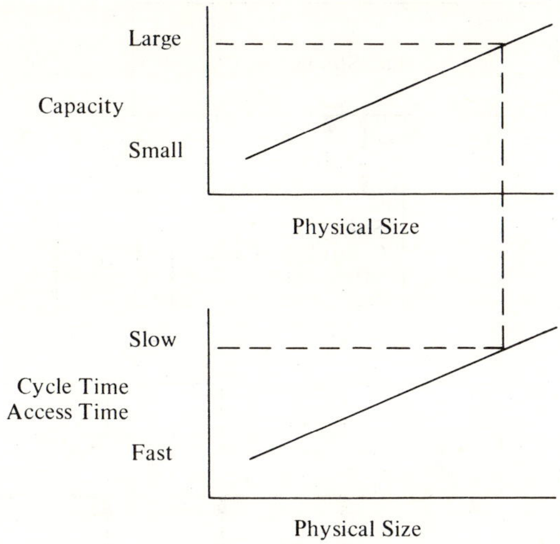

Figure C.2 The classical memory paradox.

system. The first attempt was in the IBM System/360 Model 85 (see Liptay[4]). The Model 85 uses a small fast storage buffer integrated into the CPU called the *cache*.* The cache is not addressable by a program and is transparent to the programmer. The cache is used to hold sectors of main storage that are being used and is maintained dynamically by the CPU.

In the Model 85, the cache and main storage are divided into sectors, each containing a fixed number of storage blocks. When a block of storage is referenced for the first time by the CPU, it is moved to the cache. Subsequent references to that block are made to the cache without having to access the slower main storage. Figure C.3 depicts a schematic of the Model 85. Detailed information on the Model 85 and the cache organization is available from Liptay[4] and Conti, Gibson, and Pitkowsky.[5] The concept was successful and subsequently was used in the design of the System/360 Model 195[6] and the System/370 Models 155 and 165.† The buffer system used with the Model 165 is summarized in the next section as a concrete example of the organization of a main storage buffer system.

Organization of a Main Storage Buffer System

The buffer/core storage system in the IBM System/370 Model 165 contains an 8K high-speed buffer storage unit‡ to increase internal performance. Data flow in the Model 165 is depicted in Figure C.4 with a relative access time of 9 to 1 in favor of the buffer over core storage. The CPU can obtain 8 bytes from the buffer

*In computing, a buffer is used frequently to interface two components that operate at different speeds. The most familiar example is the I/O buffer used by many programming systems to compensate for relatively slow I/O speeds.

†The System/370 Models 155 and 165 are introduced in earlier chapters.

‡An additional 8K (bytes) of buffer storage can be included with an optional buffer expansion feature (see Chapter 8).

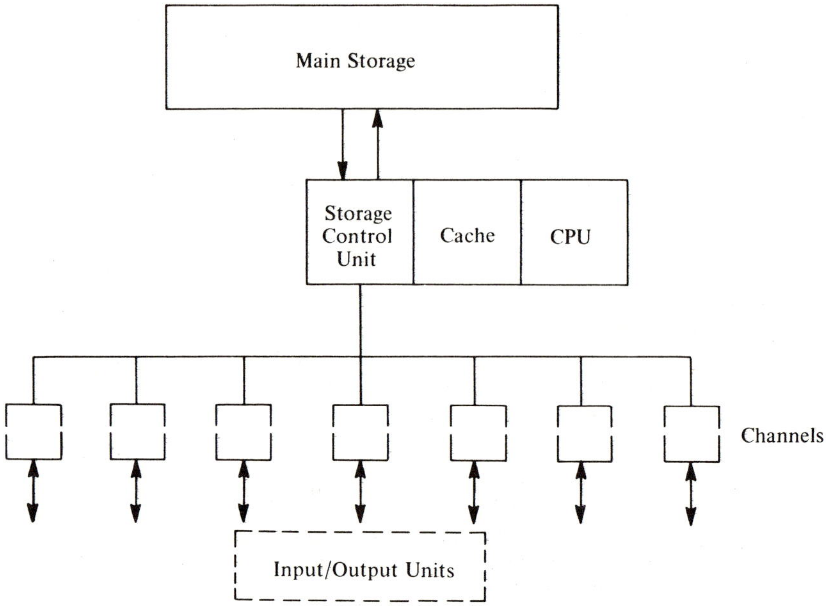

Figure C.3 Schematic of the Model 85.

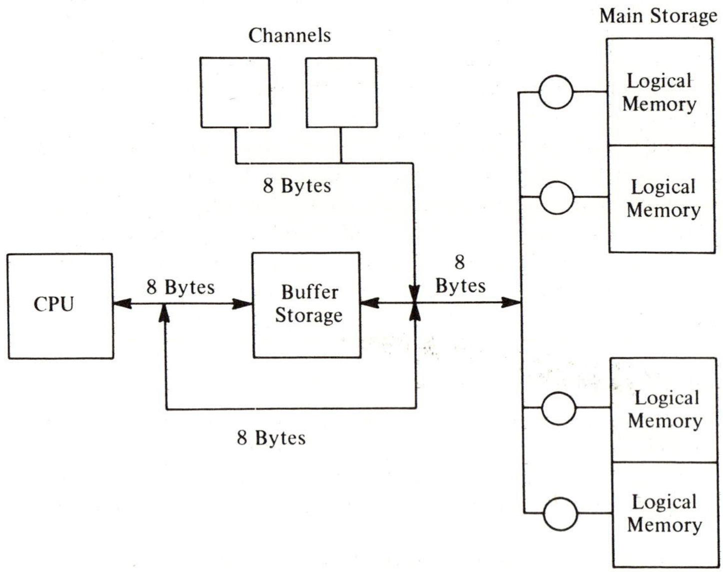

Figure C.4 Data flow in the Model 165.

in 160 nanoseconds compared with a time of 1.44 microseconds when the same amount of data must be obtained from core storage.

When a request for data is made by the CPU, the buffer storage control (Figure C.5) searches an address array of the buffer's contents to determine if the data requested are in the buffer. If they are, the data are sent to the CPU without a core storage reference. If the requested data are not in the buffer, they are obtained from core storage and sent to the CPU. The data are also assigned a buffer location and stored in the buffer. When data are stored by the CPU, both the buffer and core storage are updated if the corresponding location contains data that are currently in the buffer. The data channels always reference core storage. How-

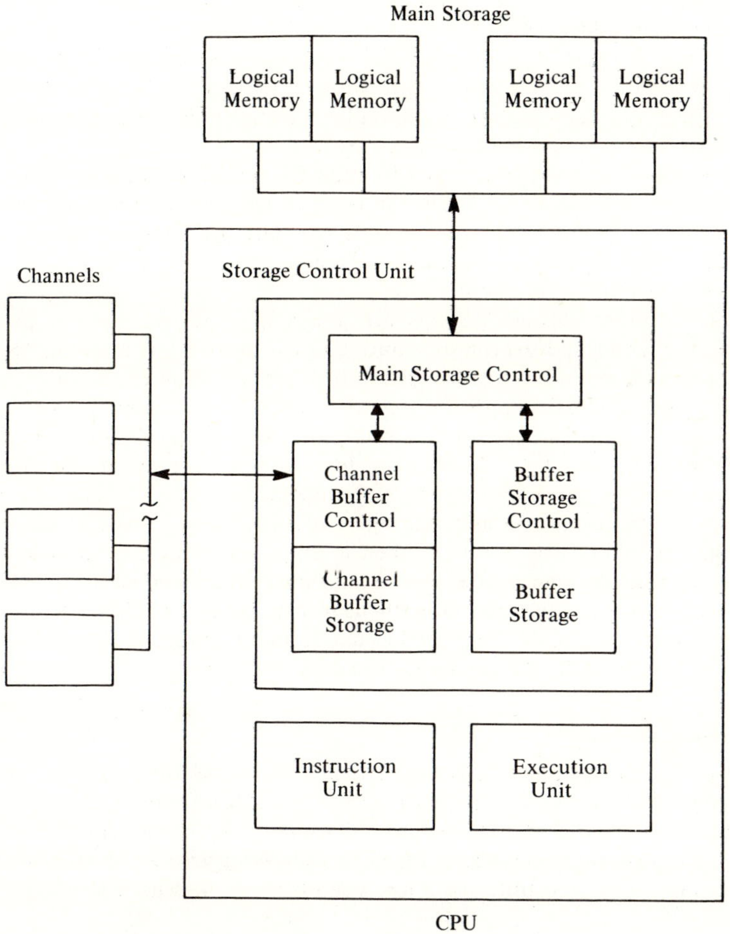

Figure C.5 Model 165 storage hierarchy system.

ever, if a data channel stores data in a core storage location that contains data in the buffer, then the buffer is also updated accordingly.*

The buffer and core storage are both divided into blocks of 32 bytes; the 8K buffer contains 64 columns, each containing 4 blocks—a total of 256 distinct blocks of information. (The 16K buffer contains 128 columns and 4 rows for a total of 512 blocks.) Each buffer block contains 32 *consecutive* bytes from core storage, which is also regarded (logically) as containing 64 (or 128) columns with the number of blocks in each column being dependent upon the size of the core storage. Any of the blocks in a core storage column can be placed in one of the four blocks in the corresponding buffer column. Essentially, a column (of 32-byte blocks) contends for a position in a 4-row column of the buffer.

The buffer storage is managed with an address array and a replacement array.† An element of the address array consists of the high-order bits of the core storage address of the 32 bytes of data contained in the corresponding position in buffer storage. When the CPU references core storage, the address array is used to determine if the requested data are in the buffer. Thus, an effective address is compared with at most four address array entries.

The buffer is managed dynamically by the CPU. Each column in the buffer is associated with a four-entry replacement array which controls buffer replacement activity. When a buffer block is referenced, it is put at the top of the list for its particular column. When a block must be reassigned, the entry at the bottom of the list is selected for replacement.

In general, buffer storage systems are amazingly effective—a fact probably caused by the tendency for programs and data to "cluster" in main storage. In sample program executions performed by IBM,[7] results showed that data fetched by the CPU is in the buffer approximately 90% of the time. Similarly, Lee[8] showed in a simulation study that even with a buffer of only 128 words, overall speed is improved by a factor of 3. Gunderson[9] gives a good survey of the effects of memory technology on computer system organization.

Clearly, the net result of a main storage buffer system is to reduce the number of references to main storage, making the CPU less dependent upon storage access times. Thus, main storage can be larger even though increased size implies longer cables and a greater access time. Other benefits also exist. The time spent in error checking circuitry and CPU degradation due to main storage cycle stealing from the CPU by high-priority data channels becomes less critical.

Large Capacity Storage

Large capacity storage‡ (LCS) is high-speed addressable bulk storage. LCS is usually combined with CPU main storage to form a hierarchy of storage directly addressable by the CPU. Addresses in LCS are regarded as an extension to main storage—although the cycle time of LCS is considerably greater. For example, an LCS with a memory cycle time of 8 microseconds is not unusual. However, inter-

*In the System/370 Model 155, a store by a data channel into locations currently held in the buffer invalidates those buffer entries.

†The address array and replacement array are described in Chapter 8.

‡Also known as large core storage.

leaving is frequently used to reduce the effective cycle time. The CPU can fetch instructions or data directly from LCS, but performance is degraded when executing out of LCS. For some applications, it is efficient to move information from LCS to main storage before it is used. In other cases, the overhead of moving the information is not justified.

LCS has been used in a variety of interesting ways. Lauer[10] describes the use of LCS at Carnegie-Mellon University as a swapping device, instead of drum, for their 360/67 time-sharing system. The use of LCS was motivated for three reasons: (1) the effective rate at which the system can deliver pages is increased; (2) response-time is decreased since LCS has no rotational delay; and (3) less main core is needed for system operation. For this application, a storage channel, which behaves exactly like an I/O data channel, was used and permitted CPU processing and core-to-core transfers to take place simultaneously. Lauer also points out the possibility of executing out of LCS directly by setting page tables to refer directly to LCS.

Freeman[11] relates an equally interesting technique used at the Triangle Universities Computation Center. At TUCC on a 360/75 system, LCS is used for checkpoint/restarts, for a technique called "hyperdisk," and for a variety of other useful functions. Using LCS for checkpoints increased the frequency with which they could be taken and provided added reliability features. Freeman also found that on a 360/75 system, only LCS was a sufficiently fast "source and sink" for system I/O to give satisfactory CPU utilization. Hyperdisk—that is, a combination of LCS and disk for overflow—effectively allowed system-type programs such as compilers, assemblers, and access routines to reside in core storage instead of being divided into multi-overlay structures.

Fikes, Lauer, and Vareha[12] describe extensions to the Carnegie-Mellon time-sharing system that effectively combine a storage hierarchy of main storage, LCS, disk and data cell. The C-MU system is further characterized by two levels of executable storage and an increased number of direct data paths from direct-access storage to the CPU. In general, the overhead problem in their system is attacked in the following way. LCS is used as a swapping device and an extension of executable core. Associated with each page of virtual memory is an indicator denoting whether that page is to be accessed by the CPU while residing in main storage or while residing in LCS. Pages that are executed in LCS use a disk as a swapping device and migrate back and forth between LCS and disk. Pages that are executed in main storage use LCS as a swapping device and migrate back and forth between main storage and LCS. The criterion used for determining where a page is executed is relatively simple (partly because of constraints on the implementation effort). All shared pages are executed out of main storage and all nonshared pages are executed out of LCS. In a university environment of small jobs with much assembly and compilation, this effectively amounts to executing system code out of main storage and user code out of LCS. It is also reported that Chen and Hsieh[13] have developed a more optimal algorithm for making the allocation between main storage and LCS.

Not all large capacity storage systems need be directly addressable or accessible by a storage channel. The CDC 7600,[14,15] for example, includes a small core memory (SCM) and a large core memory (LCM) which functions as a storage hierarchy system for programs and data. SCM is used for I/O buffers, for system overlays and tables, and for user programs. LCM is used for permanent system residence, for job swapping, and for input and output files. Only programs in SCM can be executed by the CPU, and information is moved between SCM and LCM with block transfer instructions.

Addressable Storage Summary

Collectively, buffer storage systems and large capacity storage serve the same basic purpose—that is, to increase the frequency with which accesses are made to the fast storage in a storage hierarchy system. Internal CPU performance is the key issue, and in most cases, the hierarchy of storage is transparent to the applications programmer. The methodology seeks to optimize the *overall* functioning of the system, within cost/performance constraints, by applying a functional organization to the hierarchies of storage, taking into consideration the manner in which information is accessed in a general-purpose computing system.

C.4 STORAGE MANAGEMENT

The Overlay Problem

The effective utilization of main storage is important from the standpoint of program development and for computer system performance. Inefficiencies in both categories have characteristically been resolved with the reply, "If we had more core, we could solve the problem." Although the solution is indeed partly correct, equally significant improvements have been made through advanced storage management techniques.

For the programmer, the problem becomes significant when his program is too large for available main storage. The main storage limit may be a physical hardware constraint or may be a logical constraint imposed to increase the level of multiprogramming (see Johnson and Martinson[16]). A program overlay scheme is frequently used (see Lanzano[17]) in which main storage is shared by a hierarchy of program segments. Figure C.6 depicts a program tree and a storage trace for a simple overlay.

Overlay facilities are perhaps the most elementary form of storage hierarchy for programs and are sometimes used to make addressable storage appear larger than physical or logical storage by storing unused program segments on auxiliary storage such as tape or disk. Several obvious disadvantages exist:

1. Relocation and linking are usually performed before execution is begun.
2. Overlay deck setup requires that the programmer overtly specify the segments that are overlaid.
3. Programs can not be relocated—as is frequently required in multiprogramming or time-sharing systems.
4. Storage utilization is inefficient in that enough space must be allocated for the largest core load at any point in time (see Figure C.6).

Although program overlay techniques are in widespread use today, they severely limit the programmer and the designers of general-purpose operating systems and

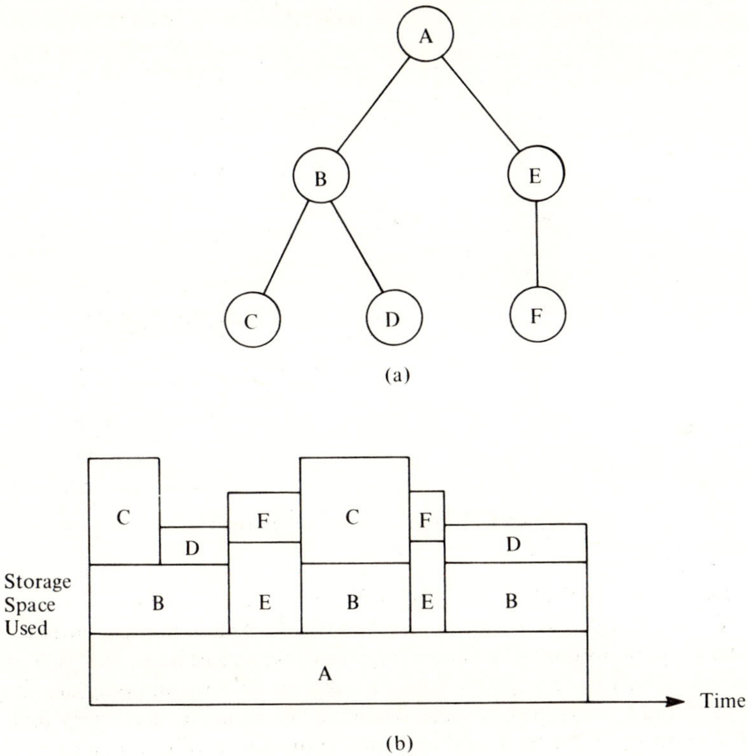

Figure C.6 Simple overlay system. (a) Program tree. (b) Storage trace.

impose unnecessary throughput limits on computing systems. The reader has probably guessed what is considered to be the state-of-the-art solution to many of the above problems—virtual memory. However, the concept first went through several stages of evolution.

Virtual Memory

Because of time-sharing operational considerations, the need for relocatability was as important in the evolution of virtual memory as was the overlay problem. The first evolutionary step was the *relocation register* used by Kinslow[18] at IBM and by Corbato, et al.,[19] with the CTSS system at M.I.T. With the relocation register method (Figure C.7), the user's program is loaded into main storage and the address at which it is loaded is placed in the relocation register. During execution, the contents of the relocation register are added to each effective address to arrive at the appropriate main storage location. Although use of a relocation register helps solve the relocation problem, it does not solve the overlay problem since the user's program must still reside entirely in main storage.

The next step in the development of a virtual memory system was to consider

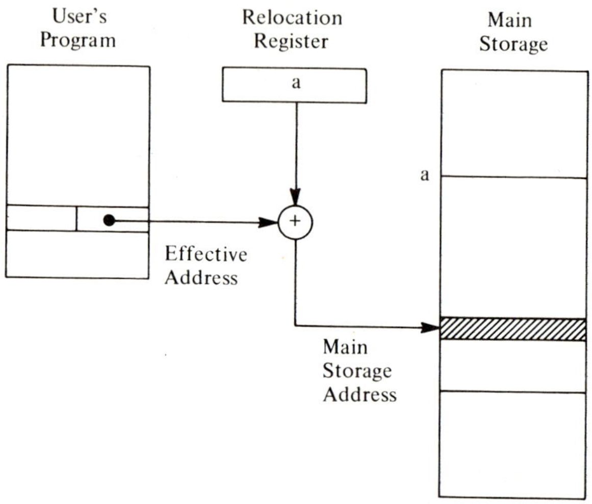

Figure C.7 Use of a relocation register.

main storage as a collection of fixed-size pages, such as 4096 bytes as used in TSS/360[20] or 1024 words as used in MULTICS.[21] The user is permitted to construct his program as though he had a large address space; however, each effective address referenced by the system goes through an address mapping, as shown in Figures C.8 and C.9 (see Randell and Kuehner[22]). In most cases, only high-order bits of an address need by translated and addresses within a page can go unchanged. This technique allows pages from different programs to reside in main storage while unused pages are stored on a direct-access device or in large capacity storage. Pages can easily be relocated by adjusting entries in a table of addresses, called a *page table*. The advantages of virtual memory are obvious (see Johnson

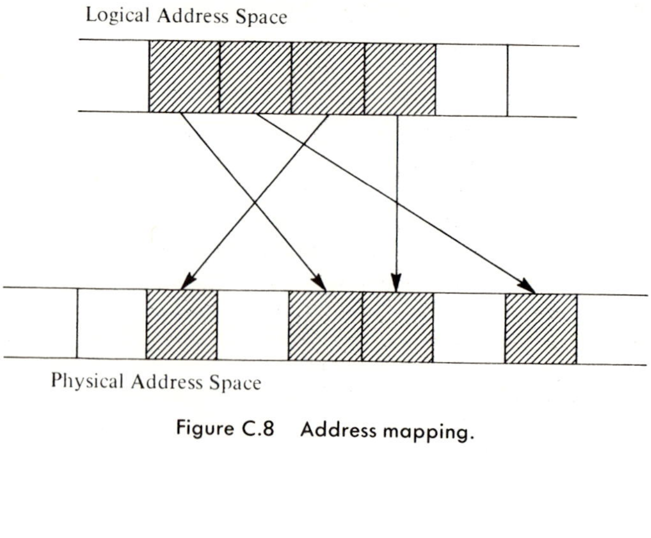

Figure C.8 Address mapping.

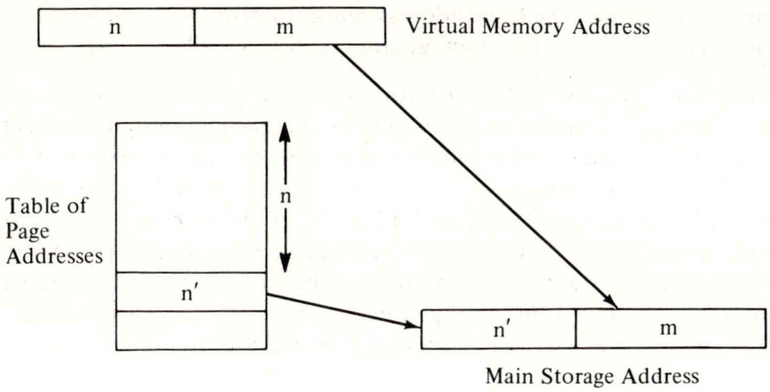

Figure C.9 Address translation (one-level page tables).

and Martinson[16]):

1. Adjacent virtual memory pages need not occupy adjacent main storage areas.
2. Not all of a user's program need be in storage simultaneously and can be retrieved when needed (called *demand paging*).

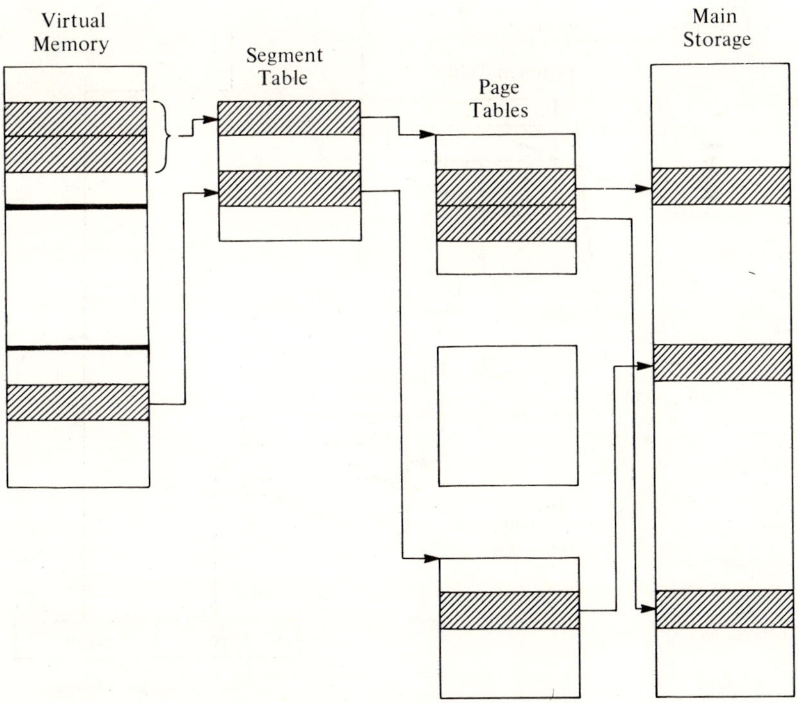

Figure C.10 Two-level page tables.

3. The user is permitted a large address space for programs and for data.
4. The operating system can manage storage dynamically.

The final step in the evolution of virtual memory achieves efficiency and versatility in storage management by defining two-level page tables and by segmenting a symbolic address into segment number, page number, and displacement within a page (see Dennis[23] and Arden, et al.[24]). Two-level page tables (see Figures C.10 and C.11) decrease page table size and allow programs to be shared by defining a shared segment of pages. The process of moving pages in and out of main storage is known as *paging* and has also been described by Flores[25] and Oppenheimer and Weizer.[26] Virtual memory and paging has been the subject of much analysis; Denning[27] gives a good summary of research in that area.

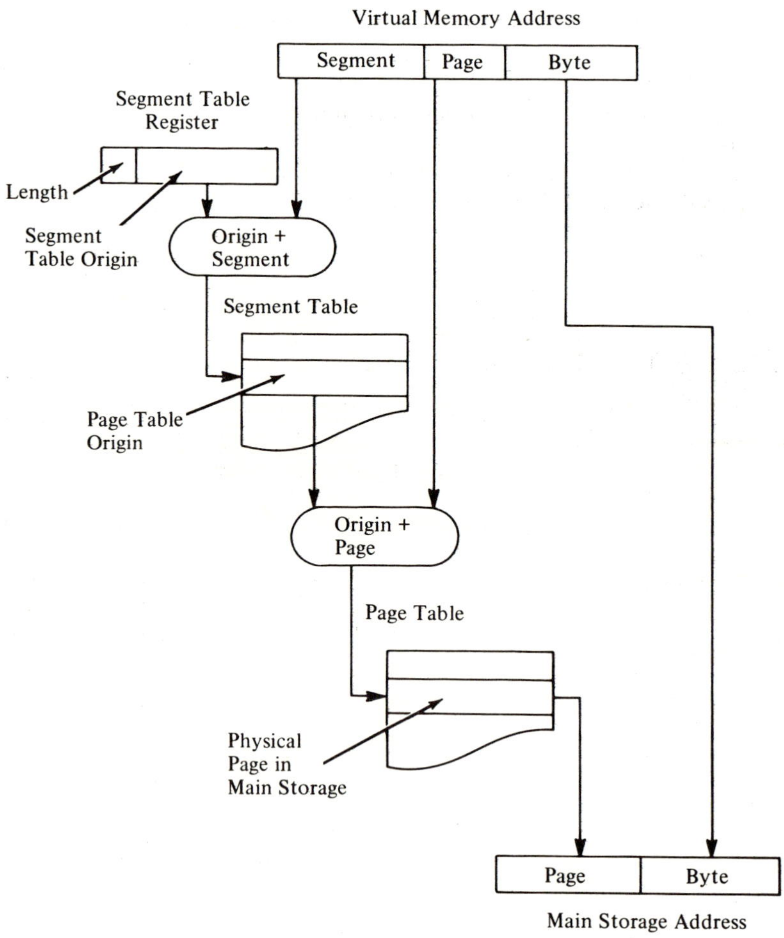

Figure C.11 Segmented addressing.

Thus, virtual memory provides a storage hierarchy system described as follows:

1. A large address space as seen by the programmer for the preparation and execution of programs.
2. Main storage containing the needed pages for one or more programs being multiprogrammed.
3. An auxiliary paging device such as drum for program residence.
4. A backup paging device to which infrequently used pages can be migrated from drum storage.

The virtual memory storage hierarchy is depicted in Figure C.12.

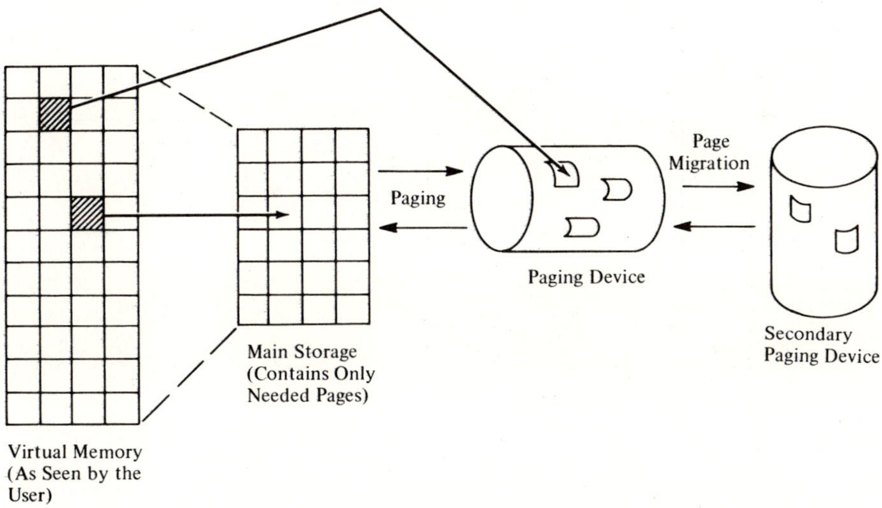

Figure C.12 Virtual memory storage hierarchy.

Uses of Virtual Memory

Unlike buffer/core systems, virtual memory storage hierarchy systems need not be transparent to the user. Virtual memory has also been used* with small computers (see Christensen and Hause[28]) to give the programmer a large address space through a combination of main storage and direct-access devices. In this instance, the user is provided with *expanded functional capability* at the cost of reduced throughput and a more sophisticated operating system.

Virtual memory has also been used to increase system throughput by improving upon conventional storage management techniques. The Boeing Company has modified OS/360 to utilize the virtual memory features of the IBM 360/67. The methodology involves overcommitting main storage by declaring more job parti-

*That is, in addition to the classical virtual memory systems such as TSS/360 or MULTICS that permit virtual memory addresses up to the addressing capability of the hardware.

tions that the computing system can support and by mapping those partitions through the dynamic address translation feature of the Model 67[29,30] onto main storage and magnetic drum. The implementation, called OS/67 and depicted in Figure C.13, increased performance because of the ability of the system to assign unused main storage to other virtual partitions when small programs are executing.

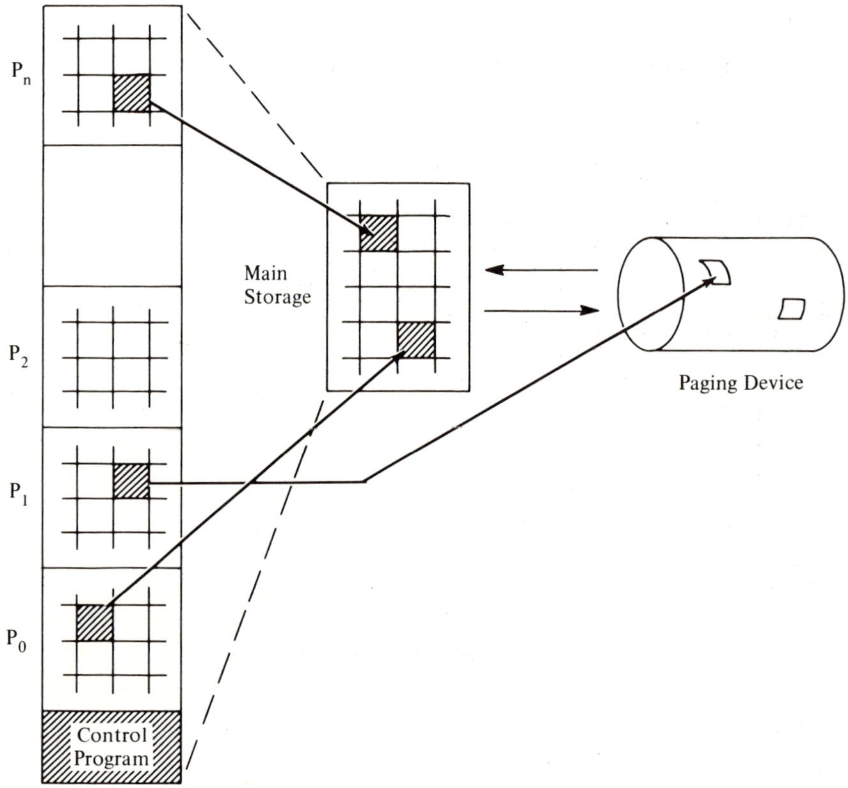

Figure C.13 Virtual memory partitioning in OS/67 (conceptual overview).

C.5 DATA ORGANIZATION AND MANAGEMENT

Hierarchy systems for data organization and management require a unique mixture of hardware features, software facilities, and user applications, and at this point in time, are not as well-defined as those previously surveyed in this paper. However, the basic objective is the same—to increase the frequency with which needed information can be retrieved from the faster device of a storage hierarchy. Hierarchical data organization also provides for efficiency of storage by reducing the amount of redundant information.

Hierarchical Data Management

The subject of hierarchical data management has been studied from different points of view by different authors. Opler[31] was concerned with the general storage assignment problem and defined four attributes of direct-access device types: flow rate, capacity, waiting time, and access time. On the basis of these attributes, he developed a hierarchy of main storage, large capacity storage, drum, disk, and magnetic strip transport systems and discussed the problems of effectively using these devices. This was the first definitive description of hierarchical data management systems.

In another important paper, Madnick and Alsop[32] discuss the levels of hierarchy in a modular file system. In this approach, the file is considered the most important unit of organization and emphasis is placed upon the logical file system as seen by the user. Madnick and Alsop define six hierarchical levels as follows:

1. Input/output control system.
2. Device strategy modules.
3. File organization strategy modules.
4. Basic file system.
5. Logical file system.
6. Access methods and user interface.

At the opposite extreme to file structures are data management systems[33,34] in which emphasis is placed on the access of individual data items. Dodd[35] surveys systems of this sort and describes structural relationships between discrete data.

Data Base Organization

Inefficiencies in both the storage and retrieval of information led several researchers (see, for example, Mealy[36] and Chapin[37]) to explore the applications of data and to recognize the distinction between data access and data organization. This work combined with the increased information needs of our society (see Aron[38]) eventually led to the data base technology and data structures that we know today.

Presently, it is customary to distinguish between data structure and storage structure in which *information* is meaning assigned to *data* and recorded on a *storage* device. Logical data, as viewed by the user, are used independently of their physical storage—which can be organized to facilitate access and conserve space. Thus, the logical data structures depicted in Figure C.14 can be stored as the hierarchical data structure, shown in Figure C.15. Although the examples are indeed oversimplified, they are indicative of the kind of information systems that are required for the interrogation and maintenance of large centralized information files. The advantages of hierarchical data structures can be listed as follows:[39]

1. Elimination of *redundant* data.
2. Use of the same data by all users of the system (*consistency*).
3. Program independence from physical storage devices.

As such, hierarchical data structures are essential for effective data base technology. The design and structure of data base systems are also described by Blier and Vorhaus[40] and the CODASYL data base reports.[41]

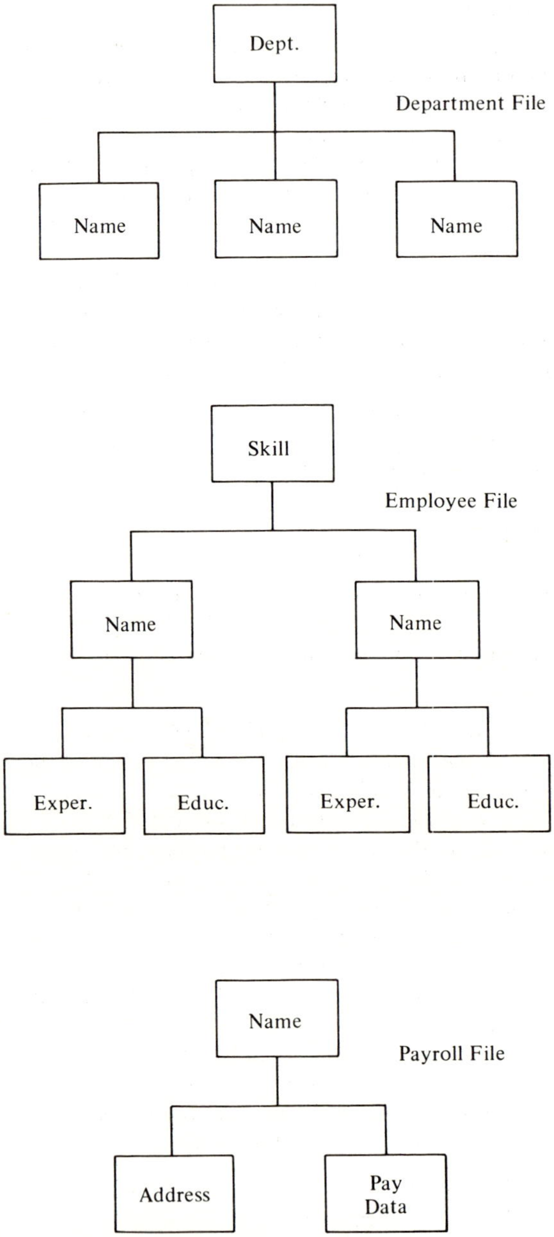

Figure C.14 Logical data structures.

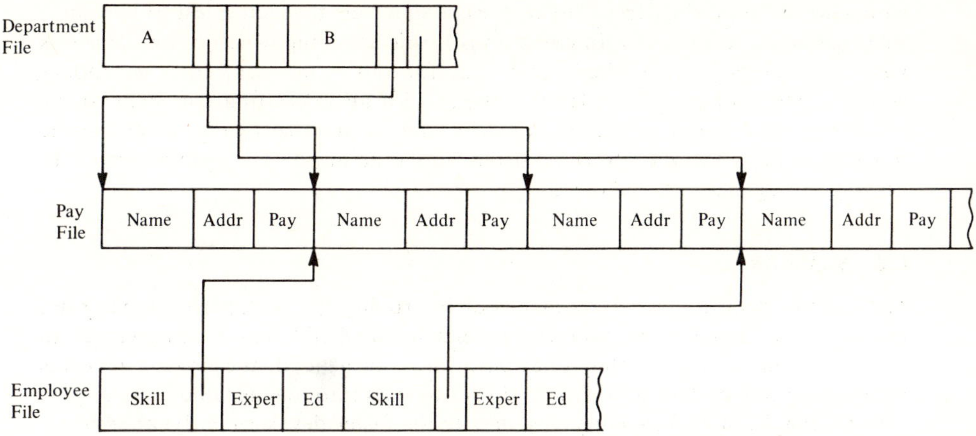

Figure C.15 Physical data structures.

Data Set Migration and Backup Storage

No survey of storage hierarchy systems would be complete without mention of the migration of data sets (files) from secondary or on-line storage to backup storage. The problem is particularly significant in a utility-class time-sharing system such as TSS/360 or MULTICS in which file storage is considered to be on-line (or public) and may be viewed as infinite in extent by the user. Obviously, on-line storage is not infinite and information stored therein must be managed carefully. Files that are no longer needed must be purged from the system and infrequently used information must be moved to backup storage—a process frequently referred to as *data migration*.

The MULTICS system at M.I.T. (see Daley and Neumann[42]) combines a file backup system with a weekly dumping procedure that effectively migrates infrequently used information. First, a copy of all files created or modified by a user during a terminal session are duplicated on magnetic tape when he signs off. These tapes, termed *incremental dump tapes*, are replaced periodically and provide a means of reconstructing file storage in case of catastrophic system failure. Another tape dump is made periodically of files used in that period. The latter process facilitates the reconstruction of on-line storage and provides a means of eliminating unused files. A file directory entry remains in the system indefinitely unless it is explicitly deleted by the user. When a user desires to retrieve a file from backup storage, the correct set of dump tapes is retrieved and mounted as requested by the file retrieval procedure in MULTICS.

The expanded use of on-line storage in the TSS/360 system at IBM Research created a need for a storage hierarchy of on-line direct-access volumes, off-line direct-access volumes, and tape volumes (see Considine and Weiss[43]). The authors developed a set of migration commands that effectively copy the contents of public storage while migrating, to archival storage, data sets that fail a test of currency. The user is also provided with commands for determining which of his data sets have been migrated and other commands for retrieving them from secondary storage. The authors conclude their paper with an interesting comment to the effect that the amount of space gained by moving data sets to archival storage more than pays for the effort involved and that most of the data moved to archival storage have stayed there.

C.6 SUMMARY

Storage hierarchy systems are a means of improving the cost/performance ratio of storage components by combining elements with different characteristics to meet the needs of a given class of applications. In general, the process involves the organization of data on fast and slower devices into manageable units and by transferring the most frequently used data to the faster device on a dynamic basis.

Storage hierarchy systems fall into three general categories:

1. Main storage buffer systems for addressable main storage that are transparent to the programmer.
2. Storage management systems such as virtual memory that are used by the programmer.
3. Data organization and management systems that permit large amounts of information to be stored and retrieved efficiently.

Collectively, storage hierarchy systems present a new approach to the storage aspects of computer technology wherein performance improvements are made through system design and organization in conjunction with improvements in the components themselves.

REFERENCES

1. H. Katzan, Jr., "Storage Hierarchy Systems," *Proceedings of the 1971 Spring Joint Computer Conference*, AFIPS Press, Vol. 38 (1971).
2. H. Katzan, Jr., "Operating systems architecture," *Proceedings of the 1970 Spring Joint Computer Conference*, AFIPS Press, Vol. 36 (1970).
3. J. Gecsei, D.R. Slutz, and I.L. Traiger, "Evaluation techniques for storage hierarchies," *IBM Systems Journal*, **9** (2) (1970).
4. J.S. Liptay, "Structural aspects of the System/360 Model 85: II The cache," *IBM Systems Journal*, **7** (1) (1968).
5. C.J. Conti, D.H. Gibson, and S.H. Pitkowsky, "Structural aspects of the System/360 Model 85: I General organization," *IBM Systems Journal*, **7** (1) (1968).
6. J.O. Murphey and R.M. Wade, "The IBM 360/195," *Datamation* (April 1970).
7. "A Guide to the IBM/370 Model 155," Form GC20-1729-0, IBM Corporation, 1970.
8. F.F. Lee, "Study of Look-aside Memory," *IEEE Computer Group Conference Proceedings*, June 17–19, 1959.

9. D.C. Gunderson, "Some Effects of Advances in Memory System Technology on Computer Organization," *Computer*, IEEE Computer Group, Nov.–Dec., 1970.
10. H.C. Lauer, "Bulk core in a 360/67 time-sharing system," *Proceedings of the Fall Joint Computer Conference* (1967).
11. D.N. Freeman, "A storage-hierarchy system for batch processing," *Proceedings of the Spring Joint Computer Conference* (1968).
12. R.E. Fikes, H.C. Lauer, and A.L. Vareha, "Steps toward a general-purpose time-sharing system using large capacity core storage and TSS/360," *Proceedings of the 1968 ACM National Conference* (1968).
13. Y.C. Chen and S.C. Hsieh, "Selective transfer analysis," *IBM Research Report RC 1926* (October 25, 1967).
14. L.I. Dinnerstein, "The CDC 7600—a giant in our time," *Data Processing Magazine* (May 1969).
15. T.H. Elrod, "The CDC 7600 and SCOPE 76," *Datamation* (April 1970).
16. O.W. Johnson and J.R. Martinson, "Virtual memory in Time Sharing System/360," TSS/360 Compendium, IBM Data Processing Division, 1969.
17. B.C. Lanzano, "Loader standardization for overlay programs," *Communications of the ACM*, **12** (10) (1969).
18. H.A. Kinslow, "The time-sharing monitor system," *Proceedings of the Fall Joint Computer Conference* (1964).
19. F.J. Corbato, et al., "The Compatible Time-Sharing System," The M.I.T. Press, Cambridge, Massachusetts, 1963.
20. A.S. Lett and W.L. Konigsford, "TSS/360: A time-shared operating system," *Proceedings of the Fall Joint Computer Conference* (1968).
21. F.J. Corbato and V.A. Vyssotsky, "Introduction and overview of the MULTICS system," *Proceedings of the Fall Joint Computer Conference* (1965).
22. B. Randell and C.J. Kuehner, "Dynamic storage allocation systems," *Communications of the ACM*, **11** (5) (1968).
23. J.B. Dennis, "Segmentation and the design of multiprogrammed computer systems," *Journal of the ACM*, **12** (4) (1965).
24. B.W. Arden, B.A. Galler, T.C. O'Brien, and F.H. Westervelt, "Program and addressing structure in a time sharing environment," *Journal of the ACM*, **13** (1) (January 1966).
25. I. Flores, "Virtual memory and paging," Part I: *Datamation* (August 1967); Part II: *Datamation* (September 1967).
26. G. Oppenheimer and N. Weizer, "Resource management for a medium scale time-sharing operating system," *Communications of the ACM*, **11** (5) (May 1968).
27. P.J. Denning, "Virtual memory," *Computing Surveys*, **2** (3) (1970).
28. C. Christensen and A.D. Hause, "A multiprogramming, virtual memory system for a small computer," *Proceedings of the Spring Joint Computer Conference* (1970).
29. W.T. Comfort, "A computing system design for user service," *Proceedings of the Fall Joint Computer Conference* (1965).
30. C.T. Gibson, "Time-sharing in the IBM system/360: Model 67," *Proceedings of the Spring Joint Computer Conference* (1966).
31. A. Opler, "Dynamic flow of programs and data through hierarchical storage," *Proceedings of the IFIP Congress* (1965).

32. S.E. Madnick and J.W. Alsop, "A modular approach to file system design," *Proceedings of the Spring Joint Computer Conference* (1970).
33. P.J. Dixon and J. Sable, "DM-1—a generalized data management system," *Proceedings of the Spring Joint Computer Conference* (1967).
34. D.B. Nelson, R.A. Pick, and K.B. Andrews, "GIM-1—a generalized information management language and computer system," *Proceedings of the Spring Joint Computer Conference* (1967).
35. G.G. Dodd, "Elements of data management systems," *Computing Surveys*, **1** (2) (1969).
36. G.H. Mealy, "Another look at data," *Proceedings of the Fall Joint Computer Conference* (1967).
37. N. Chapin, "A deeper look at data," *Proceedings of the ACM National Conference* (1968).
38. J.D. Aron, "Information systems in perspective," *Computing Surveys*, **1** (4) (1969).
39. "Information Management System; 360," Form GH20-0765, IBM Corporation, March 1970.
40. R.E. Blier and A.H. Vorhaus, "File organization in the SDC time-shared data management system (TDMS)," SP-2907, System Development Corporation, August 1968.
41. CODASYL Reports: (1) "A survey of generalized data base management systems." (2) "CODASYL data base task group." (Available from the ACM.)
42. R.C. Daley and P.G. Neumann, "A general-purpose file system for secondary storage," *Proceedings of the Fall Joint Computer Conference* (1965).
43. J.P. Considine and A.H. Weiss, "Establishment and maintenance of a storage hierarchy for an on-line data base under TSS/360," *Proceedings of the Fall Joint Computer Conference* (1969).

INDEX